ADVANCE PRAISE FOR
Material Virtualities

"A savvy, theoretically sophisticated exploration of how gender is created and negotiated in the textual environment of an online multiple object oriented interface (MOO). Based on two years of field work, this book gives a 'thick description' of the textual practices that create bodies while still being attentive to the physical activities, especially typing, that underlie these practices. The best study of online gender that I have read so far, *Material Virtualities* is a must-read for anyone interested in this fascinating and controversial area of contemporary culture."

N. Katherine Hayles, English Department, University of California, Los Angeles; Author, How We Became Posthuman: Virtual Bodies in Cybernetics, Literature, and Informatics

"*Material Virtualities* explores new ways in feminist cyberspace research. Based on a two-year cyber-ethnographic fieldwork in an online environment (MUD or multiple-user domain), this highly original and exceptional book shifts the perspective of feminist discussions of cyberspace significantly. It moves the discussion away from the stalemate between technophilia and technophobia, and between utopian visions of cyberspace as a totally free space for transgender play and the dystopy of a gloomy masculine-dominated space. Exploring the figuration of an embodied she-cyborg, Jenny Sundén contributes significantly to a convincingly balanced cyberfeminist analysis of the interplay between subjectivity, corporeality, machinic materiality, textuality, and virtuality in online interaction."

Nina Lykke, Institute of Literature, Culture and Media Studies, University of Southern Denmark and Department of Gender Studies, Linköping University; Author, Cosmodolphins: Feminist Cultural Studies of Technology, Animals and the Sacred

Material Virtualities

Steve Jones
General Editor

Vol. 13

PETER LANG
New York • Washington, D.C./Baltimore • Bern
Frankfurt am Main • Berlin • Brussels • Vienna • Oxford

Jenny Sundén

Material Virtualities

Approaching Online Textual Embodiment

PETER LANG
New York • Washington, D.C./Baltimore • Bern
Frankfurt am Main • Berlin • Brussels • Vienna • Oxford

Library of Congress Cataloging-in-Publication Data

Sundén, Jenny.
Material virtualities: approaching online textual embodiment / Jenny Sundén.
p. cm. — (Digital formations; vol. 13)
Includes bibliographical references and index.
1. WaterMOO. 2. Internet—Social aspects. 3. Multi-user dungeons—
Social aspects. 4. Virtual reality. 5. Internet and women.
I. Title. II. Digital formations; v. 13.
HM851 .S865   303.48'33—dc21   2002006254
ISBN 0-8204-6204-7
ISSN 1526-3169

Die Deutsche Bibliothek-CIP-Einheitsaufnahme

Sundén, Jenny:
Material virtualities: approaching online textual embodiment / Jenny Sundén.
–New York; Washington, D.C./Baltimore; Bern;
Frankfurt am Main; Berlin; Brussels; Vienna; Oxford: Lang.
(Digital formations; Vol. 13)
ISBN 0-8204-6204-7

Cover design by Dutton & Sherman Design

© 2003 Peter Lang Publishing, Inc., New York
275 Seventh Avenue, 28th Floor, New York, NY 10001
www.peterlangusa.com

All rights reserved.
Reprint or reproduction, even partially, in all forms such as microfilm,
xerography, microfiche, microcard, and offset strictly prohibited.

For my parents,
Gunilla Sundén and
Olle Petterson (1947–2000)

But what if my body is the disguise? What if skin, bone, liver, veins, are the things I use to hide myself? I have put them on and I can't take them off. Does that trap me or free me?

Jeanette Winterson
(2001), *The PowerBook*

CONTENTS

Acknowledgments   xiii

Introduction   1
    Female cyborgs   4
    Material textuality   8
    Shooting the typist   12
    Outline of the book   14

1. Writing a Written Culture   17
    WaterMOO ethnography   20
       Architecture   21
       MUD communication   24
       @gender (fe)male   27
       Casing the scene   30
       On the threshold   32
       Entering the field   35
       Rethinking ethics   37
       In the field   41
    Textual talk   43
       Frozen moments   46
       Virtual ethnography?   47
    Typed bodies   49
       Online corporeality   51
       Textual performativity   53

x   *Material Virtualities*

2. Reading Online Bodies   56

    Imaginative bodies   59
        Objectified bodies / Embodied objects   60
        Talking vampires   63
        Masquerading fantasy   68

    Illusions of the real   70
        Postmodern utopianism revisited   72
        Hacking masculinities on the limits of fiction   75
        The female body as exception   80

    Absent bodies   84

    Spectacle in interaction   89

3. Mapping Cyberplace(s)   92
        Home, sweet home   95
        Traveling messages   99
        Moving bodies   102
        Entrances and exits   106
        Sexual bodies, dissolving places   108
        "where you mooing from?"   111
        The relative stability of MOO places   113
        'America' as the online 'real'   115
        A realized utopia   119
        Embodied places   121

4. Corporeal Obsession   124
        "I'm still not sure she's a she"   125
        Online cross-dressing?   129
        "Sexual but sexless"   131
        Surfing tales and online betrayals   133
        The heterotextual matrix   137
        A 'lesbian' phallus?   141
        Online masochism   143
        The cybernetic bedroom   146
        Sexual textuality   148

5. The Embodied Computer Code   152
        Hypertext and postmodernism   154
        The materiality of digital textuality   156
        <help @gender>   158
        A virtual @gender order?   160
        Engendered pronouns   163
        Sexually encoded   166
        Wired incorporation   170

6. Material Virtualities 173
   To signify or not to signify 176
   Cyborgfeminist configurations 180
   A politics of sexual specificity 183
   The (re)turn of the she-cyborg 185

Notes 191

References 207

Index 221

ACKNOWLEDGMENTS

The story of this book widely exceeds its written narrative; it is merely the endpoint of innumerable encounters and discussions—face-to-face as well as face-to-screen.

To begin with, I would like to thank everybody at my home base, the Department of Communication Studies, Linköping University, in particular, Viveka Adelswärd, Lars-Christer Hydén, Per Linell, and Yvonne Waern for careful readings and commentaries. You all provided me with the kind of productive resistance that makes ideas clearer and arguments sharper. I am particularly grateful to Ann-Carita Evaldsson, who came to serve as a brilliant co-adviser, as well as to Per-Anders Forstorp, Cecilia Wadensjö, and Kosta Economou for priceless collegiality. I also would like to single out Christina Baggens, Christer Garbis, Åsa Kroon, Malin Sveningsson, and Christian Svensson, who arrived, as did I, at the department in 1996. Your support and friendship have been invaluable.

My work has, moreover, greatly benefited from my participation in the research group "Digital Borderlands," funded by the Swedish Council for Research in the Humanities and Social Sciences (HSFR), whose support has been crucial. I would like to thank the unbeatable team of borderlanders Johan Fornäs, Kajsa Klein, Martina Ladendorf, and Malin Sveningsson. My work is indebted to yet another research project, "Networds," that consists of Yvonne Waern, Maria Mattus, and Malin Sveningsson and is also funded by the Swedish Council for Research in the Humanities and Social Sciences.

I also owe a debt of gratitude to professor Raoul Granqvist, for mind-bending co-advisement and for sending me off to the University of California at Berkeley. In Berkeley, I found a temporary base at the English Department, and I am deeply indebted to Professor Hertha D. Sweet Wong for wonderful guidance and support on all levels. Other people in and around Berkeley that I would like to mention specifically are Elizabeth Churchill, David Feygin, Kim-An Lieberman, Sharon Marcus, Barry Thorne, and

William B. Worthen. You all contributed to a fruitful and thrilling Berkeley experience. Berkeley was also the site from where I first connected to and met with the inhabitants of WaterMOO. Without your openness and willingness to share your online writings, lives, and stories, this book would never have been written.

Another important academic scene is the Royal Library in Stockholm. Toward the end of the process, this place became a second home to me—and its inhabitants a second family. Brief acquaintances turned into colleagues, and colleagues into close friends. I am particularly referring to Kristina Fjelkestam, Amanda Lagerkvist, Claudia Lindén, Jesper Olsson, Cecilia Sjöholm, and Eva Åhrén Snickare. Our (sometimes very long) lunch hours have certainly shaped significant parts of my argument. I also wish to thank the competent and friendly library staff. There are a number of other important people without whom this text would have been far less clear and consistent. Among these, I want to express my deeply felt gratitude to Terry Harpold, Nina Lykke, Paul McIlvenny, Daniel Miller, Martina Tissberger, Nina Wakeford, and two anonymous reviewers at *Feminist Media Studies*. Your sensible readings and insightful suggestions have been indispensable. I am also very grateful to Professor Steve Jones and his generous offer to include this book in his Digital Formations series. It has been a true pleasure to work with Christopher S. Myers and his colleagues at Peter Lang Publishing.

One person who stands out as the most important figure for my work is my main adviser, Professor Johan Fornäs. For once, words are not enough. You are always such a challenging, curious, to the point, warm, and generous discussant and dear friend. I hope this won't be the end of our collaboration, but the beginning. I also would like to give a very special thanks to a colleague and soul mate, Bodil Axelsson. What would I have done without you? Thank you for being you, and for letting me sleep on your couch, drink your wine, and talk, endlessly. A big hug goes to two extraordinary women, Inger Pettersson, and to my big little sister, Ämma Pettersson. I dedicate this book to my parents, Gunilla Sundén, one of the strongest, most independent women I know, and to Olle Petterson, who died in 2000 and never had the chance to read this, but who never stopped loving me. This book is for you both—for teaching me self-confidence, having the guts to set me free at a very early age, and for always believing in my capacity.

Finally, I wish to thank the publishers for granting permission to reprint the following:

Sections of chapter 1, "Writing a Written Culture," and sections of chapter 4, "Corporeal Obsession," were previously published as "'I'm still not sure she's a she': Textual Talk and Typed Bodies in Online Interaction" in Paul

McIlvenny (ed.), *Talking Gender & Sexuality: Conversation, Performativity and Discourse in Interaction*. Amsterdam and Philadelphia: John Benjamins, 2002.

Sections of chapter 6, "Material Virtualities," appeared previously in "What Happened to Difference in Cyberspace? The (Re)turn of the She-Cyborg" in *Feminist Media Studies* <http://www.tandf.co.uk> 1(2), 2001.

INTRODUCTION

Type:
'COnnect <character-name> <password>' to connect to your character,
'Theme' to receive information on the theme of WaterMOO,
'connect guest' to connect to a guest character,
'CReate' for information on how to get your own character,
'Uptime' to display how long WaterMOO has been up and running,
'Version' to display the version of the current Lambda Server,
'@who' or 'Who' just to see who's logged in right now,
'@quit' or 'Quit' to disconnect, either now or later, or
'Help' for help on these commands.

The operators of WaterMOO have provided the materials for the buildings of this community, but are not responsible for what is said or done in them. In particular, you must assume responsibility if you permit minors or others to access WaterMOO through your facilities. The statements and viewpoints expressed here are not necessarily those of the wizards or Very Wet University and those parties disclaim any responsibility for them.

connect Jenny ********

*** Welcome to WaterMOO! ***

Her Office
You find yourself in the middle of a cozy messiness. The walls are covered with bookcases, filled with books and piles of papers, embracing what seems to be an awful lot of knowledge. The room is surprisingly airy, for being a hotel room, and a window reveals one of the most amazing views that you've ever seen. Next to the window, there is an old French writing desk with lots of small drawers, and probably even some secret ones behind the movable

panel. The desk is covered with books, journals and notebooks, and in the middle of all this you see an open PowerBook. In the pale blue flicker you capture a glimpse of a direct connection to . . . WaterMOO on the screen. In front of the desk, there is what seems to be a very comfortable chair. And if you were to lay your hand on the seat, you would notice that it was warm . . . as if someone a moment ago had been sitting there.
Obvious exits: Hall to Eighth Floor

Your Event Log is empty.
None of your pals are online.
@read new
You have no new messages.

This is what appears on the screen when I connect my researcher character Jenny to the text-based online world (throughout this text referred to as WaterMOO) where she is one of the inhabitants.[1] At the time of this particular moment of 'connecting,' Jenny was new in the MOO, hence all her textual message systems tell her that she does not have a life ("Your Event Log is empty," "None of your pals are online," "You have no new messages"). During this initial phase of research, empty answering machines actually seemed to be a salient element that cut across different parts of my life. I was constantly on my way to physically move somewhere else and people simply had a hard time keeping track of where I lived at the moment. It is possible that I took this feeling of continuous movement with me in my work online, because once Jenny came across the following ad in the MOO it seemed to be speaking to me directly:

> Need a warm, friendly place to live? Tired of having a room floating in limbo? If so, please check out the Hotel California. The Hotel California is WaterMOO's oldest hotel, providing a happy comfortable atmosphere for over 5 years. Every room in the Hotel comes with lots of features to make your stay more comfortable. (Type 'look $hotel' for a list) The Hotel also has a friendly staff to help you.

Who does not need a warm, friendly place to live? Tired of having a room floating in limbo? Certainly. No sooner said than done. Jenny asked for a hotel room on the top floor of "Hotel California," moved in, and turned it into "Her Office"—a text-based office space perfectly suited for a researcher of online culture. Ironically, this hotel room proved to be my most stable point of reference during the first six months of fieldwork, since my physical addresses kept changing. At the same time, and perhaps in the light of a different type of irony, it was still nothing but a hotel room, a more or less anonymous place for more temporary visits, easy to leave behind if something more tempting appeared on the scene. But in spite of this restlessness, I managed to keep this space for nearly three years, making Jenny more settled than I had ever been anywhere else.

The initial screen image that appears each time Jenny wakes up in her room (and where she helplessly falls asleep when I am not there to type her around), and in particular the description of Her Office, is significant to what online cultures are all about—as well as to the approach used in this book. The key sentence in the office description is: "In the pale blue flicker you capture a glimpse of a direct connection to... WaterMOO on the screen," which illustrates the *doubleness* that characterizes online modes of being. The online condition is fundamentally constituted through a mediation between an embodied self and a textual I, simultaneously divided and intimately connected through typed-in enunciations. In the above reflections on (online) migration, it becomes clear that Jenny and I are not precisely one and the same, but we are definitely not separated either. Perhaps one could say that we *overlap*. Cyber-subjectivity is neither coherent nor split, but digitally connects subjects through discursive circuits, making them alternately collude and fall apart according to principles that are still largely unknown. Within these loops between body and text, between fingers typing and textual characters coming to life at your fingertips, you constantly find yourself crossing the boundaries between the material and the textual in a sense that makes them blur and mingle, twist and change. The description of Her Office is an attempt to give an example of the feeling of (physically) being seated at a computer, connected to the online world. Within this world another young woman is (textually) seated by her virtual computer, which also appears to have a direct connection to the world that is being studied.

The office description can be seen as a strategy to make evident the *constructedness* of texts and subjectivity in general. Even though the border between physical and virtual locations is continuously crossed in online experiences, there is also a separating distance between the two. This distance is on one level introduced in text-based online worlds through the act of typing, and further reinforced by the mediating computer technology itself. By actively having to type oneself into being, a certain gap in this construction is at the same time created. The mediation between different realms, the very creation of texts by the means of computers, makes the interspace that always exists between myself and the understanding of this self particularly clear. Following the idea of a subject that can never have a direct and unmediated access to herself, that the I writing and the I written about can never be seen as *one*, cybersubjects are always at least *double*. This distance can in a similar way be used for methodological purposes, to form a reflexive understanding of research procedures and of the way that oneself as a researcher is always intertwined with these processes. It can be used to create room for reflection on how I, the researcher, am not only a producer of texts, such as this one, but also always a co-producer of the reality that is being written.

One of the questions that this book tries to answer is what happens with the body, conventionally thought of as not more than one, in the midst of this doubleness. At the core of this question lies the idea of the body as always sexually specific—that we can only with great difficulty imagine a body that has no sex, a body that is somehow completely sexless. Ideas of the body always hide implications of sex and/or gender (depending on which feminist tradition of thought is being used), even if these are not clearly spelled out.[2] Bodies are of course always marked, not only by sex and gender, but also by race, age, and also, but perhaps less evidently, by sexuality and class. But as will become clear, the sexed and gendered body has a particularly important role to play in online textual practices.

Female cyborgs

The relation between notions of embodiment and cyberspatial technologies has been a heated issue during the last decade. Within these discussions, ranging from high philosophy to popular culture, cyberspace is often described as completely disembodied—as a space unconstrained by the meaning and matter of the corporeal. One of the most extreme versions of the disappearing body in high-tech culture can be found in the subgenre of science fiction called cyberpunk. Cyberpunk combines punk philosophy with a vision of a highly technological future where distinctions between technology and humanity have disappeared. In this dissolution, the body, often referred to as "the meat," is left behind and the mind released from the earthly limitations of the flesh. When William Gibson (1984) in his book *Neuromancer* coined the word "cyberspace," it was described in terms of a "consensual hallucination," as an electronic alternative to physical reality.[3] This parallel world was constructed by means of human brains directly connected to a global network, inhabited by people's minds while their material bodies were left in meat space. To Gibson, this is far from a heavenly state of being.

If the concept of cyberspace was born in the realm of science fiction, it did not take long until it was turned into an integral part of many people's everyday lives; transformed, as Sandy Stone puts it, "from an interesting fantasy to a hotly contested financial, cultural, and ethical frontier."⁴ When the word *cyberspace* is used in this book, it is meant to connote this double meaning of mixed belonging to both a widespread medium for communication and a space in which to project fantasies, hopes, dreams, and desires. When cyberpunk narratives are used as a source of inspiration for cultural theorists, images of "regular" Internet users usually have to stand back for a peculiar futuristic version of postmodern theory. Ironically, this theoretical twist to cyberpunk narratives turns the dystopian dimension of the disappearing body in a high-tech future into a utopian possibility tied to the ancient dream of transcending the body:

> the duality between mind and body is superseded in a new formation that presents the mind as itself *embodied*. [. . .] Through the construction of the computer itself, there arises the possibility of a mind independent of the biology of bodies, a mind released from the mortal limitations of the flesh.⁵

In this Cartesian separation of mind from body, cyberspace is completely freed from the messiness of the physical and miraculously becomes a space of the mind. Departing from the assumption that the physical body has ceased to matter in encounters beyond its physical limits, new communication technologies open up a space for disembodied subjectivities in which the material body is something that the cyberspace traveler, at least temporarily, can leave behind. This argument dominated the scene in the early 90s and, typically, its primary protagonists were male theorists.⁶ Their flight from the body is a deep-rooted cultural theme that can, for example, be traced back to the Enlightenment and the notion of the 'individual' (i.e., the man) as a thoroughly rational creature created through intense denials of bodily un-reason.⁷ The dream of getting rid of the meat simultaneously reflects the understanding of masculinity as abstraction—of men as physically disconnected, independent and solitary individuals—which is now according to several theorists being re-mapped onto cyberspace discourses.⁸ But these discourses are, as always, dependent on the maintenance and essentializing of embodied others.⁹ Instead of maintaining an opposition between disembodied, high-tech masculinity and embodied, earthbound femininity, this book will, rather, engage in a discussion of how cyberspace and similar concepts might have been 'embodied' all along—the virtual does not automatically equal disembodiment.

The idea of the body as nothing but a passive shell for the active, virile mind—'woman' is aligned with body and nature, whereas 'man' is associated with mind and culture—is a recurring figure of thought throughout the history of philosophy.¹⁰ In feminist criticism of technoculture, one common argument has been that this (sexed) nature/culture split prevails even in intense fusions of human and machine. In 1960, Manfred Clynes and Nathan Kline invented the term "cyborg"—a coming together of the two concepts *cybernetic* and *organism*—to depict a self-regulating (hu)man-machine system ideally constructed for extraterrestrial environments.[11] Originating in the domain of military technologies and space flights, cyborg bodies have been reproduced in areas ranging from medicine and biotechnology to science fiction and cyberpunk film and literature. Machine bodies in Hollywood science fiction (as pictured in films like *Robocop* and *The Terminator*) typically illustrate an exaggerated, metallic masculinity that highlights the traditional couplings between male bodies and machinery.[12] Although a synthesis of human and machine that renders unstable the very boundaries of the human subject, the maleness of these cyborg bodies is not only left intact but strengthened through a full-body armor of virile hardness. Tricia Rose argues that "the cyborg is a masculine construct in which the technology houses all of the hard, strong, *Terminator* capacity, and the softer stuff is understood as the weak portion, the part that bleeds, menstruates."[13]

Even if such readings of machine bodies rightfully bring attention to how the sexed body does not necessarily vanish out of sight in corporeal linkages with mechanical or digital components, they seem to sidestep, entirely, the fact that cyborg bodies are haunted by contradictions. If (computer) technologies are, too hastily, seen as a male domination/denial of repressed female flesh, this builds on the problematic notion that there would exist such a thing as a (feminine) sphere untouched by technology. In a similar argument, Jill Marsden points out how such commentaries imply a "separation or distinction between technological 'agency' and the 'matter' of its operations, such that it is possible to speak of an *organic reality*, either irresponsibly wished away (in VR 'travel') or ideologically determined (as resource for exploitation)."[14] Consequently, these arguments efficiently eliminate every productive pairing of *women* and machines. For sure, female machines are a rare species. And when they do occur—as in the classic example of the robot Maria in Fritz Lang's *Metropolis* (1927)—they tend to be rather explosive incarnations of sexual danger with disastrous cultural implications. The fear of machines that become uncontrollable is entwined with the fear of female sexuality that gets out of hand.[15] As a representation of such male anxiety, the woman machine must always 'die' at the end of the story.

Therefore, it is necessary to imagine a different scene. What if she does not die? What if the female machine simply refuses to die where the narrative ends? Or, what if she even objects to narratives that *have* endings? By clearly illustrating that the connection between masculinity and machinery is not given by nature, but is something that constantly needs to be constructed, a female cyborg not only resists the alignment of woman with nature, but, following the lead of historian of science Donna Haraway, also proves impossible, tirelessly, the very division that produced this association in the first place.¹⁶

In her influential *How We Became Posthuman: Virtual Bodies in Cybernetics, Literature, and Informatics*, literary theorist N. Katherine Hayles (1999) investigates discourses of disembodiment in the history of cybernetics and shows how these exist in a complex interplay with embodied forms of subjectivity rarely accounted for.¹⁷ In a rereading of the famous 'Turing test,' from a 1950 paper entitled "Computing Machinery and Intelligence" by Alan Turing, Hayles puts forth that the first (and often forgotten) test that Turing offered was not to distinguish between human and machine, but between man and woman.¹⁸ Interestingly, the introductory man/woman setup is treated merely as an (unproblematic) illustration of the parameters in the human/machine interface. The Turing test, or, in Turing's words "the imitation game," is commonly referred to as a blind test in which a person by means of computers communicates with two other 'units' in a different room: one (hu)man and one machine (where the task of the machine is to 'pass' as human while the human tries to be as truthfully human as possible . . .). The person being tested needs to decide which is the human and which is the machine based on answers to questions s/he is posing. If no distinction can be made, this proves that machines are intelligent. Hayles shows how this line of thought depends on a notion of intelligence as something that can be extracted and manipulated independently of the body and asks:

> If your failure to distinguish correctly between human and machine proves that machines can think, what does it prove if you fail to distinguish woman from man? Why does gender appear in this primal scene of humans meeting their evolutionary successors, intelligent machines? What do gendered bodies have to do with the erasure of embodiment and the subsequent merging of machine and human intelligence in the figure of the cyborg?¹⁹

Turing never addresses these questions. According to Hayles, Turing's inclusion of gender in his test seriously questions the 'liberal subject'—the idea of the human as an utterly autonomous, rational, and unitary being that has been a dominating perception since the Enlightenment. The liberal subject is, obviously, threatened already in the confusion of human and machine in the sense that a thinking machine delineates a possible realm of *non*-human subjects. The introduction of 'gender' into this picture sheds light on yet another distinction, namely that between the material body seated at the computer and the body (re)presented on the screen. A correct answer in the 'gender test' collapses the textual and the material into a safely unified, unambiguously embodied subject. However, as Hayles makes clear, there is always a possibility that the wrong choice is made, which inserts a potential *dis*connection between the body writing and the body being written, proving "that the overlay between the enacted and the represented bodies is no longer a natural inevitability but a contingent production, mediated by a technology that [...] can no longer meaningfully be separated from the human subject."[20] It is precisely this techno-culturally produced nonnecessity of coherence—together with a profound interdependence—between different levels of embodied, sexed subjectivity that is brought to the fore in online worlds like WaterMOO.

Material textuality

The text at hand is the fruit of two years of fieldwork in WaterMOO. During my stay in this specific corner of the Net, a double-edged way of looking at online embodiment evolved. One side of this perspective consists of a developing interest in the *textual* dimension of online bodies. In regarding WaterMOO practices as texts I partly follow in the footsteps of poststructuralist literary theory. As Roland Barthes points out in his distinction between text and work: "The work is concrete, occupying a portion of book-space (in a library, for example); the Text, on the other hand, is a methodological field. [...] *the Text is experienced only in an activity, a production*."[21] A text thus traverses the bookshelf, it cuts across works, other texts, and contexts; it is itself always an intertext with allusions to other texts—a quotation devoid of quotation marks. To say that the text is always an activity, a production, is further to diminish, or perhaps dissolve, the distance between writing and reading, to tightly link them together in a process of signification that shows how the act of reading is indispensable to the existence of texts.[22]

To disengage the text from the work is at the same time a disengagement from its founder—the author. According to Barthes, "The *I* that writes the text is never, itself, anything more than a paper I,"[23] or perhaps rather a digital I in online realms, which gives readers the freedom to interpret the text regardless of who is writing/typing. This break with a textual origin shows how the author's interiority (her intentions, emotions, dreams, desires, etc.) is not only inaccessible to readers, but is likely to be inaccessible to the author herself. When transposing this thinking to the creation of online bodies, my intention is to accordingly release these texts from their authors, to not regard them as biographical imprints of authorial intentions. They will rather be viewed as contemporary fragments of networked subjectivities with certain independency. Far from being seen as straightforward replicas of their typists, characters in WaterMOO certainly have a life of their own, but one that is dependent on 'the machine.' (All online excerpts used in this book are unedited quotations and might thus contain typos).

look Raechel
High-cut rust hair and ocean blue eyes, skin no darker than fresh cream. A short lass indeed, yet trim and fit, she strolls around with her hair as mussed as it can get at that length, draped in a dark red/blue/green vertical-striped terry-cloth bathrobe, belt hanging at her sides, belly exposed, breasts barely covered, white satin panties barely visible against her skin, padding along on feet with chipping red nail-polish. She looks like she needs some sleep.

One day I met this "Raechel" (possibly named after one of the female androids in the film *Blade Runner*), who was virtually barefoot, padding along through electronic landscapes. She is one of several hundred inhabitants in this virtual world, and her textual appearance reveals a woman who has just woken up from her (cybered) sleep, "draped in a dark red/blue/green vertical-striped terry-cloth bathrobe," ready to meet the day in the wires. This text is what appears on the screen if I type <look Raechel> (words in bold indicate typed-in commands). The activity of 'looking' at each other, and of being seen, is probably one of the reasons for the common use of third-person constructions in these texts. In Raechel, there is no digital I but a digital she that meets the reader—a self-presentation ready to fit the perspective of others. In an encounter with its reader her textual body comes into being, and in every meeting, a different interpretation is performed and new meanings attached to her body. Computer technology mediates between the embodied self and the 'she' simultaneously present in the virtual realm. The interface has thus, through an act of narrativization, become a crucial site, a significantly ambiguous borderland between human and technology.

Created through strings of text that realize an openly flirtatious and seductive performance, she "strolls around" with "belly exposed" and "breasts barely covered." At the same time, she appears to wear her hair "as mussed as it can get at that length [. . .] padding along on feet with chipping red nail-polish," signaling a lack of interest in her half-naked appearance. There is really no reason for hair to be entangled and nail polish to flake off in cyberspace, and an incorporation of features like these can be understood as a resistance toward the endless number of exquisitely beautiful and mysterious female creatures wandering virtual spaces. This woman even "looks like she needs some sleep."

By mixing an exposure of a female body with ironic comments attached to it, Raechel can be read as an example of Rosi Braidotti's politics of the parody. In her discussion of the concept of parody, Braidotti emphasizes that 'woman' is not only the objectified Other tied to patriarchy through a negation, but also the very basis for female identity and therefore contains a resistance to patriarchal identity. When woman is regarded as a set of options to choose from and play with, and sometimes even avoid, it becomes possible to use traditional patterns in playful and unexpected ways to create new femininities and meanings. Self-distance and humor function as the means to, at least momentarily, dissolve the contradiction between accentuation and deconstruction of femininity, to imagine new gender identities by moving through the heart of traditional bipolar definitions of gender.[24] Thus, Raechel could be understood as a realization of a distancing strategy, as a modest displacement of the dominant gender order. On the other hand, this female figure through its openly expressed sexuality, no matter how ironic, might still be understood along the lines of highly traditional gender identities. If the irony in her (textual) voice is drowned in a silent, voluptuous body language, the emancipatory potential of the representation might be locked into a dependency to satisfy a male gaze.

In treating online bodies as texts, the purpose is not to reconstruct the world *behind* the text, to evoke its origin, but to develop a sensitivity to the world created *within*, or maybe *in front of* the text, to paraphrase Paul Ricoeur.[25] Texts are always intertextually linked to other texts, articulating innumerable elsewheres with invisible quotation marks. When examining this allusiveness in the interplay of online texts and contexts, my attempt is to discern what type of bodies, or nonbodies, take shape in the Net. Through strategic readings of these texts as cultural signs, as signifying stories of intersections between bodies, texts, and communication technologies, it becomes possible to explore online embodiment and new textualities without the limitations of illusionary originals. Anne Balsamo, in her critical examination of virtual reality discourses, formulates a similar point of view:

> In traveling through various virtual cyberworlds, it no longer makes sense to ask whose reality or perspective is *represented* in cyberspace; rather we should ask what reality is created therein, and how this reality articulates relationships among technologies, bodies and narratives. The body may disappear representationally in virtual worlds—indeed, we may go to great length to repress and erase its referential traces—but it doesn't disappear materially, either in the interface with the VR apparatus or in systems of technological production.[26]

Balsamo argues that our encounters with virtual reality technologies "no longer simply mimic or *represent* reality—they virtually recreate it,"[27] pointing out that the difference between virtual worlds and the construction of everyday realities, both being cultural and technological constructs, is a question of epistemology rather than ontology.

On the other hand, when focusing on the textual dimension of online embodiment, there is an obvious risk of completely disconnecting the textual from the *material* reality of sexed and gendered bodies, as well as from that of computer technologies. If entirely released from its physical groundings, online textuality is at risk of being reduced to a (paradoxically) free play with cultural signs and symbols. On the other side of the double edge, as a counterweight to an analytical investment in the textual creation of bodies in online worlds, I therefore intend to put forth the material dimensions of this process. The Internet is often presented as a disembodied, weightless medium—a space in which (physical) bodies have ceased to matter. Nevertheless, it is important to remember that communication technologies depend on human bodies, technologically as well as symbolically: "With tools and technologies, we can reach further away, but our physical bodies still remain the first and the last step of each communicative act."[28]

In regarding the virtual as exceedingly material, I take as a point of departure the work of N. Katherine Hayles, who consistently argues for a perspective that tightly links texts, bodies, and machines together in ways that reveal 'virtuality' as itself embodied. With Hayles as a starting point for a much needed *materialization* of cybercultural studies, my work further owes a great deal to several feminist theorists who have worked extensively on various kinds of body politics always embedded in intersections of bodies and (computer) technologies. If Hayles points out the necessity to speak of embodied virtuality, and even if she sometimes speaks of 'gender,' she does not have an explicit feminist agenda. Thus, I have felt the need to radicalize her argument through a close-up investigation of the political dimensions of the *specific types of bodies* involved. Bringing together actually rather different feminist thinkers such as Donna Haraway, Judith Butler, Elizabeth Grosz, and Rosi Braidotti, my aim has been to create a framework sensitive to flexible and sometimes perhaps surprising coalitions between the materiality of bodies, computer technologies, gender, sexuality, and sexual difference. These theoretical links and leaps within and between a range of feminist traditions may also show how not only does the field of cyberculture consist of intense couplings of (wo)men and machines, but that intellectual work itself might be rather "cyborgian" in nature. When, for example, "thinking together" Haraway's feminist cyborg with Butler's heterosexual matrix with Grosz's concept of corporealization with Braidotti's notion of sexual difference, this assemblage gradually turns into something very different altogether from the sum of its 'originary' parts. Borderland existences—in being fusions of at least two species—both resemble and differ from their originators in ways that simultaneously create alliances and make room for unexpected shapes to take on a life of their own.

Shooting the typist

Unexpected linkages between texts, bodies, and machines are commonplace in typed-in interactions in WaterMOO:

> ElBosso exclaims, "welcome!"
> You ask, "thanks . . . any place to sit?"
> You can't find anywhere to sit down comfortably.
> ElBosso says, "hmm . . . guess not. . ."
> ElBosso looks around
> ElBosso says, "sorry. ."
> You say, "that's ok"
> ElBosso says, "never bothered. . ."
> ElBosso shrugs
> ElBosso asks, "so . . . what's up?"
> You say, "oh, need to make some plans for this evening, i guess"
> You ask, "do you have any?"
> ElBosso says, "no, not really . . . am tired from the week. ."
> ElBosso says, ""
> You ask, "sorry?"
> Jenny smiles
> ElBosso says, "oops . . . the kids kept me busy this eek, am tird"
> ElBosso draws his Colt .45 and shoots ElBosso's typist right between the eyes.

In this excerpt, Jenny is visiting the virtual home of ElBosso. Many Water-MOOers have programmed objects in the shape of, for example, furniture in their rooms possible to interact with and use. The first lines in the excerpt illustrate how ElBosso's room lacks comfortable seating, which is why bodies in text are forced to remain standing. The most interesting part of this example starts when ElBosso says: "" which indicates a typing error (e.g., the utterance was sent before it was written, which results in empty quotation marks). ElBosso is apparently trying to say something, but the typist accidentally hits the return key before managing to formulate it. A couple of lines further down, ElBosso notices the mistake and says "oops . . . the kids kept me busy this eek, am tird," explaining the error by tiredness, simultaneously creating two new typos: "eek" instead of "week," and "tird" instead of "tired." These repeated slips at the keyboard result in the last line: "ElBosso draws his Colt .45 and *shoots ElBosso's typist right between the eyes*" (my emphasis), wittingly illustrating how the online condition depends on a somewhat paradoxical intersection of textual and material realities.

On one hand, a separation between character and typist is introduced when ElBosso says "oops . . . the kids kept me busy this eek, am tird," where "me" appears to point in the direction of the typist. This shift gets increasingly clear when ElBosso "shoots ElBosso's typist." In a motion that parallels the death of the author in literary theory, ElBosso's textual body performs a violent action with the material body of the typist as its target, to release itself from the dependence of the 'real' (here exemplified through several mistakes at the keyboard, which of course put ElBosso in an unfavorable light). On the other hand, the act of (metaphorically) shooting the typist is impossible, since the death of the typist implies the death of the character. In contrast to literary characters, MOO characters are continually created and re-created through their typists' physical engagement with computer technologies. As a point of departure for this study, I also would like to 'shoot the typist,' to illustrate the double gesture at work in my interpretations. In shooting the typist, the attention is focused on the world created within and between texts, without losing sight of the border between text and matter. The gesture of shooting sheds light on this border by pointing at the body of the typist, which, instead of eliminating the physical, illustrates the impossibility of its erasure. The textual world can neither be disconnected from the material conditions of its creation, nor from dominating discourses of sexed and gendered bodies. This indicates a continuous oscillation between readings of online bodies as cultural signs and symbols, but ones that are always shaped, if not fundamentally constituted, by the intense interplay between computer technologies and typists. Foucault asks us: "What difference does it make who is speaking?"[29] From the horizon of poststructuralism, the answer is, without the slightest hesitation, "none." The answer to this question given in this book is different, and not nearly as straightforward and unambiguous.

To speak of online bodies as both textual and material—or to speak of texts themselves as always materially situated—is thus not an attempt to reintroduce any (psychological) dimensions of authorship through the back door. It is, rather, an effort to put forth that both bodies and computers have everything to do with how online bodies are formulated and make sense. In using the word "typist," instead of, for example, "author," the ambition is to highlight the material activity of *typing oneself into being*. It is an endeavor to, conceptually, get rid of some of the baggage that the figure of the author is automatically dragging with 'him,' to instead focus on the processes through which online bodies are made. With a gesture that establishes a dialogue with Donna Haraway's notion of "materialized deconstruction," the text to follow balances on the very border between text and matter—to show how online bodies are neither disengaged from nor reducible to a concrete, locally situated, sexually specific body, but rather (re)embodied through prosthetic writing technologies.[30]

Outline of the book

The story I would like to tell evolves around the way human interaction is transformed when mediated by machines, and in particular in what way bodies as material systems of meaning are engaged in these interactions. The purpose of this book is to explore notions of embodiment in a particular text-based virtual world—WaterMOO—by investigating how bodies are created and rendered meaningful in this small corner of cyberspace. Based on two years of fieldwork, the main questions this book sets out to answer are: What does it mean to 'have' a body online? In which ways are online bodies typed into being? Which images of male, female, and other-gendered bodies are salient in WaterMOO? What kinds of textualities emerge from these activities? How can the body be conceptualized online while being both text and matter deeply intertwined with computer technologies and networks? In short: *What happens to (the idea of) the sexed and gendered body, conventionally thought of as not more than one, in online textual practices?* How do people handle a borderland existence of 'body doubles,' where bodies simultaneously are (textually) visible and (physically) hidden? How do they make sense of a situation in which the corporeal gets technologically extended, sometimes to the point where the body ceases to be one and becomes, at least, two?

To reach an understanding of online embodiment, careful readings of textual bodies is not enough, but a wider analysis of the cultural landscape in which these bodies come into being is also needed. Online embodiment hardly arises in a vacuum, in a "culture of no culture," but has to be understood against the background of those cultures, narratives, and technologies that continuously create and re-create online worlds.[31] In an attempt to give a nuanced image of the creation of textual bodies in WaterMOO, their culturally specific categories, patterns, and meanings, I am interested in what we can learn from these texts about the online culture of which they are part. In discourses of virtual worlds as scenes for disembodied performances, where the machine overshadows bodily groundings toward a perfect fantasy of abstractions, something very important is excluded. Left out are heterogeneities, variations, different and maybe marginalized versions. What can never be included in the discourse of a global web of information, where bodies paradoxically are made both invisible and equal, is the particular, local, and concrete, what Mizuko Ito calls "the materiality of information."[32] The problem is that this materiality is utterly absent in the interface of online worlds, efficiently erased from its surface. Nevertheless, power structures and knowledges implicated in the production and maintenance of, for example, computers and computer networks form the political conditions for our online existence, and must therefore be taken into account in critical cybercultural studies.[33] This is not an easy mission, since the virtual ethnographer in online fieldwork is part of the same systems of erasure as the people s/he studies. This difficulty, however, does not exclude an awareness of the existence of these agencies and power relations that structure the Net.

The text to follow will be performed in six chapters and will, gradually, displace the analytical emphasis: from *readings of textual bodies as signs of online cultures* to discussions that more clearly incorporate *the materiality of the virtual*. In parallel with this gesture, there is yet another motion that deals with the particularity of such materiality. This second shift moves the discussion from a concern with *sexed and gendered bodies*—toward an increasing involvement with *a politics of sexual specificity*. 'Gender' is in much cybercultural writing aligned with the realm of the virtual, mysteriously cut off from the site of the material body and its 'sex.' In contrast to the transference (and possible enhancement) of the sex/gender dichotomy into the discussion of virtual worlds, I will complicate such a division by showing how online bodies are everything but immaterial and disconnected. Along the lines of this displacement, the materiality of the virtual is disclosed as a thoroughly sexed matter.

The first chapter, "Writing a Written Culture," introduces an approach to written cultures online. It starts out with a brief introduction to MOO culture, followed by reflections on the ethnographic dimension of the WaterMOO study. As a second step, the practice of online ethnography is discussed against the background of a broader framework concerned with textual cultures and online textuality. Finally, a perspective on typed bodies will be discussed. In spaces where language, literally, substitutes for the 'real,' a wish to explore embodiment is connected not only with the way bodies can be read as texts, but how texts in a sense become bodies. How can MOO characters, in their capacity as *textual bodies*, be approached and understood?

The second chapter, "Reading Online Bodies," focuses on close readings of character descriptions in WaterMOO. The chapter is divided into three different parts. The first part, "Imaginative bodies," formulates a perspective on the writing of fiction, while focusing on the creation of (nonrealistic) fictive characters. The second part, "Illusions of the real," primarily deals with the way a certain type of turn-of-the-century realistic masculinity is being created in the MOO. In a move from the obviously fictive in the first part to striking online realism in this part, the title is meant to evoke an understanding of realism as no less fictitious, or constructed, than any other more obvious imaginative fabrication. The third part, "Absent bodies," takes a look at characters composed through textual fragments or quotes from literature and rock lyrics.

The third chapter, "Mapping Cyberplace(s)," moves the discussion from the textual world as 'itself' a place to be, to those materialities involved in the making and interpretation of a text-based online world. It sets out to investigate the interrelatedness of place-making and (online) embodiment—the fact that having a body always implies being somewhere. Drawing on recent understandings in the field of cultural geography of the activity of "mapping," in relation to which the naming of places performatively creates what is being named, this discussion of embodied place-making introduces a "politics of location." Far from being a global whole, cyberspace rather consists of innumerable, networked localities.

The fourth chapter, "Corporeal Obsession," focuses on the interplay between text and matter in the construction of bodies and sexuality in online textual talk. Letting discussions of (online) cross-dressing and notions like 'the lesbian phallus' in contemporary queer theory serve as a backdrop, the discussion mainly focuses on how bodies are typed into being through co-produced enactments of (*heterotextual* male) fantasies. Toward the end of the chapter, the story of the 'death of the Author' will be recounted in an attempt to situate (online) textuality in the wake of 'his' death—to move this poststructuralist line of thought away from its engagement with textual 'surfaces' toward a theory of texts as always materially and sexually engraved.

The fifth chapter, "The Embodied Computer Code," pays attention to how online texts are made; it focuses on the materiality of online textuality. Giving a brief overview of the main arguments in (American) hypertext theory, the discussion will turn to the increasing emphasis on the materiality of the virtual. Writing in a MOO has certainly lots of room for (individual and collective) imagination and textual playfulness, but this "writing space" is nonetheless intertwined with its coded origins of existence. Far from being a neutral tool in the hands of the typist, this investigation shows how programming is not only a cultural construction, but one that has the most intricate implications for sexually specific bodies.

The sixth chapter, "Material Virtualities," synthesizes the findings in the preceding chapters—to reground and develop the theoretical argument. One mission of this closing chapter is to introduce an alternative cyberfeminism—a cyb*org*feminism—through the conceptualization of a feminist cyborg: a she-cyborg. The she-cyborg is a figure of thought, but also a lived reality in various online spaces. She shows how (female) typists and their virtual body-doubles in no sense are separated from each other; that text and matter are intertwined in ways that give women of all kinds a diversified imaginary space, but one that is always infused with feminist politics embedded in collectivities of difference.

CHAPTER 1

WRITING A WRITTEN CULTURE

We begin not with participant-observation or with cultural texts (suitable for interpretation), but with writing, the making of texts.[1]

The production of ethnographic texts can never be a simple reflection of reality. Within anthropology, writing, nevertheless, has traditionally been seen merely as an instrument, as a tool for taking notes in the field and for completing the final report. In this perspective, the use of language is viewed as nothing but a transparent mediation of lived experiences and social relations, invisibly connected to the part of the world that is being described. The same kind of transcendence characterizes the ethnographer, the 'neutral' observer, who, without any trace of being herself a person, represents a disinterested truth. In this genre of traditional ethnographic writing, alongside objectifying descriptions, there certainly exists the telling of subjective experiences. These personal narratives, on the other hand, never stand alone, but are always preceded or followed by a formal ethnography that legitimizes them scientifically. This creates a paradoxical tension within the tradition itself, between subjective and 'scientific' voices, through which fieldwork "produces a kind of authority that is anchored to a large extent in subjective, sensuous experience [. . .]. But the professional text to result from such an encounter is supposed to conform to the norms of a scientific discourse whose authority resides in the absolute effacement of the speaking and experiencing subject."[2]

A shift within ethnographic writing, with an introduction of literary conventions and practices at the heart of ethnography, took place in the mid-80s.[3]

Anthropologists and ethnographers realized that their writing not only contained traces of, but was constituted through, literary conventions and genres. To claim transparency in a world opaque with competing meanings neglects the way texts, in this case ethnographic texts, are an integral part of, and result from, the cultural practices they describe. An ethnography never speaks for itself, and remains silent if nobody interprets it. The ethnographer had to revalue the approach to ethnographic writing, and start to read these texts as 'fiction.' Furthermore, this 'literary turn' within ethnography can be seen as part of a broader theorizing about the limits of representation itself that has appeared in different shapes during the last decades. Structuralism grew out of a desire to make texts visible, even autonomous, in relation to speaking and acting subjects. If the belief in a transparency of representation was problematic, a perspective constructed through a strong emphasis on the text and its inner logic runs the risk of completely determining the subject by textual structures. What started as a critique of a tradition claiming immediacy of experience and transparency of texts turned into perspectives without access to intersubjective relations 'outside' the text.

The point of making visible how literary conventions are embedded in the structure of ethnographic writing is rather to show how 'reality' is always constructed through narrative, or, put more broadly, through text. Ethnographic texts must thus be understood as constructs to be read against the background of the cultural framework in which they are written.[4] An emphasis on this relationship between the 'real' and the 'textual' not only tightly binds them together, but makes the distinction between them increasingly fluid. In online ethnography, the distinction between 'reality' and 'textuality' is not only fluid, but utterly dissolved, since the reality of online worlds is a textual reality. How then to start writing a culture that is already written? How to productively approach a place where life and writing are inseparable? The methodological strategy used in this study is inspired by ethnography with a strong emphasis on textual analysis—on the writing and reading of online texts. Haraway argues for an 'ethnographic attitude' when engaging with the field of technoscience. She uses the term 'ethnography' in an extended sense, which

> is not so much a specific procedure in anthropology as it is a method of *being at risk* in the face of the practices and discourses into which one inquires. [. . .] An 'ethnographic attitude' can be adopted within any kind of inquiry, including textual analysis. Not limited to a specific discipline, an ethnographic attitude is a mode of practical and theoretical attention, a way of remaining mindful and accountable. Such a method is not about 'taking sides' in a predetermined way. But it is about risks, purposes, and hopes—one's own and others'—embedded in knowledge projects.[5]

Following Haraway, I use the concept of 'ethnography' to allude to a particular mind-set in relation to which Haraway's notion of being "at risk" seems crucial (rather than describing a scientific process that more or less straightforwardly translates core practices in anthropology to the study of online cultures).[6] The WaterMOO project was never primarily about "taking sides." It was rather about exposing others, as well as myself, to critical inquiry—to engage in the making of online texts in ways that braved initial beliefs and passions.[7]

My initial focus during the stay in WaterMOO was on the writing of character descriptions. Character descriptions are relatively stable pieces of text, which are written beforehand but can nevertheless at any moment be modified, transformed, erased, or rewritten. These texts represent a certain literariness in the MOO, a type of writing both intermingled with and separated from the ephemeral, everyday-like flow of MOO dialogues. They are the point of departure for online self-presentations, the first impression on others. To me, they are interesting in their capacity as sites where bodies, texts, and computer technologies intersect, in a sense that, for example, literary characters are not. Apart from being textual, they are technological extensions of the physical bodies of typists, intimately part of a networked *social* space quite different from the imaginary worlds of novels.[8]

With the purpose of reaching an understanding of how the notion of 'having' a body is being played out in the midst of such textually networked sociality, a focus on character descriptions alone proved to be too narrow. To carry out 'readings' of these textual bodies would certainly lay the ground for an interesting study in 'MOO literature,' but it would lack the potential to analyze the type of social environments in which these texts are introduced, circulated, and interpreted. Character descriptions are the starting point of MOO activities, as well as of this book—but they are not the endpoint. A character description is like a snapshot, a picture of a textual body, whereas MOO dialogues come closer to the logic of a motion picture. These modes of stillness and movement, of posing and performing, are both important dimensions of online textual embodiment. This insight led to investigations of not only the writing of characters, but also bodily *practices* in the MOO—of how a sense of corporeality was created through typed-in enactments in WaterMOO encounters.

This chapter is primarily a discussion of ethnography in online textual cultures. It is divided into three sections. The first section, "WaterMOO ethnography," opens with an introduction to MOO culture, followed by notes and methodological reflections from the field. The second section, "Textual talk," introduces a theoretical approach to written online cultures. Which framework(s) might be useful when approaching a place where everything from interaction to architecture is created through typed texts? How can the difference between movement within online material and the type of movements that readings of texts always give rise to be accounted for? The third section, "Typed bodies," moves on to a discussion of textual bodies. It formulates a perspective that inverts the more common understanding of the body 'as text,' and instead takes a look at the possibility of viewing the text 'as body.' How do notions of sex and gender translate into discussions of online textual embodiment? What does it mean that bodies online are written?

WaterMOO ethnography

MOO descends from a phenomenon called MUD.[9] MUD (Multi User Dungeon) was originally an offspring of traditional role-playing and text-adventure computer games (where a single player, by typing short commands, could move a character through various settings and solve puzzles). This blend produced virtual worlds in which Internet users could get together and play. The term 'dungeon' was directly transferred from the genre of face-to-face role-playing games known as Dungeons & Dragons to its high-tech version online. Several multiuser games based on Dungeons & Dragons appeared in the late 70s, of which MUD1, written by Roy Trubshaw and Richard Bartle in 1979–1980, is known as the first MUD.[10] As the MUD culture spread and more and more people without previous experience of role-playing began to participate, the terms Multi User Domain and Multi User Dimension were sometimes used instead. The attempt to change the name might well have been an effort to gain respectability and to neutralize some of the gamelike and purely playful associations. These efforts were never particularly successful.

Some MUDs use graphics to visualize places, characters, and movements, but most of them are constructed entirely by plain (written) text. Put simply, there are two basic types of (textual) MUDs: *adventure MUDs* and what are often referred to as *social MUDs*.[11] Adventure MUDs are closely related to the original systems, and people can log on to the computer on which the MUD program is running to kill monsters, solve puzzles, find treasures, and interact with each other and with objects created within the program. The purpose is to gain as many 'experience points' as possible, which are transformed into power. When a player has obtained a certain amount of experience points, he or she can leave the level of the mortals and join an exclusive, immortal crowd with almost unlimited power over the virtual world. In 1988, James Aspnes of Carnegie Mellon University created the first nonadventure-style (social) MUD, called TinyMUD, which in contrast to its predecessors was more egalitarian and democratic.[12] This does not mean that social MUDs are freed from power structures, or that adventure MUDs, with their well-defined rules and hierarchies, are in some sense *anti*-social. In social MUDs, rather than aspiring to master the virtual world, people achieve status by building; they become powerful in the MUD community by mastering the programming language in which the world is built.

Social MUDs provide spaces for a kind of role-playing related to improvisational theater.[13] These MUDs are in some cases inspired by fantasy and science fiction works such as *Star Trek*, Tolkien's *The Lord of the Rings* trilogy, and the work of Terry Pratchett, to mention a few. They can also be more loosely connected to different imaginary themes, constituting more openly structured virtual meeting places. WaterMOO belongs to this latter category of social MUDs, providing its participants with a relatively open social space with the primary purpose of hanging out and socializing. In 1990, at the computer company Xerox PARC in California, Pavel Curtis created the first mother of all MOOs—LambdaMOO.[14] As of today, LambdaMOO is still up and running, as well as being the most densely populated MOO, with about four thousand inhabitants. Even though it seems as if MOO culture reached its peak in popularity during the 90s, there are still hundreds of publicly available MOO sites online, of which a growing number are used for educational purposes. It is interesting to see how text-only systems that belong to early Internet culture—predating the flashy icons and user-friendly colorful interfaces of the World Wide Web—not only survive in the Web era, but maintain a fairly strong position. In what follows, I have tried to use MUD as an umbrella term referring to all text-based virtual worlds of the multiuser variety, whereas MOO is used to point out the specificity of MOO culture.

ARCHITECTURE

A MUD can be described as an ongoing, collaboratively written, online performance. It consists of the writing of scenery, characters, movement, dialogues, and action. But there is also the writing of a wider social landscape and structures, such as public rooms and their objects; help texts; introductory texts for newcomers with guidelines of behavior, programming, and building. Building in MUDs, as Sherry Turkle puts it, is "something of a hybrid between computer programming and writing fiction."[15] A MUD is organized around the metaphor of a three-dimensional space. It gives the participants a hypertext geography of thousands of interlinked rooms that are available to navigate, explore, and inhabit, which gives the user of these systems a feeling of 'being' somewhere. Moreover, every room carries its own description. This is what scrolls down the screen if I take 'Jenny' through the hall on the top floor and up onto the roof of "Hotel California" (in which my virtual office is located in WaterMOO), walk her over the edge of the roof, and further on to one of the most frequented public rooms in the MOO, The Aquatic Dome:

hall
Eighth Floor
As you enter this hallway, you fell slightly disorientated. The walls, withtheir twisty, twirling, black, and white spirals, seem to turn and rotate. Causing you to enter a hypnotic state. A rainbow of colors float past your eyes, flashes of light blinds you. The world is becoming a rainbow blur. You better enter one of the doors in the hall quick, before you pass out! You see a button that when pressed will call the elevator.
Stairs : DOWN to Seventh Floor and UP to Roof

up
Roof
You see a large tar covered roof. As you look around you can see all of WaterMOO. . . You are awed at its vastness. . .
Obvious exits: DOWN to Eighth Floor

jump
You take a deep breath.
You walk over to the ledge and slowly walk off.

The Hotel California
You find yourself on the outside of the Hotel California. The large court-yard is covered with nice, healthy, green grass. A fountain quietly sprays a light mist into the air. The season's flowers adorn the bottom of the walls where the walls meet the ground. The tightly fitted field-stone walls are covered with Ivy and the mortor is covered with that nasty looking green moss. The walls are weather-beaten, but sturdy.
Obvious exits: south to The Water Area, north to Lobby, northwest to The Cantinia Restaurant, and southeast to Dock
You land on the ground with a bounce.
You stagger to your feet.

s
The Water Area
You find yourself on an island covered with redwood trees. Wisps of fog blow through the treetops, and a few stars glimmer overhead in the moonless sky.
* * *

Obvious exits: DOME to THE AQUATIC DOME, PAST to The Past Revisited, IDEAS to Ideas and Issues, BAP to Water Area Places, COMMONS to Water Area Commons, HOTEL to The Hotel California, Dock to WaterDock, and GARDEN to WaterMOO Memorial Gardens

dome
*** Welcome to WaterMOO! ***
OoOo THE AQUATIC DOME oOoO

You find yourself in an immense underwater dome composed of transparent, curved geodesics. All around you the dark water is penetrated by strong light-beams that illuminate a fantastic underwater scene.

The semi-opaque green beams of the WaterMOO City Hall tower over you, the tip of its central pediment touching the upper curve of the Aquatic Dome.

Obvious exits: GUEST to Guest Login Antechamber, NET to NetSpace, OTHER to Other Worlds, WATER to The Water Area, HALL to WaterMOO City Hall, HELPDESK to Help-Desk, MESSAGE to Guest Message Chamber, and Park to WaterMOO Park

The most interesting part of this textual walk is probably the moment after the command <jump> (from the top of the roof) is typed in, which evokes no less than 26 blank lines scrolling over the screen, illustrating how even virtual bodies depend on gravity. But the description of a room is only one part of its creation. For the room to be related to other rooms in the MUD, some formal coding is required. Even though MUD spaces are collectively created and constantly under construction, what remains for those who do not master the art of programming is thus to utilize what others have already built. In other words, even though the group of people who inhabit virtual worlds might be increasingly diverse, the *production* of MUDs is still dominated by a technological elite.

MUD COMMUNICATION

MUD performances are always grounded in a complex interplay between typing and responses/initiations from what could be called the 'MUD program.' This program is a special software that runs on a server to which the participants connect through a client, such as Telnet, and that everybody connected to the MUD interacts with. The following excerpts will be used to show how the most basic commands are used in MUD communication. The 'you' throughout the excerpts is me, or rather 'Jenny.' All typing errors in all online texts throughout this book have been left uncorrected. Writing in MUDs typically keeps a high pace, so there is rarely time to correct mistakes in grammar and spelling. The mode of writing is informal and spontaneous, which shows in the development of unconventional styles among the participants. What at first might look like slips at the keyboard can instead be an intentional move of the writer to create a particular voice. Various strategies of, for example, capitalization and punctuation (or the lack thereof) have particular meanings online. In a culture where everything must be typed into being, a specific way of putting symbols together not only creates a personal style, but sets the limits for whom you can be. All URLs to homepages and names of characters in dialogue examples have been changed to protect the identities of participants. Online names as part of character descriptions have been left unchanged after permission was given from their typists.[17]

> Yazmine politely knocks on the entrance to Her Office. You get the impression that she would like to come in.
> Pink Champagne on Ice
> Yazmine silently emerges from the shadows.
> You say, "hi there. . and welcome"
> Jenny smiles
> Yazmine says, "It's kind of interesting, I think, how some people will have those of themselves real life"
> Yazmine . o O (like you do)

Yazmine says, "And how others have descriptions of fictional characters, like I do"
You say, "that is interesting"
Yazmine says, "Lots of people want to do their studies online, it seems"
Welcome to The Hotel California!
You say, "yes . . . because it's still pretty new, i guess. . ."
Yazmine nods.
Yazmine says, "Too many of them ask you, "Would you fill out this big long questionaire for me?""
Yazmine bahs.

Yazmine one day knocked on the door to my online office. As usual, the song "Hotel California," by the Eagles, was 'playing' in the hotel. Fragments of the lyrics once in a while interrupt the flow of the dialogues (e.g., "Pink Champagne on Ice" and "Welcome to the Hotel California"). The written dialogue in a MUD grows out of the 'spoken' present, since there is no difference in this context between text and gesture, writing and acting. When, for example, the line "Yazmine nods" is produced, this is simultaneously the textual description of the action *and* the actual performance of the action itself. The two most common commands used in MUD conversations are <say> and <emote>. When I type "say hi there. . and welcome," the line "You say, hi there. . and welcome" is produced on my screen. Other persons present (with characters in the same room as I) will instead read "Jenny says, hi there. . and welcome." The program automatically takes care of changes in pronouns. When I instead use <emote> and type "emote smiles," everybody in the room will read "Jenny smiles." The command <say> logically realizes speech, and <emote> precedes nonverbal actions.

It is worth noticing that the MUD program makes a grammatical distinction between <say> and <emote> in relation to the creator of the text, since the command <say> uses 'you,' whereas <emote> uses a third-person construction (in this case 'Jenny'):

You say, "hi there. . and welcome"
Jenny smiles

This linguistic differentiation seems to bring the typist close to the words 'spoken,' whereas a certain distance is introduced in relation to nonverbal gestures. As soon as the textual body moves instead of speaks, a gap between typist and character is created through the use of a distancing third-person narrativization. "You say," on the other hand, makes visible another element in the process of online communication: the machine. This second-person narration is a remnant of the adventure-game genre that literary theorist Espen J. Aarseth

(1997) refers to as a 'voice'; a "narrating go-between that expedites the user's requests and commands and reports the resulting action."[18] The voice from 'within' the MUD program—indeed an intriguing ghost in the machine—turns the software into a subject that not only speaks to you but also actively guides your moves. MUD communication and narration is clearly a productive coming together of both human and mechanical agents, described by Aarseth as "'cyborg literature' [. . .] in need of a criticism and terminology with less clear-cut boundaries between human and machine, creative and automatic, interested and disinterested."[19]

> Welcome to The Hotel California!
> Jenny is a little bit tired of that song. . .
> Yazmine smiles.
> Yazmine asks, "What is it?"
> Yazmine asks, "The song, I mean, why does it do that?"
> You say, "it does that in all of Hotel California—all the time . . . i don't know how to turn it of:)"
> Yazmine says, "ick"
> Yazmine asks, "Want to come to my room?"
> You say, "sure"
> Yazmine grins.
> Yazmine grows sad, and she fades away, headed for her home.
> Yazmine mindspeaks: It's open.
> @join Yazmine
>
> A Cave
> You are standing in a huge cave. A small fire burns near the entrance, safeguarding it from invading creatures, and partially lighting the front portion. Stalagtites hang from the ceiling, reaching down to embrace stalagmites spiralling upwards. This is a living, growing cave—water drips from the surfaces, the flickering light shining across walls of what appears to be pure flowing stone. It is chill, and damp, but there are a few blanket covered boulders dragged into the cave, near the fire, have a seat.
>
> Yazmine is standing here.
> Yazmine looks at you thoughtfully as you arrive.
> Yazmine says, "Have a seat"
> You say, "a little cold . . . but nice:)"
> Yazmine climbs into the web, hanging in the elastic lines.
> You say, "thanks"
> You grab a lowhanging bit of web, and pull yourself up to where the elastic lines are thick, the ropes of the web seeming to hold onto your flesh to help support you in a comfortable embrace.

Yazmine says, "The web helps keep you warm"
You say, "that's good"
Yazmine and Jenny are hanging in the spiderwebs.
mira uses her vampiric powers to mindspeak from Hotel California.
She pages, "Hello. I am to speak to you."
mira enters with the sound of chimes.

Yazmine understands that I am tired of the MOO version of the Eagles, and invites me to @join her in her room. <@join> is a command for movement, which (as in the science fictive type of transportation in *Star Wars*) 'teleports' your character to the destination desired. In this case, I typed "@join Yazmine" and immediately found my Jenny in her room, "A Cave." She further invites me to sit down, which in this particular room, if you type <sit>, produces a line of text describing how you climb into spiderwebs and make yourself comfortable. This text is prewritten and belongs to Yazmine ("Yazmine climbs into the web, hanging in the elastic lines. [. . .] You grab a lowhanging bit of web, and pull yourself up to where the elastic lines are thick, the ropes of the web seeming to hold onto your flesh to help support you in a comfortable embrace"). Moreover, it is possible for characters to <whisper> privately, <page> each other from a distance (as when mira, a third character, toward the end of the excerpt 'mindspeaks' from Hotel California), interact with programmed parts of the scenery, and enter and leave rooms with personal, prewritten messages (such as when "mira enters with the sound of chimes"). Lynn Cherny points out: "In a MOO, all characters are technically objects, just like all scenery and all props. This means that they can be programmed and interacted with in various automated ways."[20] Interaction in a MUD is thus an interweaving of spontaneous typing, prewritten messages, and automatic responses from the MUD program.

@GENDER (FE)MALE

To become an inhabitant in a MUD, you must create a character. This initial act, which Lisa Nakamura calls "the primal scene of cybernetic identity, a postmodern performance of the mirror stage," is a site of online autobiography—a space for the writing of an electronic *persona* that against the background of the written landscape encounters and interacts with others.[21] A character consists of a name, an @gender, and a textual description. The name of the character chosen by the user appears in the interaction whenever the character is actively invoked or interpellated; the @gender attribute is most obviously revealed through the automatic use of the appropriate pronoun of the MUD program; and the user-entered description is available to other participants through the <look> command. When I type "look Raechel," the description of this character scrolls down my screen. The <look> command reaches and exposes textual appearances. Elizabeth Reid points out that the only identity trait that is always "hard coded" in MUDs is 'gender.' Some MUDs in adventure-game style do ask players to choose a racial belonging, "but the choices are more likely to be between Elvish, Dwarvish, and Klingon than between Caucasian, Black, and Asian."[22]

Choosing an @gender is more complicated than it might first appear. In WaterMOO, the following choices are available: male, female, neuter, either, Spivak, splat, plural, egotistical, royal and 2nd. The choice of @gender controls which pronouns the MUD program in referring to the player will use. 'Neuter' uses the pronoun 'it' and stands out as being the 'default' @gender. Every textual body is in the 'raw' a neuter. A neuter might, of course, be created *as* a neuter, but it might as well be a sign of being a body 'under construction.'[23] In contrast to neuter, 'either' is not an altogether gender-neutral pronoun, but evokes both (or any) side of the male/female binary in using 's/he' and 'her/him.' Spivak uses a set of gender-neutral pronouns such as 'e' and 'em.' The following can be found in the help texts on LambdaMOO:

> The spivak pronouns were developed by mathematician Michael Spivak for use in his books. They are the most simplistic of the gender neutral pronouns (others being 'neuter' and 'splat') and can be easily integrated into writing. They should be used in a generic setting where the gender of the person referred to is unknown, such as 'the reader.' They can also be used to describe a specific individual who has chosen not to identify emself with the traditional masculine (male) or feminine (female) gender.

What at first appears to allude to the postcolonial feminist theorist Gayatri Chakravorty Spivak is thus a literary creation made to realize a position 'beyond' gender. According to the help text, the Spivak @gender might be used in situations when the gendered point of textual reference is unclear, but it might also be used to more consciously challenge the Western obsession with the male/female dichotomy. If 'mainstream' cultural theory conventionally (and unreflectingly) uses the pronouns 'he' and 'him' to engender abstract concepts, such as 'the individual,' the answer from feminist theorists has often been to consistently (and consciously) replace 'he' and 'him' with 'she' and 'her.' A different tactic has been used by, for example, Donna Haraway, who instead uses 's/he' and 'her/him,' as a reminder of the ambiguity always involved in these classifications.[24]

@gender 'splat' has a set of pronouns that clearly plays with the possibilities of the keyboard ("*e' and 'h*'), and with the fact that text-based online cultures do not need to be pronounceable. Marie-Laure Ryan, in reference to hypertext fiction, speaks of electronic textuality as a type of text that can only with great difficulty be verbalized (which everybody knows who has been to a 'hypertext reading'!), and thus "could be the advent of a fully non-logocentric mode of expression."[25] The splat @gender can be seen as yet another instance of such non-pronounceable but truly 'typeable' online textuality.

@gender 'plural' ('they,' 'them'), the opportunity to be *more than one*, in a sense mirrors postmodern understandings of the subject as multiple. 'Egotistical' is simply a clearly self-centered @gender using the pronouns 'I' and 'me'; 'royal' plays with the plural form of the royal 'we' ('we' and 'us'); and, finally, '2nd' ('you') can be seen as an online allusion to 'the second sex.' In using the pronoun 'you'—the necessary flipside to the 'I' (without which the 'I' would never exist)—'2nd' is to '1st' in accordance with the same logic as woman is to man.

As an illustration of the relationship between various @genders and their pronouns, this is how the sentence "She knows her way herself" would look together with those @genders that are neither male nor female:

It knows its way itself
S/he knows his/her way him/herself
E knows eir way eirself
e knows h way h*self
They know their way themselves
I know my way myself
We know our way ourselves
You know your way yourself

The @gender command, by producing the effects it names, could fruitfully be compared to what John L. Austin designates a 'performative.' This concept "is derived, of course, from 'perform,' the usual verb with the noun 'action': it indicates that the issuing of the utterance is the performing of an action—it is not normally thought of as just saying something."[26] The notion of 'performativity' has further been remodeled and used by feminist and queer theorists, such as Judith Butler, with the purpose of showing that there is no preexisting, biological sex on which gender acts as a cultural imprint. Rather, sexed and gendered bodies are materialized through a series of reiterated acts in language. Materiality is viewed as the effect of various power relations, which is why bodies would not make sense, would be unthinkable, outside the normative practices that give them their meaning.[27] This argument is particularly fitting in relation to the @gendering of MUD characters, in which the constitution of bodies through repetitive, stylized language acts, literally, takes place. Textual bodies are language made, and as such inhabit a symbolic universe, temporarily released from the physical reality of their typists. At the same time, these online bodies can never be released from the material and cultural conditions in which they are grounded, nor from those discourses of the gendered body that render them meaningful.

CASING THE SCENE

Before choosing my 'case,' I spent some time visiting different virtual destinations. Before formally joining a MOO through the creation of a character, it is possible to take on a guest character. Guests, like any temporary visitor, are not considered full members of the MOO world. In most MOOs, the names of guests are randomly picked from a standard pool of guest names. In LambdaMOO most guests are assigned the name of a color. When logging on as a guest you might find yourself stuck with the name "Periwinkle_Guest," whether you like it or not. WaterMOO provides a certain amount of freedom in the creation of guest characters, like allowing you to choose a name, set an @gender, and write a description. The name is, nevertheless, followed by the word "guest." This gives all guests a common trait, which marks their difference and relative lack of personality compared with regular characters. Newcomers, called 'newbies' in online jargon, often start as guests to explore the world and learn some basic commands for communication and movement. It is therefore not surprising that guests are viewed not only as outsiders by the inhabitants, but also as beginners.

Being a guest is, at the same time, not only a matter of being seen as a newbie. People who are primarily interested in the communicative dimension in a MOO, and less interested in building and writing descriptions, may never leave the world of guests. Being a guest might have its advantages, especially for a researcher in the initial stage of research. Guests are pretty discrete. Guests are allowed to ask questions, even very stupid ones. Guests are allowed to hang around, observe things, listen and learn. It is true that the Internet "does greatly facilitate 'casing the scene' prior to creating a strategy for entering into active participation. It is much easier to lurk on the Internet in most cases than to unobtrusively hang out in an Amazon village."[28] Before choosing the field for my research, I visited about 50 different MOOs to get an idea of their size, activity, and atmosphere. I was looking for a world big enough to have many active characters, since I wanted a lot of character descriptions and logs of conversations as a foundational material for my project. This excluded many small worlds where there were never more than five characters connected at the same time. On the other hand, I was looking for a world small enough for me to be able to meet the same character more than once, in order to create relationships and a name as a researcher. I was also trying to find a place with a friendly feeling, since I was going to spend a considerable amount of time there.

To have the option to pick a nice place, as opposed to picking a place out of necessity, might sound like an ethnographer's dream. In *The Professional Stranger*, Michael Agar points out how the choice of area in ethnographic research is most often limited by factors outside the control of the researcher, such as problems with funding, refusals from groups in areas of interest, job opportunities in other areas, etc. Even though it might be difficult to get access to certain online communities, the online ethnographer is obviously not limited geographically. In my case, there was another type of limitation that engaged my attention, namely *themes*. As discussed earlier, some MOOs are inspired by fantasy and science fiction works, in which the creation of characters tends to be constructed along the lines of these themes. If my research interests had been more oriented toward fandom, or online re-creations of very specific texts and genres (like the novel *Snow Crash* by Neal Stephenson, *Star Trek*, or *Winnie the Pooh*), I would have picked one of these specialized worlds. But since I am more interested in what people make of themselves and each other in less predictable online spaces, this did not seem like the way to go. I wanted to explore cultural formations as lightly restricted as possible by the ideas of the founders and initial programmers/writers.

After having considered size and level of activity, as well as atmosphere and themes, I finally chose WaterMOO as my field. Ironically, this MOO is a text-based version of the San Francisco Bay Area. By the time I made my choice, I happened to physically live and work in the Bay Area. WaterMOO is a medium-sized MOO, with a population of about 1500, of whom less than 100 are active participants.[29] My first impression of WaterMOO was that it was a warm, friendly place with many helpful, interested, and curious inhabitants. It was like coming to one of those places where you, even as a newcomer, immediately feel at home. WaterMOO originally evolved around the themes "The Meanings of Water" and "The Humanities of the San Francisco Bay Area," which characterize some of the open, public areas on the level of architecture (e.g., room descriptions, object descriptions, etc.). In a help text in the MOO, the following is said on themes:

> There are two major themes that make WaterMOO unique among the all-text virtual realities on the NET:
>   1) The Humanities of the San Francisco Bay Area and
>   2) The Meanings of Water.
> These are available to all who want to explore their uses, and the janitors of WaterMOO urge you to use them. But those who feel called to other frontiers are also welcome to help build WaterMOO.
> WaterMOO has a one-word code of ethics: RESPECT
> As long as characters respect each others' feelings, WaterMOO is a wide-open textual terrain for the imagination.

The use of themes is in this sense not thought of as a way to gather a homogeneous crowd around a narrow, well-defined interest. It rather seems to be a way for those who are responsible for the MOO to express a wish to create a relatively coherent landscape. In spite of these themes, following the key word 'respect' of the San Francisco ethos, people seem to be able to build and create almost anything they want.

ON THE THRESHOLD

Before discussing how I 'gained entrance' to the MOO, I would like to give a concrete example of character creation. Even if inhabitants of online worlds are physically invisible to one another, they are not prevented from reinscribing a sense of physicality into their descriptions. This process of 'body-building' is in a way institutionalized in MOOs through the necessity to create a character. This is not to say that participants in any way are forced to inscribe bodies into their descriptions, but it does suggest that the possibility to do so is built into the system itself. The creation of a character is the first necessary move, even for the online ethnographer, before entering the field. John Suler reflects on his online self-as-researcher in the following way:

> After much internal debate, I settled on the name 'AsKi'. While I could have used my real name, I preferred to join the spirit and the fun of an online world by creating a new name that was more interesting than 'John' and/or 'Suler'—and, in fact, said a bit more about me than my real labels. [. . .] Although I chose a pseudonym and symbolic pictures to represent my identity, I must emphasize that I was always honest about who I was. As best as I can recall, I don't think I ever dissembled or avoided any member's inquiry into who or what I am.[30]

Suler further explains how "AsKi," among other things "sounds like ASCII (American Standard Code for Information Interchange), the standard computer character set for data communication. Hence 'AsKi' is a bit of a computer geek's joke."[31] Even though Jenny and/or Sundén is hardly very exciting, especially if you are allowed to combine keyboard symbols in any way you want, I choose to keep my real name in my work online. Suler affirms that choosing another name did not prevent him from being honest about who he was, and points out how creating a new name is part of the online culture. Certainly, people who keep their real names in online worlds are exceptions. On the other hand, people who explore these spaces for academic purposes are also in the minority. Suler further argues that it was important to him not only to be honest about his role as a researcher, but also to let people know that he was one of them. His character became an important means to make this process easier.

It is, of course, very important for an ethnographer to be accepted in the culture that is being studied, but it is unclear whether this acceptance is easier to gain under a name that clearly flirts with subcultural elements. To me, the main concern was not to be accepted as fast as possible, but rather, for ethical reasons, to be as honest as possible. The texts I am interested in might be experienced as personal. It is therefore important that the inhabitants of WaterMOO have confidence in me. The way I created this kind of trustful relationship was through participation in their everyday life online, and by being as open as possible about who I was and what I was doing. Since I was entering the field as a researcher to ask other participants for favors, I wanted to hide as little as possible.

However, when I was standing on the threshold to WaterMOO, ready to enter the field, I thought to myself that it would have been easier to create a character very different from my 'offline' self. Because, how do you textualize yourself? In contrast to many other texts in these spaces, I wanted my description not to deviate too much from the 'truth.' The question is how you do this, especially if you are a person who does not believe in this so-called truth in the first place. How on earth can I even start to write those strings of text that are supposed to mediate something of me, physically and mentally? Exactly what would be an efficient textual strategy in encounters with prospective informants? Who am I, anyway?

>   look me
>   Jenny a spirit
>   You see a rather Scandinavian looking woman. She is wearing laced boots, a pair of black Levi's and a dark blue woolen sweater. She has been cruising the Net for a while, and has over time developed a strong interest for virtual bodies rising from the point where flesh meets text in an ongoing, electronic dance . . . While you are looking at her, she looks back at you, curiously, piercing, in a way that makes her look like a very sensitive but at the same time strong and intelligent human being.
>   Jenny's time is Mon Dec 21 15:14:59 1998
>   Jenny appears awake and alert.
>   Carrying:
>   Cup of Cappuccino

These strings of text composed the first impression I gave people throughout the fieldwork. The first line, "Jenny a spirit," occupies the space in character descriptions where a character's belonging to a certain 'player class' becomes visible. Jenny belongs to the "Spirits of WaterMOO," which basically indicates that she can use certain features that are available to this particular group of players (like, for example, having various fairly sophisticated message systems). Other common player classes are "Cybermage Player Class," "Metaplayer," and "Vampires of Venice." During my stay in WaterMOO, I noticed that most WaterMOOers did not really care about which player class they belonged to.

To mention that I am "rather Scandinavian looking" is aimed to introduce a national background still not very common in these spaces, which at the same time can serve as an explanation of mistakes in spelling and grammar that once in a while slip into my typing. It might also be a way to give people something unusual to remember me for ("oh, yeah, NOW I remember . . . you are that *Swedish* girl doing research in here:)"). "She is wearing laced boots, a pair of black Levi's and a dark blue woolen sweater" is further taken from my own wardrobe. It is not so much the details in themselves in this sentence I find important, but rather the sense of simplicity and functionality they might give. I am there to let other inhabitants shine, while remaining somewhat in the background myself.

"She has been cruising the Net for a while, and has over time developed a strong interest for virtual bodies rising from the point where flesh meets text in an ongoing, electronic dance. . ." is meant to say something about the background for my participation, without immediately indicating its coinciding with my research interest. Early on I made the choice to not write about my research in my description. To write about my research in this text would have felt like having "I AM A RESEARCHER" written across my forehead while entering the field, before even having a chance to give this information in a more personal and nuanced way. To exclude a clear description of my research from my text had nothing to do with an attempt to withhold this information from anybody. In fact, after beginning to tell people about my project, it did not take long until I was known among them as a researcher.

"While you are looking at her, she looks back at you, curiously, piercing, in a way that makes her look like a very sensitive but at the same time strong and intelligent human being" is an attempt to assign my character some more personal qualities, a curious outlook on the world I am visiting and the people I am meeting. "Jenny's time is. . ." further indicates time and date. "Jenny appears awake and alert" is a preprogrammed stanza that tells other participants that I am currently connected and, hopefully, at my computer. The only thing I carry with me in this online world is a virtual Cup of Cappuccino, which a friend (guilty of the misspelling!) gave me to keep me awake during long sessions in cyberspace. If I, for example, type <look cup>, this text appears on my screen:

> This glass mug is filled with freshly made cappuchino- quite the relaxant after a hard day . . . the drink is topped with a liberal amount of whipped cream, brown sugar, cinnamon, and chocolate slivers. Quite appetizing, don't you think?

If I further type <drink cup>, the following textual performance, slowly, line by line, appears in front of me and everyone else (with the difference that for them the "you" is replaced by "Jenny") who in this moment is present in the same room.

> You see the deliciously tasty cup of freshly made cappuchino, with its mounds of whipped cream and delicate little chocolate slivers, and your mouth waters for a sip.
>
> You tip the warm mug of cappuchino to your lips.
>
> A bit of the whipped cream sticks to your nose as the soothing drink slides down your throat.
>
> You take a another sip of the delicious cappuchino.
>
> You take a another sip of the delicious cappuchino.
>
> You take a another sip of the delicious cappuchino.
>
> You reach the bottom of your cup of cappuchino, slurping the last little bit of chocolate sauce stuck to the bottom of the cup.

This clearly shows how interaction in a MOO is a matter of encounters not only between characters (and typists), but also between characters and objects, such as this cup. But, as will become clear, the border between human subjects and nonhuman objects is not always as clear-cut. Cyber-subjects are always partly human and partly machine (always human-created), which is why it sometimes might be hard to tell whether someone or something is 'run' by a human typist or if it is run by a computer program. The opportunity of creating humanlike characters that are no longer maneuvered by humans not only questions the border between human and machine, but sheds light on the age-old question of what it means to be human.

ENTERING THE FIELD

At this point, there are no clear, unified guidelines for online fieldwork. Nevertheless, there seems to be a violation of accepted Net courtesy to conduct research in MUDs without asking the people who are responsible for these worlds for permission. These people are called wizards.[32] After creating my character, I contacted one of WaterMOO's wizards, let us call her Fanny, to present my project and myself. I paged her and she invited me immediately to @join her in her room. She asked me to post a message to *wiz in which I presented my purposes and research strategies, since she wanted to discuss my case with the whole group of wizards.[33] I MOOmailed *wiz right away. One week passed by. Nothing. Then, I met Fanny online again and wondered what had happened to my request. She promised to have an answer for me in a few days. This didn't happen. After more than a week, I contacted her once again. At this point, she already had the answer ready for me, and told me I could start my project right away.

Persons with control over access to key resources, and sometimes even to the whole field, are in ethnographic writing called *gatekeepers*:

> Whether or not they grant entry to the setting, gatekeepers will generally, and understandably, be concerned as to the picture of the organization that the ethnographer will paint, and they will have practical interests in seeing themselves and their colleagues presented in a favorable light. At least, they will wish to safeguard what they perceive as their legitimate interests. Gatekeepers may therefore attempt to exercise some degree of surveillance and control [. . .] by shepherding the fieldworker in one direction or another.[34]

In my introductory contact with Fanny, she was not exactly unfriendly, but not particularly open and supporting either. Throughout our conversations, she was always very brief and serious. Not a single keystroke beyond the strictly professional. Repeatedly, she failed to return my requests, and it is unclear whether it was due to forgetfulness or unwillingness to actually let me start working. On the other hand, she never tried to lead me in a particular direction by suggesting changes of my approach; neither did she seem to worry about which image of the MOO I would give in my text. Overall, I experienced the whole process of gaining entry to the field as quite easy, even though it turned out to be rather slow. On further consideration, it is not surprising that my contact with Fanny was not as warm and personal as my contact with other inhabitants of the MOO. She had a completely different responsibility for the world compared with them, and she was literally holding the key to my project in her hand. By not getting back to me according to our agreements, it was quite clear that answering my request did not have top priority.

The following excerpt shows what actually happened when I entered the field:

> Jenny wonders if people in here would mind being part of her doctoral thesis. . .
> Pumpkin [to Motherfucker]: "you have to remember my wshort term memory loss!"
> Jenny smiles at Motherfucker
> Sugar appears suddenly out of nowhere.
> Knight_ingale materializes out of thin air.
> Motherfucker asks you, "is that psycholoanaklyssis?"

Motherfucker asks Pumpkin, "when did that happen girl?"
Pyrex casts his eyes down as Wolfgang passes.
He bows low, nearly sweeping the ground with his hand.
He keeps his eyes down until Wolfgang has passed.
Pumpkin [to Jenny]: "you'll get a good cross section of the freaks."
Motherfucker laughs at Pumpkin.
Jenny chuckles
Jenny [to Motherfucker]: "not really, more like communication studies"
Motherfucker. o O (true enough!)
Narrato has arrived
Jenny laughs
MegaByte [Guest] says, "Heloo . . . everyone."
Motherfucker asks you, "communication . . . what in communication?"
Wolfgang (feeding the horse) waves.
Narrato (connectus interruptus) waves.
Wolfgang says, "ay up, groovers"

Entering in the midst of a conversation (as one always does on MUDs), some utterances refer to things that happened earlier in the conversation ("you have to remember my wshort term memory loss!" [. . .] "when did that happen girl?"). Entrances ("Sugar appears suddenly out of nowhere") and greetings ("Narrato (connectus interruptus) waves") scatter sentences being 'spoken,' and speech, paradoxically, intermingles with the explicitly 'unspoken' (as in "Motherfucker. o O (true enough!)," where Motherfucker's 'thoughts' are marked with bubbles, like in a cartoon). When asking if people would mind being part of my doctoral thesis, Motherfucker asks: "is that psycholoanaklyssis?", harmlessly making fun of academic studies, or at least in an amusing way commenting on how hard it can be to spell things like 'psychoanalysis.' Pumpkin fills in: "you'll get a good cross section of the freaks," which Motherfucker finds funny ("Motherfucker laughs at Pumpkin").

RETHINKING ETHICS

Even if there is an ongoing discussion among scholars about how to remodel ethnographic concepts for online use in general, and how to treat ethical issues in particular, there is not yet any clear consensus. Nevertheless, in most online research, names as well as pseudonyms of informants have been changed, to protect the privacy of the participants. This effort to hide not only real names, but also user names, nicknames, locations in the Net, etc., reveals a respect for the realness of imaginary cyberspaces.[35] Even though identities are masked, it often remains unclear whether permission from the typists was given when logs of conversations are published for academic purposes. This confusion might be due to a difference in opinion regarding the status of online texts. For example, postings to Usenet newsgroups are most often regarded as public material, since Usenet is a public medium.[36] A posting to a newsgroup has a potential audience of millions of people, and even if the content can be very personal, these postings can hardly be regarded as private:

> Conversation on publicly accessible IRC channels or messages posted on newsgroups are not equivalent to private letters (while private, one-to-one e-mail messages of course are); they are instead public acts deliberately intended for public consumption. This doesn't mean that they can be used without restrictions, but simply that it shouldn't be necessary to take any more precautions than those usually adopted in the study of everyday life.[37]

This distinction between, on one hand, public and private material in reference to publicly accessible online conversations and, on the other, private e-mail conversations seems reasonable. The question is how this distinction applies to research on MUDs. Does a MUD consist of public or private spaces? Can MUD conversations be compared to the exchange in newsgroups, or do they actually come closer to private e-mail conversations? What about descriptions of rooms, characters, objects, etc.? Are they part of the landscape, or are they closely linked to the identities of participants?

A MUD incorporates both public and private spaces. There are public rooms open to all participants, but also private rooms more or less viewed as homes. Nevertheless, there are several differences between public spaces in MUDs and the type of space that newsgroups occupy. While reading postings to a newsgroup, nobody will know that you are there until you contribute to the discussion with your own posting. This passive participation and anonymous investigation of online material is called 'lurking,' and is without doubt the most common activity on the Web. In a MUD, lurking is not an option. First of all, it is not possible to enter a MUD without a character. The moment you enter a room, this will, immediately, become visible for everyone who is present in the room (e.g., "Jenny suddenly arrives in an unmistakable veil of curiosity. . ."). Furthermore, it might be possible to stay quiet for a while and just 'listen,' but sooner or later someone will break the silence by talking to you. MUDs in general, and MOOs in particular, are highly social, online spaces, in which the researcher has to participate in order to understand what these worlds are all about.

Conversations in public rooms in MUDs are open to everyone who is part of the community and who is present in that moment, but they are far from being as open as newsgroup postings. The expectations surrounding a MUD conversation are very different from expectations in newsgroups. Postings to newsgroups could be compared to letters to the editor, or scribbles on the walls in public bathrooms, where messages are not only likely but *meant* to be read by a lot of people. Dialogues in MUDs are not meant to be spread all over the Net, but are there to be experienced by the participants themselves. It might be helpful to make a distinction between *places* and *conversations*, since private conversations can take place in public places. Even though MUDs are much more accessible than private e-mail for an outsider, this does not mean that MUD inhabitants regard their words and actions as public property. In this regard, MUDs come close to the notion of a private club, in which you need a membership to enter, and where the same is true for the researcher. With respect to the specific atmosphere in MUDs, and to the inhabitants' perceptions and feelings for these spaces, it should be obvious that a researcher always has to ask the participants for permission before quoting any recorded conversations. Their 'real' as well as online identities should, moreover, always be masked in relation to quotes or analyses of recorded material, to protect their privacy. As mentioned previously, when I am quoting recorded conversations or events, I always change the names of the characters involved.

The question is whether character descriptions should be treated in the same discreet, cautious manner. In terms of availability, they are accessible at any time, no matter whether the character is actively connected. This could indicate that these texts, within the community itself, are regarded differently compared with direct dialogues between participants. Earlier, I emphasized how the participants might view character descriptions as very personal, and how the researcher for this reason should be very careful. What seems to be a stronger notion among WaterMOOers is that these descriptions are written with one and only one purpose, to be 'looked at' and read. This is not surprising in the type of voyeuristic environment a MUD provides, where activities such as looking at and being seen are central.[38] I noticed, for example, how almost all of the characters I met for the first time read my description and gave me comments. In this respect, to ask for a copy of a description is almost a rhetorical question, and the typist, rather than experiencing the request as a threat, takes it as a compliment. The act of asking for a description could be compared to taking pictures of people. Even though most WaterMOOers do not mind having their (textual) pictures taken by me, some of them might. Or, they might want to ask me questions regarding the purpose of the project, etc. Technically, it would be possible to collect these texts in a hidden manner, but with respect for individual wishes, I always asked for permission before copying any texts. As with the laws of copyright, the typist is the owner of the text s/he has written and has to be asked for permission.

On the other hand, I did not change any names of characters when quoting their descriptions, since the name is a significant part of the description. With the purpose of doing readings of these texts, a change of names could change the whole meaning of a text. By lending me their descriptions, the participants are at the same time lending me their names, as part of their texts. For the same reason, I did not change the names of characters when quoting their prewritten messages (such as entrance messages and page messages) in instances when these are read as isolated fragments. Similar to a character description, these prewritten lines of text are frequently obvious extensions of the character's name in terms of clever puns, something that would be lost in a name change. I am also aware of the fact that I am not making the site of my research fully anonymous (in having an interest in how America in general, and the Bay Area in particular, is constructed in the MOO). Nonetheless, it is important to make clear that these decisions are taken against the background of the nature of this particular project. It is very different to focus on the textual dimension of online embodiment, compared with, for example, the psychological and social dimensions of these characters' online lives. It is not the complexities and details of relationships, feelings, fears, hopes, dreams, and desires I intend to spread over the Net, but textual appearances of online characters, written to be seen and, maybe, admired.[39] And if the inhabitants of WaterMOO who participate in this book were to make these ethical decisions for me, they probably would have preferred full disclosure, as opposed to my own more cautious approach. Here are some reactions from them to the question of whether I could keep a copy of their character descriptions for my work:

Alex pages, "oooh. .do I win a prize? :)"

Andy smiles as he pages . . .
He pages, "and if I do, does my name come before yours in your thesis title? ;)"

(from Casa) Fata mindspeaks, "No, I don't mind at all . . . in fact, your request is quite flattering! ;-)

(from The Place) Voodoo mindspeaks, "Help yourself. It's public."

(from My Penthouse) Piggy (oui) mindspeaks, "sure . . . no problem"
(From My Penthouse) Piggy shakes your hand

Scary_Monster (.) asks you, "You want to do me?"
Scary_Monster (.) says to you, "I feel so . . . so special. . . ."

(from Private Passenger Car) Trainmaster mindspeaks, "Go right ahead and use it. At last I'll be in print. :)"

Only two participants refused me access to their texts, and neither of them gave me any elaborate answers when I asked them why. They simply did not want to be part of my work, which I, of course, respected. However, the usual response was obviously very different. I experienced a great openness; a willingness to share texts and experiences that initially surprised me. On second thought, it is not particularly surprising within a culture where there exists a widespread belief in the right of everybody to access information. This part of online philosophy ("information wants to be free"), in combination with the type of texts I was asking for (created to be looked at), might explain why it was extremely easy to collect material. The participants experienced my request as rather flattering and saw their chance to enter a new arena in which to be seen: in a PhD thesis! If their character descriptions are primarily written to be looked at and appreciated within the MOO world, they were quite thrilled about the idea of performing in yet another textual venue and thus reaching a potentially bigger (and, not least, different) audience. "Will we be famous now?" one of the participants whispered to me. "If I'm doing a good job, you might," I answered.

IN THE FIELD

Ethnographic work can never be as linear and neatly organized as some methodological reports suggest. In the textbook version, fieldwork is a well-defined period of data collection, framed by the rituals of 'entering' and 'leaving' the field, followed by analysis of data and the writing of a final report. In reality, an ethnographic process is rather circular since certain aspects tend to recur, but at the same time evolve as the meaning of these aspects changes in the light of new experiences. Online ethnography is not an exception. Maybe even the movement between narrow participation and more distant contemplation, where texts and events make sense retrospectively, appears particularly clear in the study of online cultures. In my MOO office, I have a (textual) answering machine where WaterMOOers might leave messages for me while I am gone. By 'listening' to these, the sense of actually entering the place, catching up with what has happened and continuing my work there is very tangible. At the same time, the border between 'offline' deskwork and the online field is very easy to cross, the transfer hardly recognizable, since no actual physical displacement is involved.

It is in this very borderland, between the material and the textual, that I accomplished my fieldwork. I have spent two years in the MOO, starting in spring 1998. Through Jenny, I entered, gained permission to conduct the study, and set up my office. A two-year online fieldwork cannot be compared to an equal amount of time in an 'offline' setting (where the ethnographer lives with the people s/he studies 24 hours a day). For one thing, WaterMOOers do not live in WaterMOO 24 hours a day. This venue is definitely part of their lives time-wise, but it is very rarely the most significant part. On the other hand, WaterMOO is, indeed, moving and breathing day and night, following the rhythm of people waking up and going to sleep in different time zones. I had two 'points of connecting' during fieldwork: Berkeley, California, USA, and Stockholm, Sweden, distributed according to the following periods:

Berkeley: April 1998–December 1999
Stockholm: January 1999–May 1999
Berkeley: June 1999–November 1999
Stockholm: December 1999–April 2000

This geographical variety gave me the possibility to experience WaterMOO around the clock. I had mainly two strategies for participation: 'going with the flow' and, conversely, 'going against the tide.' Going with the flow was the dominating strategy, which involved logging on when most people logged on and staying on as long as most of them did. This caught the activities during 'rush hour' (typically from early afternoon to sometime in the evening for the Berkeley connection, and late night for the Stockholm connection). To go against the tide meant being on during those hours when most people were not (morning hours in Berkeley and about any time during the day connecting from Stockholm).[40]

As mentioned earlier, my first step was to collect character descriptions. I did not choose these texts in any particular way, but asked people who were connected for permission to copy their texts. I keep copies of 184 character descriptions, of which 108 are male, 63 are female, and 13 'other.' This @gender division roughly corresponds to the division in the MOO among active characters, in which male characters are in the great majority, whereas characters @gendered as something other than male or female are very rare. In an attempt to disrupt the stability of the material body as a 'true' starting point for its textual refiguration in virtual space, I have no knowledge of how these textual bodies correspond to the bodies of their typists. I am not saying that people, myself included, are not curious about who the person is behind a certain text; I am only suggesting that textual bodies in their own universe are important. It is to insist on the realness of imagined worlds for those involved, to give these texts a certain independency, a type of freedom I intend to bring into my own readings; and it is to base my own readings on a fundamental online condition: the state of not knowing who the person is 'behind' the text.

In this initial phase of collecting character descriptions, I also kept many logs of interactions in the MOO. These logs proved to be extremely valuable, since they provided me with excerpts of bodies 'in motion' once I decided to widen my focus. It was fairly easy to, retrospectively, get in touch with characters involved in those conversations I wanted to use to get their consent. When I let them know that their names would be changed when appearing in these excerpts, nobody seemed to hesitate to give me permission to use their words. During fieldwork, it became clear that the participants' expectations about my study often differed from my own ideas and perspectives. Many of them spontaneously started to tell me about who they 'really' were, and whether their characters coincided with the way they thought about themselves or not. They took for granted that my intention was to find out how they experienced their online counterparts, and if they were lying or telling the truth. When I told them that I was rather interested in the kind of 'truth' these texts constitute in themselves in their online context, some of them seemed confused. When I went on describing my study as a study in online culture and literature, where I first and foremost was interested in them as inhabitants and authors, they understood me much better. They even seemed to like my idea a lot.

On the other hand, the notion of 'truthfulness,' no matter how critically approached, is of course an intricate issue. When WaterMOOers appear to start telling me who they 'really' are, this might well be part of a sophisticated performance of deceit. This kind of 'double' reflexivity seems to be missing in a lot of online ethnography. Even if researchers are aware of how participants in online venues might be playing with strategies of concealment against each other, they sometimes forget that they are themselves part of the same game. Once this thought enters my mind, it suddenly gets very hard to *not* think of everything that happens in WaterMOO, every time Jenny logs on, as an online serial where she is merely given the illusion of participation (while she is, in fact, the target of an elaborate plot!). With the slightest inclination for conspiracy theories, online fieldwork easily becomes the ultimate site of paranoia.

Textual talk

One difficulty in collecting various materials in a text-based online culture is that these texts look exactly like transparent representations of this culture. Since almost everything that happens in a particular moment is visible on the screen, and since there is nothing but text to build this moment with, it might seem as if a recording of this moment actually captures a piece of this culture in the most faithful way possible. To believe this is to claim the autonomy of data that supposedly interprets itself. In his online article "Getting the Seats of Your Pants Dirty: Strategies for Ethnographic Research on Virtual Communities," Luciano Paccagnella argues that "it is not safe to think of these data as some sort of objective reality frozen by the computer. Archived messages and logs are representations of the online phenomena as perceived by participants."[41] It is important to point out that these texts will remain meaningless if not interpreted and, thereby, transferred to another textual level. Ted Friedman further states that 'interactive software' (computer games, hypertext, etc.) disrupts the very categories of author, reader, and text. The question is, how can we conceptualize textual interactions where "every response provokes instantaneous changes in the text itself, leading to a new response and so on?"[42] Even though we can capture online discourses by saving texts in neat text files for our analysis, "how do we ascertain the interpretive moment in electronic discourse, particularly as it engages both reading and writing?"[43]

Online dialogues take place in a rarely acknowledged borderland between talk and text, where the ephemerality of talk is tied down by the textual practices of inscription. Most researchers have looked at MUD practices from the perspective of social interaction.[44] Elizabeth Reid points out:

> Interaction on a MUD is, after all, interactive, synchronous and ephemeral. Although sessions may be recorded using computer programs designed for this purpose, MUD interaction is not enacted to be read but to be experienced. As would spoken interaction, virtual interaction loses meaning when transposed to a computer file and reread. The pauses, breaks, disjunctions, speed and timing of virtual conversations are lost in such transposition, and such factors are a crucial signifier of meaning and context.[45]

The point that online interactions are there to be experienced, and not read or reread, needs some examination. As with spoken dialogues, online conversations exist in the moment when they develop, and then they dissolve. They do not take place with the *primary* purpose of being recorded, but of being performed and interpreted in the here and now. This might seem like a superfluous statement, but the fact that online dialogues look exactly like texts, even in the very act of 'speaking,' can lead to the conclusion that they are very similar to printed texts and therefore can be analyzed the same way. To believe this would be to seriously disregard the unique dynamics that constitute online textuality.

On the other hand, 'readings' of online sessions are not only a possibility, but a necessity to realize an analytical perspective. Aarseth states that "life in the MUD is literary, relying on purely textual strategies,"[46] and he draws attention to the fact that almost no research on MUD as literary phenomenon has yet been done. In a critique of Reid, Aarseth points out that the argument about how "virtual interaction loses meaning when transposed to a computer file," and how "the pauses, breaks, disjunctions, speed and timing of virtual conversations are lost in such transposition," parallels the ancient romanticization of presence and of the spoken word as the primary carrier of meaning.[47] Aarseth further argues that this elevation of contemporaneity is particularly out of place in discussions of MUDs, since MUD dialogues are brilliant examples of how much meaning written words can embrace. In regarding MUDs as texts, Aarseth compares MUD communication to plays:

> Like the plays of Shakespeare (and in some ways quite unlike them), MUD sessions are texts. They are to be experienced subjectively and can provide meaning without the absolute need for staging, although it usually helps. They may not be intended 'to be read as an artefact' (neither was Shakespeare's plays), but they certainly are intended to be read. This makes them textual, and the unique aspects of MUD communication make MUD relevant and interesting and well worth comparing to other types of text.[48]

I agree with Aarseth in his argument that MUD sessions, no matter how fluid, can be fruitfully regarded as texts, composed by written words, based entirely on the activity of reading and writing. If MUD practices are regarded as texts, the detour of mediation in all communication becomes particularly clear.[49] A literary perspective puts forth that online worlds are not pale copies of a fully fleshed physical reality, but imaginative universes in their own right. While relying on textual strategies of reading and writing, MUD could fruitfully be incorporated into discussions of other types of texts, instead of being compared with face-to-face encounters and constantly disparaged as less rich. Moreover, in agreeing with Reid that MUD sessions might not be intended "to be read as an artefact," Aarseth seems to safeguard his view on MUD as literature from an unnecessarily static approach. Even if MUD practices are regarded as texts, a flexible understanding of texts and readings is important so as not to lose sight of the specificity of online textuality.

But instead of regarding MUD conversations as either text *or* talk, I would like to propose an alternative path, within the domain of what I call *textual talk*—where 'textual' is meant to evoke a break in the illusion of immediate presence and 'talk' works as a reminder of the fact that these textual online worlds are social spaces. In conversation analysis, there has been a growing discussion of texts as situated productions and receptions, as an attempt to view texts as a place for dialogues, existing both within a single text ('fictional dialogues') and between texts (intertextuality).[50] Alec McHoul takes this argument one step further:

> Ironically, while ethnomethodology and conversation analysis rely upon a world in which 'actual people' interact, a theory of what is to count as 'actual' is never stated—it remains an unexplicated commonsense resource. Somehow, we are

expected to know—and we are expected to know that the category 'naturally' excludes the fictional. [. . .] In a parallel way we could say, after Derrida, that fictional talk is also an equally 'actual' happening insofar as it constitutes a trace of a culture's iteration machinery; that, in fact, 'the actual' is no longer a defensible category.[51]

Following this line of thought, a MUD appears to be an ideal site for a conversation analysis with the ambition to challenge any clear division between the language of 'artifice' and that of 'real life,' as well as that between the written and the spoken word. The inhabitants of WaterMOO would never agree that they are not in a crucial sense meeting actual people in this online world, no matter if face-to-face is replaced with face-to-screen, speaking and listening with writing and reading, and physical touch with textual imagination. At the same time, the inherent instability of the category 'actual' or 'real' is clearly expressed in online textual talk, since these typed-in enactments constantly move between a mode of everyday socializing and a type of fiction writing (even if this online fiction might be alluringly realistic. . .). This floating distinction between world and text has, as will become clear, the most interesting consequences for the typing of online bodies.

FROZEN MOMENTS

To introduce the notion of 'textual talk' is also an attempt to bring to attention the ephemeral dimension of online textuality—but, hopefully, without romanticizing the idea of 'fluidity.' When (printed) words are digitalized, their physical object bodies are transformed into changeable entities, open to what Hayles calls 'mutation.' Hayles defines mutation on several different levels, one of which is described as "what happens to the body of the text as it moves from print to computer."[52] Even if a character description is a relatively stable piece of writing compared with the volatility of MUD dialogues, this text might at any moment be modified, corrected, or rewritten. It never has to present a final version. I am not suggesting that the *meanings* of texts are any more fixated in print compared with a digital format, since interpretations of texts always make texts move, metaphorically. But I do suggest that when online texts are analyzed, the ways in which they are more easily altered than they can be in print must be seen as an intrinsic part of their meanings. The question is how this alterability can be accounted for, methodologically as well as analytically.

Once a concept like textual fluidity is introduced, sensitivity to different *degrees* of fluidity, as well as degrees of fixation, is needed. Perhaps the issue at stake is not so much one of fluidity per se, or even mutation, as it is of *supplementarity*. Even though texts in a MUD are moving, in the sense that they are never finished, in every step of typed-in appearances and movements there is fixation, breaking the flow, in which the text is liberated from the typist. Once formulated and put to use, they cannot be edited while being read by someone else. As with spoken utterances, once enunciated they cannot be made undone. This fixation of the said and done, in the moment of saying and doing, in a similar way sets the limit for the alterability of MUD textuality. These frozen moments thus form an important part of how online bodies are performed and communicated among participants. Along the lines of Derrida's notion of *supplement*, all discourses (written or spoken) are potentially unfinished, and therefore open.[53] What is already written or said cannot be altered, but can always be supplemented with new texts/utterances. Following Derrida, to speak of texts as *supplementary* could evidently be applicable to texts of any kind, but my point here is that online texts are particularly open to such additions. Texts are never finished, but constantly fixated—and liberated. This leads to a complex relation between movement and fixation, where texts in a MUD are clearly works 'in the making,' but also incessantly fixated over series of screen images, freezing them in particular performances.

In recording and analyzing these frozen moments of bodily performances in the MOO, the question is still how to take responsibility for those multiple textual journeys that online ethnography gives rise to. From within the world of WaterMOO, bits and pieces of textual bodies are captured and transported to a log file on the hard disk, then in turn migrate to a Word document, and then, finally, after considerable textual surgery, come to appear in the final product: a book. In every step of this journey, the text will look different; have different material properties and meanings. Departing from a hypertextually structured world of discontinuous jumps and linkages, these bodies in text will, gradually, be transformed into a format that fits a narrative to be told over a linear succession of pages. But, instead of arguing that the solution is to write a book that mimics a hypertext, with 'links' that invite a reading that supposedly 'disrupts linearity,' my intent is instead to take advantage of the contrast between the materiality of the virtual and that of the Codex book. One obvious example of this contrast can be found on page [X], where a rapidly scrolling screen image produced by a falling body is transformed into an almost blank page. A body falling through the screen is turned into a white void on a piece of paper that, instead of illustrating textual gravity, gives a sense of stillness—a narrative breathing-space.[54]

VIRTUAL ETHNOGRAPHY?

Another reason to speak of textual talk—to balance on the limit between literature and interaction—is to formulate a counterargument to misguided uses of the term 'virtual' in ethnographic work online. Implicit in ('traditional') ethnographic methods is the image of a physical 'immersion' of the ethnographer's body in the culture that is being studied. This bodily thereness makes face-to-face encounters with the members of the culture possible, and allows an understanding of life as it is lived and interpreted by the members themselves. What happens when this corporeality is mediated by the use of a computer? What is ethnography like in cultures created in and through on-screen textuality?

There have been several attempts to reconceptualize the term 'ethnography' in studies of online cultures. New concepts can be a way of distinguishing online spaces from physical locations. They can also be a strategy to make clear that there can be no straightforward translation of guidelines grounded in material cultures onto online worlds. Christine Hine, for example, designates her work 'virtual ethnography,' and motivates this in two different ways:

> the term virtual is metaphoric and stands in for the uncertainty in relation to time, location and presence which is evoked by the reliance on computer-mediated communication for large sections of the ethnography. [. . .] The second sense of virtual is one which is provided by my (pre-cyberspace) dictionary. Virtual, in its pre-information technology sense, conjures up a vision of something which is almost, which will do for practical purposes even if it is not strictly the real thing. I use this sense of virtual to play on the anxieties which this kind of ethnography can produce.[55]

First, the term 'virtual' is used by Hine to illustrate how the certainty of time, location, and (physical) presence in traditional ethnography disappears online. The notion of uncertainty is further connected to her second use of 'virtual,' where she stresses the literal meaning: to be almost, but not strictly, real. There is, however, something very problematic with this use of the word 'virtual' in this literal "(pre-cyberspace)" sense in the study of online cultures. Even if virtual reality is the prevailing way of describing online spaces, as being an alternative to the 'real' provided by computer technology, the concept of the 'virtual' is highly ambiguous.[56] The dichotomy real/virtual not only indicates a separation of an imagined space from a material reality, but, as most dichotomies, also implies that one part is subordinate to the other. In this case, the 'virtual,' by being less real than the 'real'—almost real but not fully—is dominated by the 'real' and its unquestioned realness. On the other hand, once the 'real,' as a basis of the definition of the 'virtual,' is questioned, it appears to be as ambiguous and unstable as its virtual counterpart. Every attempt to keep the real/virtual distinction intact is a slippery practice full of contradictions; for, what exactly is the 'real'? As well as one can insist on the very realness of the 'virtual,' of imagination, it lies at the heart of constructionism to go the other way around and put forth the constructedness of material reality itself.

As an alternative to the term 'virtual' in the naming of this particular form of ethnography, a prefix such as 'cyber-' or 'online' is more useful, since these terms do not carry connotations of perspectives in which online cultures would not matter.[57] 'Online ethnography' is the term used in this book to describe research in textual cultures that are created perhaps not in the absence, but in the *digitally mediated presence* of physical bodies in online venues. The growing field of online ethnography has, up to now, focused primarily on the creation of cultures in the 'absence' of physical bodies. Compared with 'traditional' ethnography, online ethnography went the other way around and treated the lack of bodily thereness as the key to understanding. Even if the only way to communicate online is through the use of symbols on the keyboard, this has not prevented participants from making sense of one another. On the contrary, the exclusion of bodies, voices, facial expression, and gestures has resulted in highly creative and innovative uses of symbols. The question ethnographic work online has attempted to answer is how people deal with this very absence; how specific online modes of communication develop, and how shared systems of meaning are created.[58]

Following in the footsteps of this recent tradition, online ethnography in this study concentrates on textual practices in WaterMOO as cultural production. But instead of being regarded as 'absent,' the physical body of the typist is seen as an intrinsic part of the making of these online texts. Physical bodies not only exist as textual figurations continuously brought to life in online narratives, but 'the body typing' is itself indispensable to their production. In similarity to what Haraway calls 'cyborg anthropology,' online ethnography in this sense sets out to "refigure provocatively the border relations among specific humans, other organisms, and machines," to critically intervene in textual interfaces viewed as a strategic field where humans and machines are intensely brought together.[59]

Typed bodies

In this very intersection of humans and machines, the creation and performance of characters becomes a strategic site where contemporary notions of sex and gender are played out. The question is what position the sexually specific body occupies in online domains. Is it possible to have both sex and gender in cyberspace? What exactly do we mean by 'sex' and 'gender' anyway? Not surprisingly, feminist theorists with an interest in the relation between language and gender saw early on the great research potential in text-only online environments. In these textual spaces, language and bodies are not only mutually constituted, but inevitably the same thing, since language is the only thing there is. Or so it seems. Typically, there are two versions of this discussion in online research, both organized around a separation between a 'real' physical body and its 'virtual' gender (where gender is understood as the textual figuration online, while sex is firmly anchored in the material body left in physical reality).

On one hand, there is a kind of *postmodern utopianism* in which online bodies are constituted through a dramatic divorce from every cultural implication of material bodies in virtual space.[60] Within this perspective, the virtual body moves freely through the online landscape, effortlessly performing subversive gender positions.[61] Gender is turned into 'pure' fiction, completely disconnected from the limits of the 'real,' and most obviously from the limits of language. Through a peculiar move that conceals its intimate connections with ideologies and the meaning of matter, language is made both transparent and immaterial.

Elizabeth Reid claims that in text-based online worlds, "with the body freed from the physical, it completely enters the realm of the symbol. It becomes an entity of pure meaning, but is simultaneously meaningless, stripped of any fixed referent."[62] In Reid's interpretation, the separation between 'virtual' and 'real' has gone so far as to completely disengage the former from the latter. Virtual space appears to be a place where textual bodies, freely and imaginatively, are being written with a fluidity that does not seem to have any limits. It even seems as if the physical body ceases to exist, or dies, when "the body freed from the physical [. . .] completely enters the realm of symbol." The question is how this symbolic entity can be "an entity of pure meaning" and "simultaneously meaningless, stripped of any fixed referent." This "fixed referent" is most likely the physical body that here is being left behind. How can one claim that these texts are disengaged from a culture that, somehow exclusively, belongs to the material world, and at the same time are said to exist in a purely symbolic realm? This further implies that the boundaries between online and the material realities in some sense are absolute, without leakages, as if the online culture actually is a 'culture of no culture' where bodies are performed under the illusion of transparency.

On the other hand, there is a discussion that almost inverts this argument. Instead of claiming full freedom for language-made online bodies, several theorists have criticized this view for ignoring the ways in which gender inequalities are far from erased when we go online, but rather reproduced, and possibly even fortified.[63] They argue (as have 'offline' linguists!) that men and women have different communicative strategies online, and that this communication is both male dominated and male oriented. Male participants are said to accomplish this by "ignoring the topics which women introduce, producing conversational floors based on hierarchy instead of collaboration, dismissing women's responses as irrelevant, and contributing a much higher percentage of the total number of postings and text produced."[64] While certainly being most valuable for pointing out that online worlds are not separated from discourses of gender difference and sexism, these analyses reproduce the problematic idea of language as something gendered (or rather, sexed); that inequalities produced in and through language are somehow biologically grounded in sex differences.

This understanding of language and gender seems particularly out of place in online environments, since the sex of the typist, of the physical body at the keyboard, is literally an ambiguous matter. Even though women might be confronting the same problems online as they do elsewhere, my point is that in reducing online practices to straightforward effects of (an unknown) physical reality, language is not only turned into a simple extension of a certain sexed body, but this time without any knowledge of this body and its sex.

ONLINE CORPOREALITY

I would argue for a perspective on online textual embodiment that is not limited to one side of the real/virtual divide but that complicates this distinction. This understanding is the fruit of a long-term participation in everyday practices in WaterMOO, in which clear distinctions between 'real' and 'virtual' are both articulated and contested. It is a perspective that does not believe in the 'real' as an underlying truth, nor dismisses the 'virtual' as a mysteriously disengaged fiction, but is rather interested in how participants' understandings of 'real' and 'virtual' are typed into being through textual enactments of sexed and gendered bodies. It is an attempt to explore how people handle an online borderland where they meet without seeing each other, how bodies come to matter, textually as well as materially.

In transferring only 'gender' to discussions of online circumstances, the classical distinction between biological sex and cultural gender as immutable properties is repeated, and possibly fortified. The way a body comes into being in MOOs occurs through the @gender command. By typing <@gender female>, the character is programmed as female, and the pronouns attached to this character are automatically set to she, her, hers, and herself. Ironically, the @gender command points not so much in the direction of gender, but rather of sex, even though sex in this case must be understood as immaterial. The @gender command refers to the *sexual specificity* of typed bodies. I prefer to understand online bodies (as well as material bodies) as both sexed and gendered, but not in a sense that makes sex a passive, natural foundation on which gender is culturally inscribed. Instead, I agree with Elizabeth Grosz in arguing that the body, or rather, bodies, cannot be adequately understood as ahistorical, pre-cultural, or natural objects in any simple way: they are not only inscribed, marked, engraved, by social pressures external to them but are the products, the direct effects, of the very social constitution of nature itself. It is not simply that the body is represented in a variety of ways according to historical, social, and cultural exigencies while it remains basically the same; these factors actively produce the body as a body of a determinate type. I will deny that there is the 'real,' material body on one hand and its various cultural and historical representations on the other. It is my claim [. . .] that these representations and cultural inscriptions quite literally constitute bodies and help to produce them as such.[65]

To regard the sexed body not as a biological base, but as an active materiality, as a site for political, social, and cultural struggle, the body is no longer opposed to culture, but is itself a cultural product. Grosz suggests that the category of 'gender' (which she otherwise avoids) can be understood not as the cultural shaping of a biologically given sex, but as connected much more intimately to the specificities of sex, to *sexual difference:* "Gender is not an ideological superstructure added to a biological base. [. . .] it becomes clear that the 'masculinity' of the male body cannot be the same as the 'masculinity' of the female body, because the kind of body inscribed makes a difference to the meaning and functioning of gender that emerges."[66] In focusing on bodily differences, between the sexes and between members of the same sex, an analysis of a diversity of bodies and significations becomes possible that neither reduces sex to essence, nor ignores its material existence.

In an attempt to extend this thinking to incorporate the (quite literal) textualization of cyberspatial bodies, one useful strategy could be to turn to the metaphor of the body as a writing surface, on which 'texts' are inscribed. When bodies are viewed as systems of writing, different techniques of inscription and encarving (social, juridical, medical, disciplinary etc.) constitute bodies as culturally and historically specific. In her striving toward a corporeal feminism, Grosz is skeptical of the view of the body as a blank, passive surface, as a neutral page open to societal intextuation: "If the writing or inscription metaphor is to be of any use for feminism, [. . .] the specific modes of materiality of the 'page'/body must be taken into account: one and the same message, inscribed on a male or a female body, does not always or even usually mean the same thing or result in the same text."[67]

In a similar manner, I regard online bodies as bodies that are being written, but simultaneously bodies to write *on*. The writing and meaning of messages appearing in character descriptions and interactions, what could be called *virtual gender*, is intimately related to the specificity of *virtual sex*, constituted through the @gender command.[68] The same description ascribed to differently @gendered textual bodies will, of course, take on entirely different meanings. Even if it is easier to see that virtual sex, compared with material sex, is not something outside of and beyond processes of inscription (since it, literally, has to be inscribed), it is important to point out that the @gender command serves as an underlying structure in bodily practices in MOOs not reducible to the writing of other texts/utterances. Intimately connected to the code of the MUD program itself, automatically determining the pronouns being used in typed-in interaction, the @gender command comes as close as one can possibly get to a material existence of immaterial bodies. Thus, @gender gives the textual body a sex, in relation to which other texts are rendered meaningful. It provides the online world with some stability, without being a natural given, but itself impregnated with cultural meanings.

TEXTUAL PERFORMATIVITY

Judith Butler, working in the interspaces of the relation between feminist and queer theory, has spent considerable time on the deconstruction of not only gender, but sex itself. In her writing, any clear distinction between sex and gender is seriously put into question: "If the immutable character of sex is contested, perhaps this construct called 'sex' is as culturally constructed as gender; indeed, perhaps it was always already gender, with the consequence that the distinction between sex and gender turns out to be no distinction at all."[69] Far from being understood as the essential raw material upon which gender acts as an active, cultural imprint, sex in Butler's thinking has been constructed all the way. Within the system of compulsory heterosexuality, the myth of sex as origin makes sex appear as something completely natural, which in turn conceals the very operation of this construction. Gender is understood not only as the cultural signifier of sex, but also as the cultural means by which a 'prediscursive' sex is produced and reproduced, as the performative machinery by which the illusion of a sex/gender dichotomy is maintained. The performativity of gender is thought of in the sense that gender inscribes the fantasy of a true, stable gender identity on the surface of the body, which simultaneously naturalizes the normative fiction of heterosexual coherence.

In *Bodies that Matter*, this argument of gender performativity is taken further, so as to clearly incorporate the process through which bodies are materialized:

> Performativity must be understood not as a singular or deliberate 'act', but, rather, as the reiterative and citational practice by which discourse produces the effects that it names. [...] what constitutes the fixity of the body, its contours, its movements, will be fully material, but materiality will be rethought as the effect of power, as power's most productive effect. And there will be no way to understand 'gender' as a cultural construct which is imposed on the surface of matter, understood either as 'the body' or its given sex. Rather, once 'sex' itself is understood in its normativity, the materiality of the body will not be thinkable apart

from the materialization of that regulatory norm. 'Sex' is, thus, not simply what one has, or a static description of what one is: it will be one of the norms by which the 'one' becomes viable at all, that which qualifies a body for a life within the domain of cultural intelligibility.[70]

Butler's radical critique of the stability and naturalness of material bodies stands in sharp contrast to the theories of gender online discussed above. These were either grounded in the illusion of the 'real,' or constituted by a drastic divorce from every cultural implication of material bodies in virtual space.

Butler has, nevertheless, been criticized for disregarding the material reality of bodies, for excluding the suffering woman in feminist thought by viewing her body as merely a 'construction.'[71] Butler's response is that an understanding of the body as constructed requires a reformulation of the meaning of construction itself. As it appears in the quote above, it is not the materiality of bodies *per se* that is being questioned, only the naturalness of this materiality. The material is viewed as the effect of various power relations, which is why bodies would be unthinkable outside the normative practices that, in a fundamental sense, make them intelligible. At the same time, unthinkable bodies are needed to maintain these practices. This is why construction must be understood as something painfully real, in the way it contains a violent force of erasure and exclusion of bodies that do not yet matter. On the other hand, where the stability of matter is being disrupted, the cultural meanings through which bodies are constituted might very well be subject to change.

In a transposition onto the online world, Butler's theory of gender performativity could be very useful in formulating an alternative framework for a study of online bodies. Butler's notion of gender performativity goes against the idea of boundless gender play, freed from every constraint of the meanings always already embedded in the body. In her theory, there is no subject who decides its gender, but the subject is, rather, partly constituted through gender. One reason to work with Butler's ideas in research on online worlds is to demonstrate how the construction and enactments of characters can never be as conscious and free as they might seem. The performance of a character can never be regarded as disconnected from dominating discourses surrounding sex and gender. Construction, on the other hand, should not be seen as something opposed to agency, but rather its necessary assumption. The construction of the subject is never final, and its subversive potential lies in the way norms can be performed in new directions.[72]

Even though it might be hard to envision how and when these performative moments of variation might occur—considering the almost compulsory structures of cultural repetitions—to look for displacements and disturbances of these repetitions seems like a mission well worth undertaking. In the continuous construction of cyber-subjects, reiteration is certainly the ground rule. The challenge is then to identify ruptures and inconsistencies that, in unguarded moments, might trouble the self-evident and familiar. In the chapter to follow, the initial act in the creation of cyber-subjects—the writing of character descriptions—will be the focus of such an investigation. These first steps in the online world are the narrative beginnings of the continuous, collaboratively written story of WaterMOO. All inhabitants in the MOO write a unique story of their own. This follows not only from shifting perspectives and interpretations in their different readings of online texts, but also from the fact that these texts in their actual construction make every character the main character of their own story (through the way of the MUD program to incessantly attach the pronoun 'you' to the person typing). The text I am writing might differ from the others in the sense that it does not as clearly have a main character. On the other hand, I would never deny that this is my—and Jenny's—way of telling the tale of WaterMOO.

CHAPTER 2

READING ONLINE BODIES

While all those of us who have been poststructurally trained undoubtedly begin from a position that the textual character can never be responded to or analyzed as though s/he were a 'real person', it seems to be equally problematic to deny that this is—on occasion—part of the reading fantasy.[1]

Imagine yourself sitting at a(n online) sidewalk café, watching people passing by, busy hurrying to a meeting or more slowly strolling down the street. All of a sudden, in the midst of this stream of flaneurs, there is an unusually tall, slim figure that catches your eye. E walks down the street as if e were striding down a catwalk, putting eir feet (in dangerously high-heeled green sandals), carefully, on an invisible straight line, softly moving eir hips from side to side as e does. Eyes covered by designer sunglasses, a bright yellow plastic bag hanging nonchalantly from one shoulder, e slowly stops, almost in front of your table, as one hand digs deep in the bag (to get out some money for coffee?). From this close-up angle, you notice that eir cheekbones are more distinctive than most women's (aren't they?), and eir legs unnaturally tall, giving the impression of never ending as they disappear up under a short, bright red sundress. Who is e? A transvestite? Well, the contours of eir breasts do not look fake (or do they?). On the other hand, a woman would never dress like that in broad daylight (or would she?).

Whatever e 'is,' such border existence intensifies processes of meaning construction in making the cultural limits of 'sex' visible. In a moment like this, taken-for-granted categories tied to the idea of recognizable, mutually exclusive male and female bodies unexpectedly collapse. The question is how these mechanisms of categorization—through which (most) bodies are becoming culturally intelligible—can be approached. This was a question that I initially carried with me in my investigation of embodiment in text-based online worlds. I was curious about the potential in these environments to create ambiguously sexed and gendered characters. Within the invisibility of material bodies, I imagined these spaces to contain a possibility to challenge cultural limits and to, at least momentarily, stop making sense the usual way. Taking ambiguously embodied characters as an explicit point of departure, I wanted to question the almost self-evident notion of the body as an easily categorized entity. With the aim of exploring how bodies are communicated in online worlds, I wanted to focus on these characters as textual transgressions of not only gender, but sex itself. What does it mean to enter a virtual world 'without' sex? How are 'sexless' characters understood within the online culture where they operate? How are they textualized? Do they have bodies at all? Do they express any kind of sexuality?

Driven by a desire to view the Net as a place for transgressions and textual (de)constructions of the physical body, I was increasingly inspired by a growing discussion in the field of cybercultural studies. In *The War of Desire and Technology at the Close of the Mechanical Age*, already a classic, Sandy Stone (1995) states:

> In cyberspace the transgendered body is the natural body. The nets are spaces of transformation, identity factories in which bodies are meaning machines, and transgender—identity as performance, as play, as wrench into the smooth gears of social apparatus of vision—is the ground state.[2]

After participating in several MOOs for a while, I noticed that the number of ambiguous textual bodies was relatively restricted. And strikingly often I found questions like these scrolling down my screen:

> OpAqUeNeSs says, "so how old are you and what do you look like"
> [. . .]
> Kramer (((show me))) pages, "ahh. .where are u right now? how old are u btw?"[3]
> [. . .]
> Necromancer asks, "How old are you, if I might ask?"
> [. . .]
> You sense that Carlo [Guest] is looking for you in Introduction to WaterMOO. It pages, "Hey . . . are you a *real* woman?"
> [. . .]
> Swordman (Scabbard) pages: "Ok. What isyour real name? Jenny? Or is that fake?"

By an explicit focus on deviant characters, and their potential to transgress and threaten cultural boundaries, I not only limited myself to my own theoretical inclinations, but I limited the whole project to a utopian view of cultures that I did not know at this point. From the always present possibility of playing with sex and gender, it does not necessarily follow that this is a common activity. The fact that a creation of an online character of the opposite sex (compared with the typist's) is only a few keystrokes away does not automatically constitute the 'transgendered' body as the online 'ground state.' Or as Lori Kendall puts it in a critique of Bruckman, Dickel, and Turkle: "[They] confuse limited gender *exchangeability* (the ability to *represent* oneself, with variable success, as a different gender identity from one's offline identity), with gender *malleability* (an understanding of gender as constructed, fluid and changeable)."[4]

Typed-in notions of 'having' a body in WaterMOO soon proved to be textual projects that did not smoothly follow postmodern expectations of fluid gender performances effortlessly inscribed on digital bodily surfaces. In fact, corporeality in the MOO is of a different kind altogether. The following analysis aims at giving a nuanced image of character creation in WaterMOO, its culturally specific categories, patterns, and meanings.[5] How are characters written in WaterMOO? What can we learn from these texts about the online culture of which they are part? The readings are organized around the meaning of the body. In what way is the body conceptualized and communicated in these texts? Which images of sexed and gendered bodies are salient? These readings will be divided into three parts.

The first part, "Imaginative bodies," explores the creation of nonrealistic fictive characters. It begins with characters in the shape of (nonhuman) objects or phenomena, but focuses primarily on humanlike characters inspired by science fiction and fantasy literature. How far are bodies 'fictionalized' in WaterMOO? Are object-bodies able to constitute speaking subjects? Is it possible to be disembodied in a world built on the notion of moving a (textual) body through virtual space? How can a concept like 'transgender' be understood in online immaterial environments? How are ambiguously gendered fiction bodies interpreted when interacting with others in the MOO?

The second part, "Illusions of the real," deals primarily with the way a certain type of 'realism' is being created in the MOO. As if the writing of the ongoing fiction of WaterMOO were interrupted, the writing of realistic characters seem to render the text transparent, to transform the online fantasy into a story of people's everyday lives. The question, is in what ways is this being done? What constitutes online realism? How does it operate? What perspective/ideology is reflected in realistic (re)presentations in WaterMOO? Which images of male and female bodies emerge in this writing? In what ways is the border between the textual and the material illustrated/crossed/threatened in these texts?

The third part, "Absent bodies," takes a look at characters composed through textual fragments or quotes from literature and rock lyrics. What does it mean to, in this sense, put oneself on the margins of online body-writing? Does a missing corporeal description leave the character 'without' body? In what ways can textual transitions that move from performances 'on-stage' to character writing 'on-screen' be understood? What does a 'disembodied' character look like? Does a descriptionless character leave the watcher with a blank screen, a digital void in which the body that was never written could have been typed into existence? Or does this refusal of 'taking shape' take shape in a sense beyond the control of the typist?

On one hand, my ambition has been to present dominating tendencies that have emerged after many readings and rereadings of the texts. This becomes visible, for example, in the division of the analysis into four culturally specific themes. To give an idea of how the descriptions are distributed over these themes, I would say that one half of these texts are versions of what I call *online realism*, about one fourth consist of *imaginative bodies*, and one eighth each represent *quotations* and *disembodied* characters. I have tried to let different written voices be heard, sometimes at the cost of clean lines. "Ethnographers have generally refrained from ascribing beliefs, feelings, and thoughts to individuals. They have not, however, hesitated to ascribe subjective states to cultures [. . .]. All the voices of the field have been smoothed into the expository prose of more-or-less interchangeable 'informants,'" James Clifford argues.[6] Statements containing the homogenizing "WaterMOOers. . ." throughout this text are guilty of this type of seamless unification, emphasizing the general in an erasure of ambiguities and oppositions. Apparently, ethnographic texts would be very difficult to grasp if written completely without this type of 'controlling' discourse. The challenge is, rather, to find a balance between unity and diversity, to not only lift particularities to the level of the general, but "read against the grain of the text's dominant voice, seeking out other half-hidden authorities."[7] All texts are composed of an interweaving of voices, which cannot be fully controlled or finally structured. The readings presented in this text are the provisional result of a struggle between many possibilities. Left open for continuation, dialogue, and critique, they invite competitive alternatives instead of creating closed endings.

Imaginative bodies

"The age old desire to live out a fantasy aroused by a fictional world has been intensified by a participatory, immersive medium that promises to satisfy it more completely than has ever before been possible," writes Janet Murray in her compelling *Hamlet on the Holodeck: The Future of Narrative in Cyberspace*.[8]

Even if one might wonder whether online worlds have the potential to satisfy our fantasies "more completely" compared with other types of fictional worlds in, for example, film and literature, the idea of sharing an unscripted imaginative space with others in constant negotiation of the narrative is incredibly intriguing. In the metaphor of the body as a writing surface, a 'page' on which various social and cultural discourses are inscribed, material bodies are in a sense fictionalized. In MUDs, this fictionalization is taken one step further, since in these spaces bodies are already textual. If human flesh is seen as a resistance to how far the (material) body can become a fiction, what meanings it can possibly incorporate, then the limit of fiction in a MUD might be of a different kind. As a collaboratively written, never-ending online narrative, WaterMOO opens up a world that is both different from and very similar to the (physical) world as we know it. In its most convincing moments, this fiction works toward an inversion of terms to the point where physical surroundings turn pale and the story of WaterMOO takes on a life of its own. When carried away by this absorbing, contemporary fairy tale, transported to an alternative universe, WaterMOO hides possibilities of creating bodies that do not immediately obey the strict rules of the 'real.' In this section, I will start with the most fantastic of these bodies, to gradually move in the direction of the next section on online realism.

OBJECTIFIED BODIES / EMBODIED OBJECTS

> look Orac
> A small box constructed of clear plastic. The box is crammed full of various electronic bits and pieces. It flashes and sputters intermittently.
> It is awake and looks alert.

In the borderland between embodiment and disembodiment, in which the contours of a human body are erased, something very different materializes. In what appears to be a bodily denial, the gendered body is dissolving. Orac is a neuter, and as such not only transgresses the male/female dichotomy, but goes beyond its organizing principle and carves out an alternative way of being. 'Orac,' supposedly from "oracle", is the name of the future-predicting computer that appeared in the BBC-based science fiction series *Blake's* 7. Based on a vision of computer technology and design, Orac is built as a "small box constructed of clear plastic," which "flashes and sputters intermittently." Orac is a fascinating example of what an alternative body in computer-based cultures might look like. By representing a nonorganic object, it does not have a humanlike appearance, but certainly a nonhuman object-body that in the MOO comes to life and brings a different type of materiality into motion. Compared with the idea of the (human) body as essential to the understanding of ourselves and others, a self-presentation of a plastic box "crammed full of various electronic bits and pieces," can be read as a liberation from the limits of the physical and its classification system based on gender.

On the other hand, the fact that computers are human-made gives them certain anthropomorphous qualities. This becomes even more evident in the case of 'Orac' in *Blake's* 7, who is not an ordinary computer, but rather a mind—a brain—that can access unlimited sources of information from other computers. On the basis of this infinite knowledge, 'Orac' makes predictions of the future. The last line of the character description (added automatically by the MUD program), "It is awake and looks alert," ascribes the character with human, or at least animal features. A computer can be 'on' or 'running,' but the state of being awake and alert seems hard to apply to (lifeless) objects. By being part of the text, these qualities are metaphorically transferred to Orac, which further contributes to its anthropomorphization. This line, automatically ending all character descriptions (if not actively removed), clearly gives characters the status of being *subjects*, even if objectlike presences are created in the text.

In the following example, even matter is disappearing. Paradoxically, in the midst of this material disappearance, gender is being reintroduced:

look Fluorine
Fluorine (#17217) *MetaElement*
A pale yellow, flammable and irritating gas. Are you sure you want to be around her?
She leans towards you and whispers, "First, do no harm. . ."
Fluorine appears to be awake.

Fluorine, from the Latin word *fluere*, which means 'to float,' is a chemical compound characterized by being a highly poisonous gas. This is the most reactive of all elements, positioned on top of the group of halogens in the periodic system. Fluorine in very small doses exists naturally in, for example, nails and teeth, and is added for tooth protection in many types of toothpaste. The WaterMOO population at large might not be familiar with the 'fluorine-lady' phenomenon, an acquaintance Swedish schoolchildren in the 60s and later had to make. The fluorine-lady wandered the schools with small plastic cups filled with the most disgusting sludge one could imagine (fluorine) for us kids to gargle. 'Fluorine,' by being a female character who does not seem very pleasant to hang out with ("Are you sure you want to be around her?"), corresponds to qualities of fluorine that we ascribed to the fluorine-lady. The last line: "She leans towards you and whispers, 'First, do no harm...'" can be read as a redeeming feature, a way of ensuring the reader that she is not as difficult to be with as she might seem. The description as a whole can be understood as a commentary on the way female characters regularly are being paged and invited to @join male characters for a chat (and possibly more). It seems to be a well-known (but little-used) strategy in the MOO to exclude physical features in the creation of female characters, to avoid this type of attention. In Fluorine's case, an "irritating gas" that symbolizes a more inflammable femininity replaces a potential female body.

No matter if gender online operates as a *double construction*, it seems to serve as a fundamental organizing principle in interactions between characters in the MOO. An understanding of online gender as doubly constructed departs from the way gender, in general, can be viewed as a historical, cultural, and social construction. Online, stories of gendered bodies are brought into the picture through *textual* constructions (on several levels), in relation to which the physical body of the constructor, of the typist, often remains unknown. Gender as constructed is not merely an empty fiction, but sometimes painfully real in the way narratives and cultural meanings of the body structure our (online) lives. The fact that very few characters in WaterMOO are @gendered 'other' possibly indicates that it is very hard to imagine a way of being beyond gender. Even Fluorine, who has a very unconventional online 'body,' is still @gendered female. If the description attached to this character is meant to keep male characters at a distance, would not a more efficient strategy be to avoid (human) gender completely?

The wish to leave the body behind, through the writing of alternative, disembodied beings, remains a never quite fulfilled dream. Even if the matter of (human) bodies is avoided, these characters still contain humanlike features, like being awake and alert or having the ability to lean toward 'you' and whisper things in your ear. These qualities might not in themselves inscribe physicality, but they nevertheless imply a bodily grounding, an imagined body that provides these allusions with their necessary foundation. This becomes even more obvious in typed-in interactions where everybody has a voice and an ability to move themselves between virtual locations.

As mentioned previously, discourses of disembodiment in contemporary cyberculture has been criticized by (cyber)feminists for repeating the age-old figure in which the position of the 'disembodied' mind is a male privilege, but one that is completely dependent on embodied females for its own bodily erasure. The question is whether textual performances in a place like WaterMOO are not the *inversion* of the very same problem. If the act of leaving the body behind is a disguise of male abstraction, then having a body in virtual space does not seem less problematic. In WaterMOO, by being entirely structured around the notion of having, using, and being a body, there does not seem to be a way out of schemes of thought structured around (sexually specific) embodiment.

TALKING VAMPIRES

The question is how ambiguously gendered and/or textually disembodied characters are being performed and interpreted when interacting with others in the MOO. Is it possible, even in the act of 'speaking,' to rest within this gender fluidity and disappearance of physical contours? Or are these interactions limited in a way that circumscribes the type of bodies that can be performed? There seems to be a shift in the understanding among Water-MOOers between 'writing' and 'speaking,' or between character creation and interaction, because no matter how fantastic the characters may be, the conversations between them are most often very mundane. This creates an interesting tension between character descriptions and textual talk, which becomes especially visible in the case of 'nonrealistic' characters. In what follows, the journey among characters in WaterMOO will explore the composition of humanlike bodies, inspired primarily by science fiction and fantasy literature. The question is how the relation between MOO conversations and the writing of these bodies can be understood. Is it even possible to distinguish the 'everyday-like' from the 'imaginative'? Or do these different types of writing intermingle in a way that makes them inseparable?

Considering the historical development of MUDs, in which (face-to-face) role-playing games inspired by fantasy scenarios played a major role, it is not surprising that this type of writing is a major trend in the creation of characters. In her work on global youth culture and role-playing games, Anne Scott Sørensen discusses the influences of horror and SF (science fiction) in these games. Drawing from literary Gothic, film noir, and splatter and horror movies, role-playing narratives within the horror genre build on "the horror which arises when something changes character and challenges the boundaries between the human and the inhuman (bestial), or between the human and the superhuman (divine/paranormal) and thus spreads doubt as to elements such as identity, body and gender."[9] A central figure in this genre is the vampire, which in the MOO forms a 'player class' of its own and takes on different shapes:

> look Ilyenna
> Ilyenna is a tall, spare-framed woman with unnaturally high, sharp cheekbones on an angular face. Black hair streaked with white frames the face, partly hidden by a net hood of silver studded with tiny sparkling gems at each

> crossing of threads. Their icelike gleam is matched coldly by black eyes, their lids painted silver.
>
> Tattered black rags partially conceal the gleaming skin of her body, leaving glimpses of only the occasional jutting hipbone, shoulderblade, knee. As she moves, it can be seen that her forearms and hands are covered in spidery black tattoo, symbolic gauntlets. Similar markings crawl up around her throat, disappearing under her hair to be seen only at the curve of her ear.
>
> Her lips are dark, and if she uses her mouth to speak, she displays onyx teeth slightly more pointed than a human's. Her teeth and lips are not the only dark parts of her mouth; her tongue and all the rest of what can be seen is also a dark blue-black. This allows the silver bar piercing the centre of her tongue and the multifaceted clear crystal ball to shine, catch light as she speaks in a way that is a distraction from the low hoarseness of her speech.
> She is awake, but has been staring off into space for a minute.

In the form of a "tall, spare-framed woman," 'Ilyenna' "displays onyx teeth slightly more pointed than a human's," symbolizes vampiric powers bordering the unhuman and the monstrous, as well as the superhuman and an eternal state of being. With detailed precision, this female character might not immediately challenge the concepts of 'gender' and 'body,' but elements such as "unnaturally high, sharp cheekbones," and the way her "teeth and lips are not the only dark parts of her mouth; her tongue and all the rest of what can be seen is also a dark blue-black," create a female body with rare qualities, belonging to a time and place different from our own. At the same time, the appearance of Ilyenna is highly androgynous in the sense that almost all female pronouns easily can be changed to male pronouns: "Tattered black rags partially conceal the gleaming skin of [his] body, leaving glimpses of only the occasional jutting hipbone, shoulderblade, knee. As [he] moves," etc. In the absence of explicit references to a female body shape and other features hard to incorporate in a male body, Ilyenna shows a vampiric belonging by being indefinable in character, and, as such, questions the nature of the sexed and gendered body.[10] Haraway points out that vampires "are narrative figures with specific category-crossing work to do. [. . .] The existence of vampires tropes the purity of lineage, certainty of kind, boundary of community, order of sex, closure of race, inertness of objects, liveliness of subjects, and clarity of gender."[11] In describing boundary creatures on many levels, vampire narratives resist categorizations, rendering unstable the idea that bodies do not come in more than two sexes.

This questioning of the sexually specific body is in the following interpretation of a MOO vampire taken a few steps further:

> look leighloo
> delicious sadist; Unseeling faerie perched angelicly atop the 666 building
> peering down upon the frantic streams of idiocracy flowing through the viens
> of the metropolis.{so much blood} Tightly clad in a suit of metallic blue, flut-
> tering eir fiber-optic razored wings; E is entranced by the faint whisper of a
> pulsar star . . . somewhere . . . somewhere . . . its calling. . . . . .
> leighloo's vampiric powers wrap em in shadow. You can see no more from
> here.
> E is sleeping.

'leighloo' is @gendered Spivak, which becomes visible in "*E is entranced*" and "leighloo's vampiric powers wrap *em* in shadow," etc. (my emphasis). In a colorful, fragmented imagery of a fairy's perspective of the pulsating madness of humanity, the text refuses the reader's search for innocent wholeness through its dissolving of clear boundaries. "Tightly clad in a suit of metallic blue, fluttering eir fiber-optic razored wings," e resists from its in-between, unfixed position any singular determination of gender. In her article "Coming Apart at the Seams: Sex, Text and the Virtual Body," Shannon McRae argues that a choice of one of the alternative genders that some MOOs offer can be a way to avoid traditional gender assumptions. In her investigation of virtual bodies and sexuality, she has found that, for instance, the Spivak @gender "has encouraged some people to invent entirely new bodies and eroticize them in ways that render categories of female or male meaningless. [. . .] a spivak can have any morphological form and genital structure e devises for emself."[12] Rather than being a crucial part of human identity, gender is altered into a mere abstraction, one of several features of the bodies that are written.

MOO characters @gendered 'other' in a sense wander virtual spaces as textual incarnations of Haraway's mythical cyborg, offering alternative ways of seeing and being in the world. In contrast to the use of cyborgs in mainstream science fiction as an illustration of a hardened masculinity through the fusion of the (hu)man and technology, Haraway reads the cyborg as transcendence of the dichotomous categorization male/female toward a genderless utopia. A cyborg is a fusion of human and technology, of machine and organism, combining elements that are both organic and inorganic in a sense that blurs the boundary between areas that are traditionally thought of as separate. In Haraway's understanding, 's/he' is a social reality as well as a fiction, where the boundary between real and virtual is an illusion. Haraway uses the cyborg as an alternative figure of thought, a powerful political fiction that shatters the dichotomous categorizations of Enlightenment epistemology, such as mind/body, organism/machine, public/private, culture/nature, civilized/primitive, and centrally, man/woman, male/female, masculine/feminine.[13] The strength of a cyborg understanding of textual characters in computerized environments lies in the way cyborgs, through their constantly moving borderland bodies, are both flesh and imagination, nature and culture. There are at least two ways of interpreting cyborg imagery. First, the connection between human and machine might be located within the body, surgically refigured through technological inscriptions. This fusion is vividly imagined and illustrated in SF cinema, but it is also part of everyday life in the shape of transplants, implants, artificial limbs, etc. But cyborgs could also be understood in reverse, through an inscription of physicality into the immaterial reality of textual beings. In this second sense, the cyborg is integrated into an abstract flow of information, and the border between a physical body and its prosthetic extension through technologies is rather socially and culturally constructed.

The question is how far alternative narratives and utopian images of transgressive cyborg bodies can take us in the examination of (other-gendered) bodies in WaterMOO. Sandy Stone argues that the transgendered body is the cyberspatial 'ground state,' but she never quite clarifies what counts as 'transgender' in cyberspace.[14] There is certainly something paradoxical in the use of a concept like 'transgender' in the online context. If a performance of a character @gendered male by a female typist is viewed as 'transgendered,' this presupposes that 'gender,' on both sides of the screen, neatly follows the cultural expectations of sex. Gender is actually being reduced to sex. Moreover, the online 'transgendered' body is in this case *trans*gendered only as long as the person who performs the character can be proven to have a different 'gender.' Online bodies are largely constituted in the invisibility of the person at the keyboard, which makes such verification problematic. On the other hand, 'transgender' can also be used to describe certain gender performances *within* the online world, without reference to the body of the typist. If temporarily released from its physical anchorage, 'transgender' can fruitfully be transformed into an intratextual strategy in the MOO. Characters like Orac and leighloo, both @gendered 'other,' could be described as 'transgender' by transgressing the limits of gender as a bipolar construction. Nevertheless, being @gendered 'other' can neither be the only nor a sufficient condition for determining online bodies as 'transgender.'

One reason for this is that several characters @gendered male or female can also be interpreted as 'transgressive' in relation to dominant gender performances in the MOO (like Fluorine). For example, central themes in SF and related genres (such as cyberpunk) evolve around highly unstable, but unambiguously sexed male and female bodies. The human subject in the horror genre is constituted in direct relation to a threat from the inside of the body, to something that at any moment might break through the skin and absorb the individual. In classic SF, the threat is instead external and invades the body from the outside. In the development of SF as cyberpunk, the invasion from the outside by computer technologies, smart drugs, and microchips results in a cyborg fusion of mechanical and organic parts to the point where it is no longer possible to distinguish between humans and technology. Against the background of these narratives, in which not only the body is dissolving, but the human being as a natural, self-evident category, WaterMOO characters with cyberpunkish elements rest on relatively modest incarnations of human/machine hybrids:

> look &ru
> &ru is a rather tall, skinny person with black hair falling in clumps and tangles across his eyes and high cheekbones to his shoulders. His eyes shine sharp and dark from behind the slightly greasy curtain, an aquiline nose seems almost out of character on the thin, sensitive face, but speaks to the sneer across &ru's woman's mouth by the crookedness of its having been broken.
> &ru has multicolored telephone wire wrapped around his neck and his arms, bright patterned bands against the plain black clothes he wears. From the open collar of his black silver-buttoned shirt, a slender length of tubing runs up to coil along with the wires to disappear into the unkempt hair, the clearness of the tube leaving one to wonder whether the liquid being transported inside is oil for a machine, or blood.
> He is awake and looks alert.

'&ru' is a male morph of a female character named 'Izha,' which 'she' is occasionally transformed into. Morph, as in "morphology," refers to the possibility of online shape shifting, of moving between different characters that belong to the same typist. This might explain the name &ru, which illustrates the status of merely being an appendix to the 'regular' character. &ru sounds almost like "Andrew," or even more interestingly for the character in question, like "andro," as in a short version of "androgynous." &ru has an unusually detailed face, which seems to mix both male and female features in an interesting interplay: "an aquiline nose seems almost out of character on the thin, sensitive face, but speaks to the sneer across &ru's woman's mouth by the crookedness of its having been broken." At first, there does not seem to be anything special about this black-clothed, tall, and skinny male person. But toward the end of the description, the alert reader will notice how from "the open collar of his black silver-buttoned shirt, a slender length of tubing runs up to coil along with the wires to disappear into the unkempt hair, the clearness of the tube *leaving one to wonder whether the liquid being transported inside is oil for a machine, or blood*" (my emphasis). In these last lines, the cyborg dilemma of not knowing how to relate to hybrid others is exposed, since it is unclear whether this creature is 'natural' or 'mechanical,' flesh-made or technologically constructed.

MASQUERADING FANTASY

The question is how these stories of vampiric and science fictive bodies relate to the construction of 'everyday' socializing in the MOO. In chapter 4, "Corporeal Obsession," I will take a closer look at the content and meaning of textual talk in WaterMOO. For the moment, it seems sufficient to point out that these conversations do not explicitly lay the ground for encounters between medieval knights and futuristic hardwired machine bodies, between elves and vampires. The discrepancy between WaterMOO conversations on one hand and character descriptions linked to imaginative worlds with ancient or futuristic connotations on the other may best be described in terms of *masquerade*. The way these descriptions at first might be conversational starting points and thematically evoked in interactions, but after a while merely dispatched into the background, comes close to the use of a masquerading disguise. This does not render character descriptions transparent or meaningless, since masks and costumes can be understood as simultaneously concealing and accentuating subject positions in interesting ways. Terry Castle (1986), in working on the (literary) history of 18th century English masquerade, puts forth how the

> masked assemblies of the eighteenth century were in the deepest sense a kind of collective mediation on self and other, and an exploration of their mysterious dialectic. [...] New bodies were superimposed over old; anarchic, theatrical selves displaced supposedly essential ones; masks, or personae, obscured persons. [...] The pleasure of masquerade attended on the experience of doubleness, the alienation of inner from outer, a fantasy of two bodies simultaneously and thrillingly present, self and other together, the two-in-one.[15]

Online bodies, written against the background of fantasy and science fiction novels, are in a similar way played out in the midst of this dialectic between self-presentation and self-concealment. Always moving between levels of disguise and exposure, these texts are "a fantasy of two bodies simultaneously and thrillingly present," the one always tightly bound to the other. This superimposition of the theatrical (over the supposedly original) not only shows how masks are always cultural constructs, but how the meaning of the body 'being masked' at once is significantly altered. The meanings of these 'body doubles' cannot be found other than in their contrasting overlappings—in those instances when their seams and stitches are revealed through fissures in the costumes. Such ruptures of masquerading fantasies occur constantly in the MOO. Nonrealistic MOO characters are constituted through several layers of meaning, moving between the level of textual talk and the creation of extraordinary bodies. Naturally, all WaterMOO characters are part of this masquerade, but my point at the moment is to put forth the play between 'person' and 'persona,' or between various levels of masking, when one of these levels is apparently constructed or fictionalized. It is to point out how different textual modes make the constructedness of the 'real' in general, and of WaterMOO reality in particular, more or less obvious.

On one hand, there is a gap between the tone in MOO conversations and the mode of writing in the case of 'nonrealistic' characters, which becomes especially urgent in those cases when the (human) body and/or recognizable gender positions are dissolving and replaced by floating entities of indeterminable nature. I have argued that this textual difference is significant even in the case of fantasy and SF-inspired characters, since conversations in the MOO constitute a form of 'everyday' socializing from which fantastic figures deviate. On the other hand, even if the subject in SF potentially inhabits a universe not immediately determined by dichotomies such as human/nonhuman, embodied/disembodied, and man/woman, most characters belonging to this literary domain in the MOO have clearly gendered, human bodies. In the development of SF as cyberpunk, the fundamental assumption is that the physical body has ceased to matter. The body is referred to as 'the meat,' as something disturbingly inert that surrounds and limits the active and spiritual mind.[16] But as Anne Balsamo notices: "Fictional accounts of cyberspace play out the fantasy of casting off the body as an obsolete piece of meat, but, not surprisingly, these fictions do not eradicate body-based systems of differentiation and domination."[17]

In WaterMOO, these body-based systems are articulated through the creations of fantasy characters, which, in contrast to high-tech incarnations of SF and cyberpunk, rely on alarmingly conventional gender classifications:

look Phantom
Golden ethereal mists circle the Phantom, as he stands, shadowy, before you. A stream of golden vapor flows out from his sleeve and spirals up his arm. A cloud of golden smoke whisps around his waist, then floats around his head. All you can see of Phantom himself is his cloak. You look at his face, under the hood, but the longer you look at it, the more blury it gets . . . A whisp of golden steam spirals through the air away from him, almost as if governed by some intelligence far beyond the understanding of science today.
He is awake and looks alert.

look madri
Raven-kissed silk reflects only the deepest of plum in the sun's direct light; strands are fine, but not frizzy, cascading to just past shoulder's height and encompassing a small elven face. Eyes so blue and pale as to be like liquid crystals in a fading light, shimmering to near silver at times while light autumn

skin ripples with summer's inner warmth and passion. Her features and movements contain a near cat-like grace: delicate in appearance, but quick, agile and strong when the need arises.
Madri's vampiric powers wrap her in shadow. You can see no more from here. She is awake and looks alert.

"Golden ethereal mists" circle around him, the 'Phantom,' "as if governed by some intelligence far beyond the understanding of science today." Strong and intelligent, his body veiled in a cloak, not even his face visible under the hood. With "[r]aven-kissed silk [. . .] Eyes so blue and pale as to be like liquid crystals" is she, 'madri,' coming into shape with "features and movements [that] contain a near cat-like grace." Pleasant, pleasing, and elfin-faced, her hair cascades in shimmering light. Instead of altering recognizable categorizations of sexed and gendered bodies, fantasy literature often depends on simplified worldviews of easily discernible dichotomies of good and evil, Man and Woman. Transposing these literary tendencies into the creation of characters has introduced numerous bodies that read like textbook examples out of fantasy novels. Even if these fantasy characters carry elements of a supernatural fairy-tale world ("A stream of golden vapor flows out from his sleeve and spirals up his arm," etc.), they simultaneously inhabit a universe in which men are brave and women beautiful, which reproduces, even fortifies, 'traditional' gender positions. In contrast to character descriptions where the (human) body is disappearing, these fantasy-novel bodies rather allude to the archetypal, which, instead of creating a gap between the fantastic and the mundane, bridges this difference.

Illusions of the real

look Speedy
Speedy a spiritprogrammer
OK! Here's briefly what I look like:

I'm 5'11.". . . 175lbs, mousy hair green/grey eyes, have all my own hair and teeth, and it covers all my head. . . . hair that is, not the teeth. . . . . I'm English and try to keep a suntan for most of the year, although our weather tries to thwart my attempts!

I live in England, a place called Manchester, which is an inner city. I am considered to be intelligent, but this doesn't stop me from making mistakes from time to time, so, I also qualify for the classification of being human after all. I enjoy cultured, interesting and stimulating conversation but have no time for infantile banter. . . . . so you chose to which category you belong to before entering into any verbal intercourse!!!

If there is anything else you wish to know then do not be afraid to ask. . . . I don't bite. . . . . . well not too much these days!

I finally succumbed to getting something up on the WWW so go check out my web site at http:\\www.tjoho.tjolahopp.uk and make me happy that my hard work has paid off. . . .:)

You can never be sure of whom you are meeting. In every encounter, there is always uncertainty. This feeling of insecurity is intensified online, where you, apart from not being sure of whom you are meeting, can neither see nor hear the other person. Eye contact, voices and gestures are replaced by text, and the activity of writing and reading is the only means by which you can come to terms with the physical invisibility of yourself, and of others. This state of uncertainty, within a culture where a sense of being exposed can be very strong, seems in WaterMOO to have created an obsession with ways of determining the 'real.' This becomes evident in conversations between participants, but can also be traced at the level of character construction. If conversations on the topic seem to circle around the question "Who are you *really*?" the creation of characters goes the other way and states, "This is who I am." In Speedy's case, this is formulated in: "Here is briefly what I look like: I'm. . ." Obviously, 'realistic' textual bodies might or might not correspond with the bodies of the typists. My point is that these texts, within the online context, are normally interpreted as enunciations of 'realness,' as representations of the way the 'real' is communicated within this culture.

Speedy can also be read as a way of introducing a touch of Englishness within an overall American WaterMOO culture. This American dominance can be viewed as a hidden subtext in many descriptions, and in Speedy it becomes specifically clear in the lines "I'm English and try to keep a suntan for most of the year, although our weather tries to thwart my attempts! I live in England, a place called Manchester, which is an inner city." Americanness as the norm runs like a silent stream through a majority of the texts, where, for example, not a single description contains "I'm American. . ." In Speedy, it becomes clear that WaterMOO, if 'located' anywhere, is not to be found anywhere near Manchester. Not only is geographical place explicitly stated, but it is also implied that the reader is not already supposed to know that Manchester is an English city. A certain English flavor can even be found on the subtle level of spelling, in the eyes being described as "green/grey." In American English, they would have been green/gray. By introducing a geographical location, the text is anchored in the physical world. This not only gives it a material connection; it also creates a point of reference within a culture with diffuse origins. By further incorporating a connection to a personal homepage, the text is also tied to a person in a way that makes this person morally responsible for his or her actions. Regardless of whether the homepage belongs to the typist or not, the text communicates a gesture toward disrupting the facelessness of the text-based virtual world.

POSTMODERN UTOPIANISM REVISITED

In the creation of characters, practically anything can be written and brought to life. Many WaterMOOers, when confronted with this 'limitless' opportunity to textualize themselves, choose to present themselves in a very down-to-earth and ordinary manner. In letting the text appear as if it is revealing more than it is hiding, these descriptions rather allude to a recognizable reality that stands in sharp contrast to assumptions among several theorists working with bodies and notions of identity online. With arguments similar to the postmodern utopianism found in discussions of virtual bodies, they state that online, you can be anybody, or anything, since nobody knows who you are. Sherry Turkle suggests:

> The anonymity of MUDs—one is known on the MUD only by the name of one's character or characters—gives people the chance to express multiple and often unexplored aspects of the self, to play with their identity and to try out new ones. MUDs make possible the creation of an identity so fluid and multiple that it strains the limits of the notion. Identity after all, refers to the sameness between two qualities, in this case between a person and his or her persona. But in MUDs, one can be many.[18]

In WaterMOO, characters might have several names, and sometimes even several descriptions, but this does not automatically lead to a widespread notion of identity as 'multiple' in this context. There is a difference between the *possibility* to create "an identity so fluid and multiple that it strains the limit of the notion," and the *actual* performance of such an identity, or a general widespread understanding of identity that contains these qualities. Furthermore, what at first sight may look like expressions of multiple identities can be interpreted very differently in particular online contexts. In WaterMOO, for example, most characters are known under a certain name. Even if several descriptions and/or supplementary names are being used, this does not seem to disrupt the understanding of the character as a coherent whole. Alternative names and descriptions might be used as alterations and transformations of a main theme, as features in a textual masquerade, but among online friends there is rarely more than one 'true' version of a character:

Pyrex [to Jenny]: "i shall donate my description. . ."
Sugar says, "I'm outta here."
Pyrex quickly. . . . . . morphs into Emcee
Sugar. o O (but of course I'll be back. . . .)
Sugar rolls her eyes.
Jenny [to Emcee]: "you will?"
Sugar goes home
Emcee nods.
Emcee [to Jenny]: "i have several. . ."
Jenny [to Emcee]: "i see. ."
Emcee [to Jenny]: "this is my true form however. . ."
Emcee quickly. . . . . . morphs into Zebro

In this excerpt, a character momentarily named Pyrex "morphs into Emcee," which in turn is transformed into Zebro, after mentioning that "this is my true form." The anonymity of MUDs does not seem to lead to limitless play in WaterMOO. On the contrary, the writing of many characters points in the opposite direction, and typically puts the gendered body back into the picture:

look NiceGuy
5`9. . . jet black hair . . . black eyes . . . fair complextion. . check me out
Http://tjohoo.hopp.com/~blabla
He is awake and looks alert.

look Tulip
A cute but short female. I have long black hair and deep dark eyes. I love to meet and talk to new people. . .
. . . so whatcha waiting for, silly?! Page me ;) Oh, btw, my homepage is http://tjoho.edu/~hopph, lemme know whatch think:) and, if you look within the depths of my page, you'll see a picture of me there. . but you'll have to find me first, hehehe. . ;)
Tulip's vampiric powers wrap her in shadow. You can see no more from here.
She is awake and looks alert.

'NiceGuy' and 'Tulip' invite to a kind of 'stepping through' the textual world out into a 'real' world behind it, through the references to personal homepages. Allusions to URLs serve as keys that guarantee that the brief, textual descriptions online (e.g., "5`9. . . jet black hair . . . black eyes . . . fair complexion. .") stand in a verifiable correspondence to the physical body of the writer. The ". . ." separating different bodily features in NiceGuy introduces a certain seductiveness, which quickly leads over to the "check me out" part, as if indicating a gaze moving from body part to body part. As if the text were constructed as a hyperlink, it gives a sense of being 'clickable' by hinting at what might be found on the page of reference. That page is actually mostly image based, revealing a Pakistani young man in several close-up shots, with exactly "... jet black hair ... black eyes ... fair complexion..." The relatively anonymous text of NiceGuy is linked to a place, a face, and a name, which fills or compensates for bodily invisibility with image-based visibility.

The description of Tulip is divided into two parts. The first part starts with a straightforward description, but then turns into an explicit invitation to dialogue: "... so whatcha waiting for, silly?! Page me ;)." The winky face ;) at the end of the sentence makes clear that the tone of this written voice is humorous, with a hint of irony. The second part invites to an exploration of the online but extra-MOO Web habitat of the typist. The text is filled with pauses . . . emoticons :) and textualizations of spoken language, as in "lemme know whatch[a] think," which makes it come through as informal and spontaneous. If captured by the "long black hair and deep dark eyes" in the first line, toward the end of the text the reader will find an ironic comment on this expected desire: "if you look within the depths of my page, you'll see a picture of me there. . but you'll have to find me first, hehehe. . ;)." Where NiceGuy was linked to a page full of images, Tulip instead transfers the reader to a page dominated by text and links to other pages, containing both personal and professional material. The information given reveals a Pennsylvania-based young woman, working in software engineering. In contrast to many other homepages of women, this page does not contain a picture of its creator in an easily discernible place. After a lot of clicking, one header appears to hide a directory filled with pictures. In one of these there surely is a dark-haired, dark-eyed 'me.' But unlike the construction of NiceGuy, with an intimate linkage to a face, Tulip is related primarily to personal interests, friends, and competence. Through an inversion of traditionally expected positions, in which women are reduced to their bodies, whereas men are equated with their minds, Tulip and NiceGuy show off male vanity and female brains.

In contrast to the belief in boundless creativity, Don Slater points out that the deconstruction of embodied identity online—far from resulting in experimentation and free play—is experienced as practical and existential problems by IRC participants:

> participants operated within a dialectic of cynicism and belief: they experienced their online world with a mixture of cynical detachment on the one hand (a refusal to believe anything online and therefore a refusal to treat events or relationships there as serious), and on the other hand a desire to trust and invest in online relationships which depended on pursuing strategies of authentication (and a constant concern about being deceived, ripped off and otherwise hurt by others' inauthenticity). Significantly, these strategies [. . .] were attempts to fix

the other in a body or body-like presence, one which persists over time and is locatable in space.[19]

Slater describes a tension in which participants on IRC constantly find themselves, between suspicion and confidence, between never wanting to trust anybody online and the craving to give oneself to the other (and to be met accordingly). In contrast to this difficult balance between cynicism and trust, the mode in WaterMOO is very little characterized by skepticism and doubt. On the verge of naiveté, participants seem to believe in each other, at least as long as the other's performance is coherent. Nevertheless, even though a MUD character has the ability to persist over time and to be locatable in space, the fundamental issue of the typist's physical invisibility remains unsolved. As in Slater's depiction of authentication strategies on IRC as "attempts to fix the other in a body or body-like presence," WaterMOOers spend considerable effort on the seemingly hopeless project to expose the body 'behind' the text. Irrespective of how bodylike their presence in text is, what sometimes seems to be of more interest is where in the world the material body is located—its sex, appearance, age, etc. This does not imply that the textual performance becomes transparent or loses its importance, but it is in fact the only means by which the impossible but irresistible project to reach the physical can proceed.

HACKING MASCULINITIES ON THE LIMITS OF FICTION

> look anarchy
> anarchy (#13227) *Metaprogrammer*
> Ready with a joke and a laugh, Anarchy lives up to his name in a few ways, not the least of which is the amount of time he spends online. He has way too much work to do to be here, but likes it too much to give up . . . Oh Well. If you tell a really obscure joke or reference, he'll likely get it, or be challenged into asking what you meant. Physically, he's about 6'5, blue eyes, borwn hair bordering on black, in OK shape except for the hint of a spare around his middle. Ask him about computers and he will also likely know the answer, especially if it's a PC/Mac kind of thing. Almost always interested in a dep discussion. Excuse his typing; the current telnet doesn't have a baskpace.
> anarchy (So what's up?) is sleeping

In the text 'anarchy,' the name refers to online hacker ethics, a belief in a deregulation of the Net, and everybody's unlimited access to information. The first lines, "Ready with a joke and a laugh, anarchy lives up to his name in a few ways, not the least of which is the amount of time he spends online," hint at the sometimes endless sessions in front of the computer, not only common, but proudly referred to within these circles. The longer the sessions, the more impressive. Eric S. Raymond, in *The New Hackers' Dictionary*, puts forth that within hacker culture, "Dry humor, irony, puns, and a mildly flippant attitude are highly valued—but an underlying seriousness and intelligence are essential."[20] This fusion of competence and wit is running through the text, in sentences like "Ask him about computers and he will also likely know the answer, especially if it's a PC/Mac kind of thing. Almost always interested in a dep discussion," where the seriousness is efficiently weakened by the (involuntary?) misspelling of 'deep.' The text as a whole gives the impression of fast and slovenly writing, with spelling mistakes in every other sentence. This is explained in the end: "Excuse his typing; the current telnet doesn't have a baskpace," where the misspelling of 'backspace' appears suspiciously conscious, as an ironic meta-comment on the problem of not being able to erase anything of the already written.

anarchy is a pretty good example of a mainstream male character in the MOO, which gives an idea of the nature of this mainstream. Even if the percentage of highly skilled computer professionals (or students) online is shrinking, as the Net grows and the World Wide Web gives more and more people easy access to computer networks, tech people still seem to be highly present in MUD populations. In WaterMOO, judging from online conversations alone, advanced tech skills are the rule rather than the exception. Technical knowledge is not always explicitly expressed in the writing of characters, as in anarchy, but the appearance of several (male) characters points in the direction of technical faculties and (California) computer companies:

> look Ragabash
> Shapeshifter Ragabash (why do I bother?)
> A six and a half foot man, with cobalt blue eyes flecked with slate. His eyes slit down, and the deep wrinkles betray his youthful physique. His body, seemingly forged in steel, is adorned by a tattered black shirt with the phrase "why do I bother?" stencilled on it, and a pair of cutoff baggy pants of indeterminate color. His long black hair, shot with bolts of iron grey, is tied off behind him in a ponytail. A single thick braid, terminating in a bright blue stone, hangs off the side of his face near his ear. He looks at you, and seems to be weighing how you will react.
> He is awake and looks alert.

Swedish computer geniuses working for hot consultant companies might still have to follow a pretty strict dress code, but this is far from the reality in the 'Valley.' Worn-out jeans, T-shirts, and long hair are part of the regular outfit, which is why California car dealers long ago learned to treat young men looking like 'Ragabash' as potentially very rich. Without implying that this man could not be found in the hallways of, let us say, a department of literature, it is more likely that he belongs to the laid-back crowd of skillful programmers and system designers. His "tattered black shirt with the phrase 'why do I bother?' stenciled on it" ("why do I bother" recurs in his @mood) is a splendid example of the type of humorous symbols spread around in these circles. On the other hand, what separates Ragabash from most male characters in WaterMOO is the way his body is marked by time: "His eyes slit down, and the deep wrinkles betray his youthful physique. [. . .] His long black hair, shot with bolts of iron grey." Age, if present at all in the MOO, is most often the age of youth. In many texts, age is not even thematized, which in itself might be a silent expression of an underlying youth, of the period in life when time is not a problem and life seems to go on forever.

The by far most common impersonation in WaterMOO is the 'realistic' male character. Not only do these characters introduce and define a gendered reality, but this is often formulated in a mode that could be called *online realism*.

look ACW
ACW (#22747) *Metabuilder*
A thin bald guy with a mustache, 41 years old. His sweatshirt has an emblem of three pine trees on it. The back of the sweatshirt is smudged with green chalk. He knows a fair amount of math and linguistics, and is interested in everything. Page him and strike up a conversation.
ACW appears awake and alert.

The point is not to speculate about whether this text mirrors the body of the typist or not, but rather to point out that a "thin bald guy with a mustache, 41 years old" who is wearing a sweatshirt "smudged with green chalk" has been created in a place where everybody can be young, beautiful, clean, and athletic. This is not to say that everybody necessarily would *want* to be all of this when going online. Rather, it is to pay attention to a tendency that goes against the often assumed idealization of bodies in cyberspace. As an ironic comment to commercials telling us that we do not even have to get dressed before going online, how we can do serious business in our pajamas since nobody can see us anyway, 'ACW' expresses an explicit lack of interest in holding even the online appearance together. The irony in this arises out of the difference between, for example, 'real' hair and online hair, since many men, unavoidably lose hair as an effect of increasing age. In the MOO, this is obviously not the case. Online hair, or the lack of such hair, must be typed into being to exist. To mention that everything online must be constructed to exist might appear to be a superfluous statement, but it can be useful to point out that no matter how 'ordinary' and 'everyday-like' a character might look, it is the product of a certain (more or less conscious) selection and creation. What at first glance might look like an ingenuous expression of the 'real' is no less a construct than something more obviously 'unreal' and imaginative, only harder to reveal as such.

Such perspective is certainly nothing new or unusual in the study of literature, where realism is a fictive genre, only more naturalistic than, for example, fantasy or romance. Realism is usually thought of as a transparent mode, in which its discursive constitution is hidden by processes of naturalization: "It is characterized by an inability or a refusal to know itself as writing; illusionism, a kind of willful self-blindness destined to induce in its reader a reciprocal self-blindness."[21] It appears to be natural rather than culturally constructed, as if it were a simple reflection or an unmediated image of reality:

> Realism involves a fidelity both to the physical, sensually perceived details of the external world, and to the values of the dominant ideology. [. . .] Realism's desire to 'get the details right' is an ideological practice, for the believability of its fidelity to 'the real' is transferred to the ideology it embodies. The conventions of realism have developed in order to disguise the constructedness of the 'reality' it offers, and therefore of the arbitrariness of the ideology that is mapped onto it.[22]

The genre of realism is traditionally related to literature from the Renaissance and onward, characterized by its focus on individual experience, bounded by its mission to represent the 'real' conditions of social existence. While being driven by the same philosophy as underlying bourgeois materialism, the reality of the realist novel is first and foremost the reality of the bourgeoisie.[23] But instead of making visible class references, realistic texts proceed as if their ideology were not there, as if their reference were nature itself. Thus, the question that needs to be asked is not *"whether* realism of this kind is an adequate mode of expression, but *for whom* it is adequate."[24] If in literature realism is the characteristically 'bourgeois' mode of representation, the realism online in general, and in WaterMOO in particular, might be of a different kind. Or rather, online realism can be read as middle-class representations of our time, as an imagery of the (already) privileged, connected, and computer literate.

With tattered shirts, cutoff baggy pants and dirty hair as illustrations of 'realism' in the MOO, a certain type of masculinity oriented toward interests and knowledges is slowly taking shape. In sharp contrast to the idealized macho-maleness of swelling muscles and conspicuous strength present in much fantasy and science fiction literature, most male characters do not incorporate muscularity at all. (Ragabash with "his youthful physique" and his "body, seemingly forged in steel," is one of few exceptions). Instead, a visitor in the MOO is likely to encounter numerous nice, seemingly inoffensive characters, ready with a smile as they gaze back at their observer:

look Alen
Through gold rimmed metal glasses, bright smiling blue eyes glance up and gaze back at yours. Alen strokes his chin thoughtfully as he regards you, then his slender face broadens with a warm smile, as he nods to you.
He is awake and looks alert.

look Musiu
 Musiu (#22547) *Musiu of WaterMOO*
A quiet man, with a ready smile and a warm, affectionate nature. His eyes are quite blue and rather intense, but he's mostly harmless.;-)
Musiu (asleep) is sleeping

They express innocence without boredom, and invitation without danger. Blue-eyed and smiling, warm and friendly, 'Alen' and 'Musiu' manage concisely to capture the typical WaterMOO ambiance. More revealed than hidden, a stroke of sensibility and consideration is breaking through the lines, pointing toward a masculinity seemingly more connected with affection than with reason. One thing that these male characters have in common is that they can be very hard to grasp. The fact that they are cultural constructs, as much as any knight in shining armor in the same online spaces, might at first glance be concealed by their very ordinariness. As if they were translations of a reality not possible to interpret differently, they tend to be rendered invisible, and revealed only through deviant others surrounding them.

Stone, in analyzing how we easily forget that online communication requires sophisticated skills for participation, looks at a slightly different type of naturalization:

> In observing social interaction in cyberspace we find that while some aspects of meaning production escape traditional cultural codings, many things in the nets are in fact naturalized; and this more subtle naturalization can easily pass unnoticed. For example, entry to the world of virtual community requires high levels of skills in the English language and a high level of technical proficiency, but this annoying fact usually passes unremarked. [. . .] Of course to believe that in cyberspace everyone is equal merely because the codings that have attached themselves to voice quality and physical appearance have been uncoupled from their referents, and that this uncoupling provides a sensation that might be perceived as inherently liberatory, is to misunderstand how power works.[25]

Under the erasure of the illusory equalizing interface, in which those skills and requirements necessary for participation are wiped out, everybody seems to have the same access to online means of representation. But under this surface, a wide range of knowledge and cultural belongings are being hidden, of which English language skills and technical knowledge are indispensable.

Participation in online cultures demands access to computers and computer networks, which efficiently excludes an overwhelming majority of the world population. Furthermore, concrete access is evidently not sufficient, but knowledge of how to engage with the technology, and an understanding of online cultural codes, is crucial. Following Stone, this material and cultural foundation of online life easily disappears on the screen, at least for those participants for whom access to computer technology, advanced tech skills, and familiarity with online cultures are all natural.

Stone's analysis of naturalization online focuses primarily on how participatory prerequisites are being hidden through the process in which the textual representation is disengaged from the 'real.' As far as my readings go of character descriptions in WaterMOO in general, and of 'realistic' male characters in particular, necessary competencies for online participation are not disengaged from, but rather *reinscribed* in the online text. Mechanisms of erasure and obscured exclusion at work to disconnect the 'virtual' from the 'real' can be said to be working in reverse on the level of online textuality in WaterMOO, as to *reconnect* the 'real' to the 'virtual.'

If I understand Stone correctly, it is, first and foremost, already privileged bodies who can enjoy the liberatory sensation of the 'virtual' in its uncoupling from the 'real.' When she wrote this, the most numerous participants in cyberspace were white, middle-class, well-educated, computer savvy, English-speaking men, who because of all these components could afford to set themselves free from their own groundings, to move through virtual space under the illusion of equality and emancipation.[26] Even if some Internet demographics since then have pointed toward an increase in, for example, female participation, the above characteristics seem to be the elements that, more or less clearly pronounced, constitute the 'realistic' male character.[27] He is a turn-of-the-century reconfiguration of middle-class masculinity organized around the art of mastering the 'machine.' By being more or less young, white, well-educated, and computer knowledgeable, the 'realistic' male character is the visible and, at the same time, efficiently modest incarnation of the most successful cyberspace traveler.

THE FEMALE BODY AS EXCEPTION

In contrast to the position of postmodern utopianism in theorizing online bodies, ethnographic studies of MUDs rather go the other way and put forth the inertness of dominating gender discourses. This perspective takes on different shapes, but all of them point toward the belief that online bodies are gendered in ways that not only introduce gender conventions operating among physical bodies, but clearly fortify these rules. In her brief analysis of female characters on LambdaMOO, Caroline Bassett notices that the "female gender on Lambda is an exaggerated phenomenon. Hyper-femininity takes various forms. These 'women' display themselves in third person, with a battery of physical features. They tend to present themselves as objects of a sexual gaze."[28] In WaterMOO, rather than constituting a norm, this type of 'hyper-femininity' belongs to the exception. Many female characters might contain physical features, but few give the impression of being shaped as objects for a sexual (male) gaze.

> look Kerri
> Kerri (#22308) *Metadreamer*
> She looks at you with brown, sparkling eyes. She is almost always grinning mysteriously, but she'll never tell why. She wears a silver silk blouse and black pants. Her black hair cascades over her shoulders like dark, special chocolate.

In this regard, 'Kerri' is certainly a borderline case, dressed in "silver silk blouse and black pants." With "brown, sparkling eyes," she meets the eye of the reader, ready to toss her black hair while it "cascades over her shoulders like dark, special chocolate." These lines fit neatly within a heterosexual Western frame of beauty, where female bodies are molded to please male fantasies. Through the writing of a distanced third person, Kerri is herself being created within this very reflection. By creating a perspective in which she appears to watch herself through an imagined (male) gaze, the body in the text unfolds in a somewhat objectified manner, ready to be admired. The only element that might disturb this image of ingratiating femininity lies in the way she "is almost always grinning." Along the lines of female passivity and becoming moderation, it would, probably, have been more appropriate with a smile.

In her online article "Cyberfeminism," electronic media artist Nancy Paterson describes how a 21st century Pandora, a powerful bitch/goddess and android, infiltrates the imagery of the Net. The number of erotic representations of women, textually or visually floating around in cyberspace in a way in which sex and danger are linked to women and machines, are countless, but their presence has seldom been more obvious than in the era of the Internet. Or as Paterson puts it: "Cyberfemmes are everywhere, but cyberfeminists are few and far between."[29] Patriarchal representations of femininity occupy the space where women could define both themselves and their own relationships to new technologies. Nevertheless, fusions of female sexuality and high technology very common in, for example, computer games are hardly present in WaterMOO.[30] Even if gender appears to be a core issue for the participants, the exaggeration of gender in the creation of the online body does not seem to be as prevalent here.[31] Rather than alluding to the type of hyperbolized images of women discussed above, shaped through an openly sensuous, erotic vocabulary, 'women' in the MOO are usually written in a very different mode:

```
look Suzanne
Suzanne (#22424) *Suzanne of WaterMOO*
A 29 year old, who neither looks nor feels like her age. Nor acts it (see, you
can interpret that two ways). Slender, dark-haired and dark-eyed, her perma-
nent half-smile seems to suggest she knows or has secrets she isn't likely to re-
veal. And if you can't take sarcasm or cynical wit, you better stay away from
this lady.
She leans towards you and whispers, "Real women don't have hot flashes,
they have power surges."
You see Suzanne (tough cookie) here, but is she *really* here?
Carrying:
Official Dykes of WaterMOO badge
```

Embodying self-confidence, humor, and wit, 'Suzanne' proceeds through the MOO as the "tough cookie" she is. A certain ambivalence is introduced between her inscribed age, "29 year old," and the hint at "hot flashes" (here transformed into the more positively loaded "power surges"!), normally associated with older women. The sense of doubleness that follows online participation by simultaneously inhabiting both material and textual realms is implied in: "You see Suzanne (tough cookie) here, but is she *really* here?" Suzanne of WaterMOO is certainly here, in text, but the question seems to be: Where does she end? As communication technologies might be viewed as prosthetic extensions of physical bodies, MUD characters can be interpreted in the opposite direction. They could be seen as prosthetically extended in text in the direction of the keyboard and the typist. From the point of view of virtual beings, the material body is the extension (and not the starting point).

By carrying an "Official Dykes of WaterMOO badge," this text marks a different sexuality in the overall (silently) heterotextual spaces of WaterMOO. In her investigation of bodies in cyberspace, Nina Wakeford shows how 'textual bodywork' is performed on 'Sappho,' a discussion list with a majority of lesbian-identified subscribers. In contrast to a view of cyberspace as disembodied, the participants on Sappho inscribe their physical bodies and cultural identities in several ways in their postings. One way to perform a lesbian body on the list is through the use of feminist and/or lesbian signatures at the end of the message. The signature might include personal information, such as name, address, and a quotation from a central character in lesbian culture. Through interpretation of these postings, "bodies on Sappho actively subvert the norm of dominant heterosexuality in computer-mediated communication by the use of references to lesbian cultural practices."³² Textual activities on Sappho thus do not only introduce the physical bodies of its (supposedly) female users, but also create a space of resistance at the margins of cyberspace. In a similar manner, Suzanne, by deviating from an unspoken heterosexual norm in the MOO, makes this norm visible.

In comparing male and female characters in the MOO, male characters are overall more similar to each other than female ones. Moreover, the fact that male characters are more numerous makes this tendency toward uniformity clearer. Being in the majority, the male character constitutes a visible norm from which other characters, more or less automatically, deviate:

> look Izha
> Izha is a slender woman of medium height, with long black hair and eyes like cinders. Her skin is dark, arabic, and her face is painted in the style of Aegypt. Silver pierces her ears, her nose, her tongue, and dangles from her throat in a liquid seeming chain set with black stones.
> &ru's vampiric powers wrap her in shadow. You can see no more from here.
> She is awake and looks alert.

'Izha' not only differs from the male norm by being a woman, but is also different by being a 'woman of color,' or at least not completely 'Caucasian.' The fact that her "skin is dark, arabic" stands in sharp contrast to the overwhelming (virtually) 'white' population in this particular online world, marking otherness, but also making visible a differently 'colored' participation. The constitution of WaterMOO as textually white is not grounded in frequent, *explicit* references to whiteness in the descriptions (even though this occasionally occurs). Instead, this creation of characters with what seems to be a fairly pale complexion is accomplished on a more modest symbolic level, through logical implications of hair and eye color. Put differently, the color of their skin might not even be mentioned, but in formulating these bodies as either blue-eyed and/or blond, this most often presupposes white bodies.³³ Not a single character (implicitly or explicitly) is black. Even a character described as a model called Naomi turns out to be completely white. In *Race in Cyberspace*, Kolko, Nakamura, and Rodman point out that race seems to belong to those binary switches that, departing from the fundamental logics of zeros and ones, permeate cyberculture: "Either it's completely 'off' (i.e., race is an invisible concept because it's simultaneously unmarked and undiscussed), or it's completely 'on' (i.e., it's a controversial flashpoint for angry debate and overheated rhetoric)."³⁴ WaterMOO seems to be one of those places where the 'race switch' is off. In contrast to @gender, it does not have a property of its own, hence (virtual) race needs to be inscribed in a character's description—or evoked in conversations—to exist.

The writing of difference in the creation of female characters points in several directions. More or less hidden categories in most descriptions, such as sexuality, race, and age, are explicitly exemplified in these texts. To perform readings of male and female bodies is a tricky practice, not least in an attempt to avoid predefined categorizations and assumptions. To liberate oneself as a reader from dominating cultural understandings of 'traditional' femininities and masculinities on one hand and of 'new' and 'unexpected' ones on the other is very hard, if not impossible. Nevertheless, a world of multiplicity is never clear-cut, and once an interpretation seems to do the text justice, something new comes up that demands a new reading, a different perspective. As if texts, constantly, were resisting, they always keep moving and invite readings of both coherences and ruptures.

The fact that a creation of an online body @gendered 'other' is only a few keystrokes away does not necessarily lead to this being a common creation. Neither is the writing of an other-gendered body automatically subversive, leading to a notion of gender as fluid in the online world. On the contrary, the naming, @gendering, and writing of characters in WaterMOO rather seem to point toward notions of stability through the construction of non-surprisingly @gendered male and female characters. Instead of using the Net as a place for liberating transgressions and textual deconstructions of the physical body, most WaterMOOers tend to use the text to put the gendered body back into the picture, inevitably dragging a whole battery of cultural meanings with them. At the same time, characters in WaterMOO are also concerned with conversational strategies. These texts often invite the other not only to acts of interpretation but to *participation*. Instead of turning themselves into physical or literary objects to be gazed at or read in solitude, they actively disrupt such understandings by embodying speaking subjects.

Absent bodies

In an analytical movement away from a disparate range of online bodies written either in the mode of (nonrealistic) fiction or in the slippery domain of on-line realism, this final section is somewhat different from the others. If many character descriptions in WaterMOO are clearly physical, enhanced by the notion of 'having a body' inherent in the MUD program, there is a textual tendency that strives in the opposite direction. Instead of enforcing the way characters physically inhabit the world of WaterMOO by textually introducing physicality in the descriptions, these texts rather read as refusals of the constantly present possibility of body-writing. This takes place on at least two different levels: through textual performances in the shape of literary and lyrical quotes and through fragmented or completely absent descriptions.³⁵ Among characters who employ quotes as descriptions, there is a blend of 'popular culture' and 'high art' ranging from rock lyrics to Virginia Woolf and William Shakespeare:

> look Rosencrantz
> Rosencrantz (#14813) *Metaprogrammer*
> What a piece of work is man! How noble in reason! How infinite in faculties! In form and moving how express and admirable! In action how like an angel! In apprehension how like a god! The beauty of the world, the paragon of animals! And yet to me, what is this quintessence of dust?
> Rosencrantz appears to be dead on his feet.

When I asked 'Rosencrantz' about the source of this text, he answered: "Shakespeare, I would hope. Hamlet. First act, if I recall correctly," which comes through as a very different way of speaking compared with most Water-MOO conversations. This reply was a voice from within the play *Hamlet* itself, or at least from a character very much 'in character.' Dressed in Shakespeare's words, Rosencrantz moves through the MOO, interpreting a personal Shakespearean drama along the way. (The quote in question is actually from Act II, which might be of minor importance. On the other hand, considering the unmistakable English flavor bordering on cultural snobbism in the response, this 'mistake' might turn out to be no mistake at all. Instead, this could be an expression of pride in knowing, but not really caring, about the details.)

The name Rosencrantz is taken from *Hamlet* as well; he is a minor character in the play. Rosencrantz, together with his companion Guildenstern, are sent to kill the prince. The problem is that they are not clever enough to follow through before Hamlet reveals their intentions. Interestingly, the quote chosen for the MOO character does not contain Rosencrantz's lines; it reflects a famous passage in which Hamlet utters these words *to* Rosencrantz. This further strengthens the notion of the quotation as a paraphrase; a somewhat vulgarized classic take-off rather than a more sincere expression of knowledge. The name Rosencrantz could also relate to a renewed interest in this character, born of Tom Stoppard's play and screenplay *Rosencrantz & Guildenstern Are Dead*. In Stoppard's surreal examination of the underlying themes of *Hamlet*, the whole story is retold from these two characters' points of view. Knowing this, a use of the name Rosencrantz not only alludes to Shakespeare's play; it also takes on meanings from within a framework of contemporary film and popular culture.

Rosencrantz is @gendered male, but this gender position has also been given the more specific assignment "Serendipitous." It is possible to have a character @gendered, let us say, female, and then in a more personal manner to 'name' this position something else, for example "cybergrrrl." There is no @gender called cybergrrrl, but it is still possible to assign one's character with such a supplement. The activity of naming has no effect on what pronouns the MUD program uses for a certain character 'in action,' but these names can be seen as part of the description, as ways of giving the online body another dimension of meaning.

Serendipity, the faculty for making desirable discoveries by accident, as an @gender assignment could point toward the ability of the reader to (accidentally) discover for herself the gender of Rosencrantz. "Gender: Serendipitous" could indicate a playful awareness of how gender was a shifting, many-layered construct in Shakespearean productions. Performing Shakespeare was traditionally a task for male actors only, whether they enacted male or female characters. Given that female actors at the time of Shakespeare were unthinkable in his plays, cross-dressed male performers were not only common, but indispensable. When viewed from a contemporary perspective on cross-dressing as a strategy to make visible the body as a cultural construct, the classical Shakespearean drama has been turned into a playground of gender politics: All physical bodies on stage were male, but their staged performances can be seen as an exploration of a wide range of gender positions, which in turn opens up a variety of interpretative possibilities for the audience. Through the character of Rosencrantz, the complex interplay between 'real life' and 'play,' between bodies and masks, is translated into the world of WaterMOO. His online body is hard-coded as male (i.e., the MUD program will automatically attach male pronouns to Rosencrantz's utterances and movements), but the name assigned to this body in the online drama is highly ambiguous ("Serendipitous").

Rosencrantz might not be a radical refusal of the notion of having a body online, since he is conventionally @gendered. Since being a man or a woman is indissolubly connected to the idea of being embodied, it might be hard to imagine a character @gendered male as bodiless. Nevertheless, descriptions like Rosencrantz's can be read as negations of the many detailed descriptions of sexed and gendered bodies in the MOO while rejecting any explicit inscriptions of physicality. A few characters have taken this strategy a few steps further, excluding descriptions altogether:

look Rita
She is awake.

When I asked for this 'description,' 'Rita' appeared to be very surprised, since she does not really have one. But by saying: "I have no objections to you using my lack of description as part of your dissertation," she seemed to agree with me that absences might be as interesting as textual presences for my purposes. The absence of a character description is not necessarily an active counter-statement against the almost institutionalized activity of description writing in the MOO. The lack of description could, for example, stand for a lack of interest. But taking into consideration how unusual it is to *not* have a description, it is tempting to read these textual voids as strategies of resistance to the always present, if not imposed, 'possibility' of description writing.

Moreover, not to introduce a textual body already in the character description can also be understood as a wish to reach beyond the bodily surface, to be defined in accordance with words and opinions rather than with (online) looks. In a culture where the physical surface is increasingly important, it is tempting to produce places based on the *invisibility* of the physical body. In WaterMOO this absence of appearance is however constantly challenged through textual introductions of the categories excluded by a text-only interface (such as sex and age). Against the background of the reintroduction of the physical in spaces where physicality seems to be excluded, the absence of a character description comes through as an effort to resist the game of the gazes. In relation to Rita, this can even be seen as an attempt on her part to avoid being turned into an object of a male gaze, to be the one who comes into existence by, passively, being looked at. When typing <look Rita>, one might expect a text alluding to the actress Rita Hayworth—a voluptuous femme fatale with tall gloves, tight dress, long, flowing hair, and a piercing, seductive gaze. Instead, the reader is met with a typed silence, an emptiness or absence, with a non-text or a non-body.

Brief or missing character descriptions might in this sense offer a temporary relief from the terror of the body, a momentary solace in relation to the meanings embedded in matter. On the other hand, even if a description is never written, what appears on the screen when a 'descriptionless' character is looked at is not a blank screen, but most often a few lines produced by the MUD program. If the character belongs to a certain player class, this information will show (i.e., "Jenny a spirit"), as well as the 'awake'/'asleep' line (which automatically adds certain corporeality to all characters if not actively removed by the typist). What might have started out as an attempt to deny the watcher the possibility to watch has instead turned into a fairly mechanical construction (the necessity to consist of preprogrammed text). The body is still excluded, but it is replaced by nonsurprising machine lines. These lines are of course always present in character descriptions, but they become particularly obvious if the self-composed text itself is lacking.

It might be useful to point out that the lack of description in Rita is not the result of a lack of activity. The command connected to description writing ("@describe me as. . .") needs to be typed, followed by the return key that ends the (absent) description. The result will then be a missing description. In other words, a non-description is not what automatically occurs in the absence of action, but it rather has to be actively created to exist. If instead *nothing* is done, the character will look like this:

> look lennon
> You see a player who should type '@describe me as . . .'.
> He is awake and looks alert.

The line "You see a player who should type '@describe me as. . .'" is given from the MUD program to all characters, and will stay as part of the character if not removed with the "@describe me as. . ." command. This indicates how the program itself hides some cultural implications in relation to description writing as something one *should* do. The character lennon is thus the result of a choice of a name and an @gender (male), but nothing more. For being a MOO character, lennon comes very close to the mode of self-presentation common in chat rooms. On IRC, for example, participants are represented through their nicknames only, since the possibility to create more complex characters in these spaces does not exist. Names might therefore be more important to these participants than character names in a MUD, since your 'nick' in combination with your conversational skills define who you are to yourself and others. Your name might even be the reason why people start talking to you at all. In a place like WaterMOO, character creation is in a similar manner important for how conversations and relationships begin and unfold, but in this setting lennon stands out as being nothing more than a name. lennon, as a textual (re)incarnation of John Lennon (but with the common computer-culture lowercase beginning), inevitably leads to thoughts of the Beatles and early pop music, the political awareness of the 60s, etc. In the absence of an accompanying description, the importance of the name increases as the only means to make a first impression.

lennon can also be understood as a radical denial of online embodiment, not only by lacking a description, but more importantly, by being born in the outskirts of the MOO institution of "@describe me as. . .". When leaving the preprogrammed line "You see a player who should type '@describe me as. . .'" intact, characters often get the question why they do not have a description. In fact, nondescriptive characters often seem to be questioned on this point, as if they were withholding some important information from others. The crucial thing for WaterMOOers does not seem to be whether a textual body is a 'sincere' reflection of the body of the typist or not, but the fact that a body in text is *there*. Physical performances in WaterMOO are about coherence, and possibly, reliability. If a bodily characterization is coherent and reliable enough, it will not be questioned. A missing body is then, per definition, unreliable.

Spectacle in interaction

In her *Feminism and the Politics of Reading*, Lynne Pearce (1997) treats the act of reading as a romance with a 'textual other.' In contrast to the idea of the reader as somebody in search of something to interpret, an understanding of the reader 'as lover' emphasizes not only the emotional dimensions of the reading process, but also sheds light on the impossible task of ever 'understanding' a text/the other: "The textual other, then, is whoever or whatever causes us to engage with a text in a manner that is *beyond the will-to-interpretation*."[36] To use languages of love is thus an attempt to break with more instrumental models of reading that do not have room for the intensity of a love affair; it is an endeavor to release oneself from textual theories that cannot accommodate "the reader as lover, whose object is not to understand the text but to engage (with) it."[37]

This perspective on reading practices seems particularly fitting for the (writing and) reading of texts in WaterMOO in general, and perhaps of character descriptions in particular, since these texts explicitly act as textual others in inhabiting a space that brings together writing and social interaction. In speaking about the tension between poststructuralism and the capacity of imagination to (partly) erase the divide between sign and referent, the introductory quote puts forth something very interesting. Even if the poststructuralist point of departure in readings of character descriptions—as well as of my own analysis—begins from a place where textual characters are nothing but signs of their own universe, the understanding among WaterMOOers appears to be of a different kind. As part of the online 'reading fantasy,' these texts are rather responded to and engaged with as textual others—as subjects in texts to encounter and to perhaps even fall in love with.

The main question that this chapter tried to answer was what kind of sexed and gendered bodies are typed into being in character descriptions in WaterMOO. In "Imaginative bodies" and "Illusions of the real," a wide range of online bodies took shape, reaching from the writing of nonrealistic fiction to the ambiguous domains of online realism. In "Absent bodies," the lack of descriptions in the creation of characters did not make the character textless; it rather emphasized characters' dependence on prewritten machine lines. In contrast to the myth of the Net as a place where the most fantastic bodies are created (that *still* seems to circulate among certain scholars as well as in popular culture), character creation in WaterMOO proved to be of a different kind. It became clear that most textual bodies in the MOO are not only unmistakably human, but unmistakably humangendered (even in the case of fantasy and SF-inspired creations) in rather nonsurprising, toned-down manners. Avoiding implications of the fantastic, as well as of sexed and gendered hyperbole, these texts rather vacillate between the practices of *writing the self* and *making conversation*.

Character descriptions incorporate a mode of autobiographical writing; a typing of a virtual 'I' that is never the same as the 'I' typing, although materially intersecting. Texts (broadly speaking) are indispensable to understand—or perhaps rather to *engage with*—identities. It is only through signs and symbols that we become visible to others (and to ourselves), through which we can show who we 'are' or who we wish to be.[38] According to the French philosopher Paul Ricoeur, texts are not only vital to an approach of identity, but also necessary for the very constitution of the subject.[39] Similar to the impossibility of having an unmediated, immediate access to the world and to others, it is equally impossible for the subject to have that kind of closeness to herself. Rather, she constantly needs to make a detour over the other (which in Ricoeur's case means the text) to, again and again, find herself anew.[40]

In an online world populated by textual others, character descriptions are often written in a mode that incorporates both self-presentations and conversational strategies, very much along the lines of a lonely-hearts column. Textual bodies are displays of bodily contours and surfaces, lending themselves to the pleasure of being looked at and admired. They are costumes and disguises to be mise-en-scène that simultaneously expose and conceal various levels of online embodiment. WaterMOO is primarily a *visual* culture. Gazes are repeatedly exchanged, which bring textual bodies into being through an ongoing interplay between the activities of watching and of being watched. In a similar vein, Castle shows how 18th century masquerade

> had its undeniably provocative visual elements: one took one's pleasure, above all, in seeing and being seen. With universal privileges granted to voyeurism and self-display, the masquerade was from the start ideally suited to the satisfaction of scopophilic and exhibitionist urges. Bodies were highlighted; other personal features were subsumed. The event put a premium on the sensuality of the visual.[41]

But to look, and be looked at, is rarely the only point in (online) masquerade. Even if much joy is taken in the visual, this seems to be only the beginning of the show. Castle discusses "the obsessive verbal return to the question of identity" in masked encounters, and notices how several "unusual or bizarre features of verbal behavior appear frequently. [. . .] A sequence of set phrases—usually beginning 'I know you' or 'Do you know me?'—was often used to initiate conversations between masks."[42] In WaterMOO rather phrased as "Who are you?" in its various subversions ("where are you?," "how old are you?," "are you really a man/woman?," "what is your real name?" etc.), such invitations to similar conversations explore the mysterious field of intersections and discrepancies between those bodies that are both revealed and obscured in the mask/description. Character descriptions are spectacles of the self, in which textual bodies are turned into sights to be explored through the <look> command, but ones that at the same time explicitly invite others to interact with them. The question of identity is certainly bound up in a dialectic of the social: no audience—no spectacle—no-body, so to speak. Character descriptions in WaterMOO repeatedly bring together this notion of being on-stage (or rather, on-screen) together with attempts to reach out and establish contact with others.

CHAPTER 3

MAPPING CYBERPLACE(S)

Shall we repeat with the logicians that a door must be open or closed? And shall we find in this maxim an instrument that is really effective for analyzing human passions?[1]

If the previous chapter was primarily concerned with readings of character descriptions in WaterMOO, as a way of discerning cultural themes with a particular interest in the construction of sexed and gendered bodies in these texts, this chapter flows in a different direction. It moves from a discussion of online *bodies* to an analysis of *online embodiment.* When participating in textual activities of WaterMOO, with an interest in textual embodiment, it soon becomes clear that there is a whole range of spatial, or rather *placial* practices that shape and structure online embodiment. This chapter therefore sets out to investigate the interrelatedness of place-making and embodiment—the fact that having a body always implies being somewhere, as well as this 'somewhere' not making sense apart from embodied positions, trajectories, traversals.[2]

The Internet is often presented as a placeless medium, an infinite, abstract electronic space located everywhere and nowhere, rendering every conception of 'place' meaningless. In *The Fate of Place*, Edward S. Casey (1997) performs an impressive investigation of outspoken, as well as unspoken, conceptualizations of 'place' in the history of philosophy. During this fascinating journey ('journey' is certainly the word to describe such an examination!), Casey shows how the notion of place, long a repressed philosophical matter, is slowly gaining ground, so to speak, in discussions of subjectivity and society. Obscured in Western thinking under the universalism of infinite space—an abstract 'everywhere' that does not easily give in to a particular 'somewhere'—place, along with a politics of the particular, vanishes out of sight.

A parallel tendency can be found in discourses of cyberspace, in which images of 'global' connectivity promise that the *where* is irrelevant as long as you are 'connected' and thus part of the giant network that collapses distance into nothingness. But to erase the where of location, even in a seemingly placeless space where typed-in thoughts travel with the speed of light, obviously has its price for those who do not occupy positions from which to be heard. In romantic discussions of 'the global village' incorporating dreams of revitalized democracy and obliterated hierarchies, something very important is excluded.[3] Left out are all those differences grounded in diverse localities. What can never be included in the discourse of a global web of information, where bodies and their in-placements are made both invisible and equal, is the material conditions of computer technologies and the impact of the particular, local, and concrete. Sandy Stone has noted that only already privileged and powerful bodies, for whom the concepts of gender, race, class, and sexuality have never been problems, seem to be able to move around in cyberspace freely and unchallenged.[4] This argument similarly applies to the meaning of place, since only for those who already speak from privileged locations does 'placelessness' have a liberatory potential. They have nothing to lose if their referents are dissolved. But, in parts of the world where computers are rare, or where accounts are shared with twenty of your friends or siblings, if there are any accounts to share at all, place makes all the difference.

It is important to remember that the contemporary myth of networked globalization always hides its own opposite. When WaterMOO typists connect to the MOO world, rather than dismissing place as irrelevant, or erased in a striving toward a world where place no longer makes sense, this technological engagement creates another sense of place, a virtual place.[5] Being in WaterMOO is not to be nowhere, but rather to reside in a very specific somewhere, a place that, like Foucault's 'heterotopia,' is "at once absolutely real, connected with all the space that surrounds it, and absolutely unreal, since in order to be perceived it has to pass through this virtual point which is over there."[6] The question that needs to be asked is how place comes to matter in online practices in WaterMOO, and in what ways the sense of 'being in a place' ties into the sense of 'having a body' and vice versa.

The analytical strategy that will be used for this purpose can be understood in parallel to the cartographic activity of 'mapping.' Neil Smith and Cindi Katz describe mapping (here understood as a both material and metaphoric procedure) as "an active process whereby the locations, structures and internal relations of one space are deployed in another. [. . .] There are many ways to map a given space—none automatic, all requiring a substantive translation from the mapped to the map."[7] Mapping is, far from being an effortless, transparent transmission of the area being studied to the map being made, a complex process of translation, and thus of interpretation and selectiveness. Closely related to this understanding of 'mapping' is the concept of 'topography.' Topography, from the Greek words *topos* (place) and *graphein* (to write), means 'the writing of a place.' But, as J. Hillis Miller clarifies, the word 'topography' today is the product of a triple figurative transference. 'Topography' originally meant the creation of a metaphorical equivalent in words of a landscape. Then, by another transfer, it came to mean representation of a landscape according to the conventional signs of some system of mapping. Finally, by a third transfer, the name of the map was carried over to name what is mapped.[8]

If at first topography meant the description in words of a place, it then came to refer to the practices of mapmaking by graphic signs, to finally sidestep 'representation' altogether and create a more direct link to places being mapped. This third figuration, which according to Miller is the most common today, shows how "the conventions of mapping and of the projection of place names on the place are so great that we see the landscape *as though it were already a map*."[9] In this sense, the naming of places performatively creates what is being named. This notion of topography has proved to be very useful in analyzing online 'topoi,' since these are places that *are* their names, and conversely, these names are inseparable from their own 'making':

@join Evelyn
back garden
A wilderness. Nothing but weeds. Garden tools in a makeshift shed near the house. Hmm, looks as if someone has plans here . . . The sun is shining, the birds are singing.
Obvious exits: inside to Truthful Lie
You join Evelyn.
Evelyn is sitting on the floor.
Evelyn smiles welcomingly at your arrival.
Evelyn says, "hi :)"
Evelyn stands up from the floor.
Jenny blinks
You feel the warmth of Evelyn's embrace as she hugs you with affection.
You say, "hi there:)"
Evelyn says, "find some grass to sit on :)"
Evelyn sits cross-legged on the floor.
You sit cross-legged on the floor.

A place like WaterMOO might seem strange in the sense that some parts are very realistic, with strong correspondence to physical architecture, whereas most parts constitute a blend of different styles of building/writing within this vast collective project of individual construction work/storytelling. The writing of these textual surroundings, the creation of characters, their entrances, exits, and interactions within virtual rooms, are all *communicative strategies of a simultaneous mapping and creation of online places*. These rooms, locations, or destinations would not make sense, or not even exist, apart from the physical movements of characters within and between them.[10] In the above excerpt, there are several examples of the simultaneous creation of 'body' and 'place.' Greetings ("Evelyn smiles welcomingly at your arrival. Evelyn says, 'hi :)'") mark the entrance of a textual body into a room. Physical interaction between characters ("You feel the warmth of Evelyn's embrace as she hugs you with affection"), as well as between characters and the scenery ("Evelyn sits cross-legged on the floor") further reinforces the sense of being together in a particular place. It is in this very intersection between WaterMOO architecture and 'textual talk' that Evelyn's "back garden" becomes meaningful.

The topographic analysis of WaterMOO place-making and embodiment to follow departs from the most intimate level of individual construction work—the creation of private rooms. It then continues with modes of communication that tie the bodies of characters together while physically located in their separate virtual homes, 'speaking' to each other from a distance. Finally, the analysis follows how bodies leave the safety of their nests, to enter, move around in, and dwell in virtual locations together. In this sense, the analysis follows a motion from solitude to community, as well as from 'distance' to 'closeness.' But while certainly being a place 'in itself,' a world where text *is* matter, and virtual ground a place to stand, WaterMOO as place has at the same time proved to be a leaky construction where assumed localities of the typists' bodies, as well as cultural implications of a certain geographical taken-for-grantedness, are central features. Therefore, as a second step in mapping the world of WaterMOO, the interwoven references that link textual imagination with the politics of physical geography will be incorporated in the analysis.

HOME, SWEET HOME

>***Izobelle from Simplicity asks most politely if you would @join her.
>page Izobelle coming. . .
>@join Izobelle
>Simplicity
>A spacious room with a fire place on the west wall and lots of pillows thrown about in a haphazard way. There is a large bay window with green velvet drapes covering most of the window. They are pulled back with silver cords. To look out the window fills you with a sense of peace and serenity. There is a large wraught iron framed bed in the corner with mosquito netting over it. All

around the walls are prints of artists ranging from H.R. Giger to Bosch to
Monet. You feels a sense of peace as you enter. You know that in the roughest
of times, its the simple pleasures that always make you smile.
Izobelle is standing here.
Obvious exits: up to Solitude, door to Oak Forest, and down to This Corrosion
Welcome to uneasy happiness.
Izobelle goes up.
up
Solitude
A small, secluded room for reading and thinking. There is a comfortable chair
againt the far wall. Next to the chair, is a small table where you can place
your book when you're done. All around are blazing candles in tall holders of
wrought iron. The scent of flame and sandlewood envelops you, caressing
your senses. The walls are covered with shelves of books, more than any mortal could read in a lifetime. But isn't that all we have?
Izobelle is standing here.
You see SmallWoodenBox and Reverend's Tip of the Day Machine here.
Izobelle goes down.
[. . .]
Izobelle says, "here is another room. . ."
Izobelle goes down.
down
This Corrosion
You carefully make your way down the rickety stairs to find yourself in surrounded by darkness and the closing feeling of lonliness. The only light comes from a bare bulb that swings freely from a thin wire. The muskiness surrounds you and closes in like a thick, wool cloak in the spring. Your ears ring from the clamouring silence. Your eyes adjust to the light, or lack thereof, and you peer around the room in curiosity. The swinging bulb casts shadows cloaking most of what is surrounding you. The shadows never stop wavering. All you can make out are walls and barriers built up around different sections, perhaps hiding what's behind them. You can't decide whether or not to let your curiosity get the best of you.
Izobelle is here.

WaterMOO architecture is a confusing mix of a relatively coherent core structure around the Dome and a bewildered mix of thousands of individual constructions. The 'central' parts of the MOO world are public rooms, written primarily by those who founded this world, while most other rooms are private rooms, usually with diffuse connections to the core areas. Public rooms are linked to each other in a way that makes it possible for WaterMOOers to 'walk' between them with simple commands. Private rooms, on the other hand, can rarely be reached on foot, but need the more unconventional move of 'teleportation' through the command "@teleport me to. . ." or "@join. . .," which in an instant transfers the character to the location desired.

In the above quote, Izobelle asks me to @join her to take me on a tour of inspection in her virtual home. The first room, "Simplicity," welcomes the visitor with detailed warmth. This is the entrance room from which other rooms can be accessed ("Solitude," "Oak Forest," and "This Corrosion"). <Up> is, for instance, "Solitude," a private getaway for reflection surrounded by books and bookshelves. <Down> is "This Corrosion," a room in what appears to be the basement. If "Solitude" carries a sense of harmonious solitariness at peace with the world, "This Corrosion" brings frightening darkness to loneliness, a shadowland that appears painful to explore. A virtual home away from home gives WaterMOOers an opportunity for individualized place-making, for personal participation in the vast collective project of making the world of WaterMOO inhabitable and inhabited. These are the locations where characters wake up (connect) and go to sleep (disconnect), where they invite friends and lovers away from more trafficked parts of the MOO.

One way of approaching virtual homes, these microcosms of online life, is through a Bachelardian 'topoanalysis.' In *The Poetics of Space*, Gaston Bachelard (1958/1994) explores the interconnectedness of poetic imagery and the psyche, and he uses the term 'topoanalysis' to sketch out a field where the placing, or perhaps 'placedness,' of images in dreams becomes visible: "Topoanalysis, then, would be the systematic psychological study of the sites of our intimate lives."[11] To Bachelard, the primary site for such an analysis is the house and consists of an exploration of houses room by room as imagined and remembered. In contrast to an autobiographical understanding of self as narratively constructed through time, topoanalysis accentuates the meaning of places that one has inhabited and experienced, for "localization in the spaces of our intimacy is more urgent than determinations of dates."[12] In his approach to poetic and literary houses and rooms, Bachelard conveniently talks about the 'writing' and 'reading' of rooms in a way that is easily related to online textual architecture. But perhaps even more interesting from the horizon of WaterMOO is how the imaginary to Bachelard—as reflected in images of rooms: garrets, cellars, stairs, corners, drawers, wardrobes, etc.—is anything but chaotic and diffuse. On the contrary, the way dreams and memories are structured are rather 'placial' in orientation. This way of thinking about the imaginary is highly persuasive, since a place like WaterMOO in a sense is a dream world, but one that is carefully structured with 'rooms' and directions.

Bachelard talks about "the dramatic tension between the aerial and the terrestrial,"[13] about the house as an illusion of stability. This stability has to do with the house being imagined as a vertical entity, something that rises upward. The notion of verticality is tied to the opposition between cellar and attic, where the 'rationality' of the roof is opposed to the 'irrationality' of the cellar. As in the home of Izobelle: "Up near the roof, all our thoughts are clear," whereas "the cellar [. . .] is first and foremost the dark entity of the house. [. . .] When we dream there, we are in harmony with the irrationality of the depths."[14] Bachelard formulates a phenomenology of the daydream that approaches the complexity of mixed reverie and memory, the polarity between light and darkness, day and night: "In the attic, the day's experiences can always efface the fears of night. In the cellar, darkness prevails both day and night, and even when we are carrying a lighted candle, we see shadows dancing on the dark walls."[15]

This tension between aerial and terrestrial is highly present in the writing of WaterMOO, especially in the private homes of characters. These places have both light and dark sides, vertically arranged along the dimensions of directions like <up> and <down>. Bachelard says about stairs that we "always *go down* the one that leads to the cellar, and it is this going down that we remember," but "we always *go up* the attic stairs, which are steeper and more primitive. For they bear the mark of ascension to a more tranquil solitude."[16] In the home of Izobelle, the attic even bears the name "Solitude," a room with only one chair and one small table for books already read. In the entrance room ("Simplicity"), in what appears to be the most 'public' room of the house, the guest is met by the motto "Welcome to uneasy happiness." The notion of "uneasy happiness" beautifully embodies the tension between the 'aerial' and the 'terrestrial' by pointing toward the borderland between lightness and depth, that inhabiting happiness always implies difficult struggles. At the same time, there seems to be a way out of the house, or at least a temporary getaway out the <door> to "Oak Forest":

> Izobelle leaves for the door.
> door
> Oak Forest
> You walk out the door to a vast expanse of woods. The trees grow together thick and surrounding. The tall oaks tower above you, sheltering you and enveloping you in their fierce green and brown armor. Through some of the breaks in the leaves, you can see the moon shining brightly. The soft ramblings of a stream calms your mind and draws you closer. You hear the sounds of the residents of woods chattering and conversing, not even noticing your presence. You feel calm and safe.
> Izobelle is here.

A Bachelardian topoanalysis not only explores imagined houses in their verticality, but is also developed through the relationship between 'outside' and 'inside'—where the symbolics of doors and thresholds play important parts.

When "you walk out the door" you leave the house for a comforting "Oak Forest" that embraces you and makes you feel at peace with the world. It is exactly this 'walking out the door,' along with the possibility *to dwell in the doorway*, to rest in an in-between that is neither inside nor outside, that to Bachelard signifies how the notion of 'place' is not easily captured in static opposites. He shows how outside and inside form an absolute divide that blinds us to the shades and nuances of the in-between, the neither/nor. The division between outside and inside

> has the sharpness of the dialectics of *yes* and *no*, which decides everything. Unless one is careful, it is made into a basis of images that govern all thoughts of positive and negative. [. . .] Philosophers, when confronted with outside and inside, think in terms of being and non-being. Thus profound metaphysics is rooted in an implicit geometry which—whether we will or no—confers spatiality upon thought; if a metaphysician could not draw, what would he think?"[17]

The question is how, for example, daydreams can be forced into this razor-sharp split of on or off, here or there, this side or that side, absence or presence, being or nonbeing. Exactly where are dreams—or the unconscious for that matter—located? And conversely, how is *location* pictured in dreams? Bachelard calls such place-structuring oppositions "these unfortunate adverbs of place [. . .] endowed with unsupervised powers of ontological determination."[18] As much as these adverbs are unfortunate in relation to place and images of place in general, they are equally unfortunate in discussions and images of online places. Together with Bachelard, I am asking: "Shall we repeat with the logicians that a door must be open or closed? And shall we find in this maxim an instrument that is really effective for analyzing human passions?"[19] To inhabit the world of WaterMOO is to be both outside *and* inside, here *and* there, visible *and* hidden, text *and* body. The door to this place is neither closed nor open—but, as Bachelard would have put it, *half-open*. The entrance to a virtual world provides the possibility of residing in an extended state of dreaming wakefulness, transgressing simple metaphysical determinations. The door to the virtual world is a dream that points in two directions, toward text *and* matter, without asking the typist to pick sides. The trick is rather to develop an ability to simultaneously walk both ways and through typed-in enactments embody the state of neither/nor.

TRAVELING MESSAGES

If the private homes of characters can be seen as individualized place-making that in a sense incorporates imagined bodies of others, then when characters reach out to each other through typed messages that travel through MOO space, this more openly adds a communicative dimension to the relationship between place-making and embodiment. The following will focus on how locations are rendered meaningful through communicative actions, and in particular how bodies come to mean different things depending on where they are located and how they are typed into being. The most common mode of communication in WaterMOO is through the use of the <page> command, which makes possible communication from a distance. If you type @who, you will get a list of all characters currently logged in along with their current location. This list usually looks something like this:

@who

Player name	Connected	Idle time	Location
Jenny	19 seconds	0 seconds	Hotel CA: Her Office
Miriya	14 minutes	6 seconds	Miriya's Mysteries
Ventura	19 minutes	6 seconds	Koffie Place
Diablo	a minute	8 seconds	Alhambra [mailing]
Fistandantilus	14 minutes	10 seconds	Miriya's Mysteries
Doha	13 minutes	16 seconds	oOoO The Aquatic Dome OoOo
Starstruck	12 minutes	22 seconds	oOoO The Aquatic Dome OoOo
alexandria [Guest]	6 minutes	31 seconds	oOoO The Aquatic Dome OoOo
Ace!	4 minutes	a minute	Mac_Daddy's_Palace
Nash	12 minutes	a minute	oOoO The Aquatic Dome OoOo
shrimp	14 minutes	a minute	Just Another Reef
Dusk	13 minutes	2 minutes	Johnny and Dusk's spot.
Erin	an hour	2 minutes	Hotel CA: Erin and Alla
SweetHeart[Guest]	6 minutes	3 minutes	Guest Login Antechamber
Ringer	18 minutes	4 minutes	The Reading Room
Christy	5 minutes	4 minutes	Christy's Pad
Masked	an hour	6 minutes	Cloud Thirty-Two
Fluorine	25 minutes	17 minutes	Light Booth
Anla'shok_Winslow	21 minutes	20 minutes	The White Star
Torkain	57 minutes	57 minutes	My House

Total: 20 players, 16 of whom have been active recently.

"Connected" shows how long characters have been connected; "idle time" is how long characters have been inactive (if it is only a matter of seconds, this most likely indicates that typists are giving their next move some thought); and "location," finally, reveals where characters are located. According to the list, there are four characters in "oOoO The Aquatic Dome OoOo," but all the others are apparently alone in a room (most often their private room). This might mean that their typists are busy doing something else (Diablo in Alhambra is, for example, "mailing"), while perhaps waiting for a friend to log on. But it might also mean that they are in fact having intense conversations with each other—in 'pages'—sending messages across the MOO. Dialogues in pages are always entangled with automated page messages that accompany typed-in sentences. As most automated elements in MOO communication, these messages, if not actively changed, have standard appearances. Standard messages for incoming pages (messages coming your way) and outgoing pages (messages that you send) look like this (standard elements in bold):

(from Butt Ugly Farm) Jed **mindspeaks**, "hi, how's it going?"
page jed just fine thanks . . . you?
Your message has been sent.

But many characters have more personalized messages attached to their page activities. These texts can at times be extensions of the character description, as with Rosencrantz and his literary quotes:

page rosencrantz hi there:) are you busy?
Now are thoughts thou shalt not banish. Now are visions ne'er to vanish; from thy spirit they pass no more like dew-drops from the grass –
[. . .]
Take this kiss upon the brow. And, in parting from you now, thus much let me avow-
Rosencrantz pages, "not all that busy, why?"

They might also be functions of a particular player class, as in messages from characters that belong to the vampires of the MOO:

page slyvia hey . . . do you have a minute?
Your message travels through the darkness to its destination.
Slyvia uses her vampiric powers to mindspeak from OoOo THE AQUATIC DOME
oOoO.
She pages, "Sure"

But most often they are physical descriptions of how messages are transported back and forth between senders and receivers in a way that gives the MOO a sense of being a vast communicative territory: "Your message slides into an antique bottle, and you throw it into the sea," "A bottle of Spring Fresh TOILET DUCK flies in, takes up your message, and delivers it to Papagayo," "A small white dove arrives to carry your message away to Elasandria," "Small furry creatures scamper away with your message clutched in their tiny paws," "From across the miles, through a dozen network hops, you hear. . . ," etc. In the last example, the image of a physical world that is being bridged by a messenger (a bottle, a dove, etc.) is turned into an image of a networked social space across miles of physical distance. If most page messages are concerned with the world of WaterMOO as itself physical and with a geography of its own, then this last example rather speaks about what this textual world depends on, as meta-commentary that focuses on its construction through wires and computer networks.

Unlike group conversations in public rooms, conversations in pages are always one to one in a more private mode, and thus not possible to monitor unless you are in the conversation yourself. While often being more intimate compared with a 'noisy' environment like the Dome, paging nonetheless carries a feeling of physical distance, fortified by messages that describe textual transportations across the MOO world. While being more private than conversations carried out in a public space, where anybody might pass by and eavesdrop, paging is shaped around the distance between textual bodies securely located in different places.

MOVING BODIES

After a certain amount of paging, a common conversational move is to invite the other to @join you in your private room (or wherever you happen to be), which certainly adds an entirely new dimension to the notion of being 'face-to-face' with someone:

> You sense that Billy is looking for you in Billy's Castle.
> He pages, "do you want it all in pages or face-to-face?"
> page Billy face-to-face? you in Berkeley??
> Your message has been sent.
> page Billy do you want me to @join you?
> Your message has been sent.
> You sense that Billy is looking for you in Billy's Castle.
> He pages, "*grin* no, I meant join me or I can join you. Paging is awkward
> ... yes! =)"

This exchange took place at the beginning of fieldwork, which is why I was caught by surprise when asked whether I wanted to meet up 'face-to-face.' For a second I thought that Billy's typist wondered if I wanted to meet up in the flesh, so to speak. Then I realized that this was exactly what Billy meant, only that 'in the flesh' in the MOO is a textual affair. While paging contains sometimes disturbingly long page messages, lines of automated text that constantly intermingle with lines of instantly written dialogue, these extra layers of text are immediately removed when characters instead pay visits to each other. As if page messages not only mark distance, but simultaneously conceal textual faces and bodily expressions, this physicality is instead exposed when characters travel to 'face' each other. On a different occasion, I kept another character, Pascal, waiting for a few minutes while finishing up a few other conversations (in pages). But as he didn't have much time himself, he showed up in my office anyway, only to find Jenny all alone:

> Pascal knocks politely and wonders if he may @join.
> Pascal joins you, looking around, and then orients himself.
> Pascal smiles
> Pascal asks, "talking to your cappucino ?"

To teleport oneself to someone's room is, technically, only a matter of using a simple command (<@join. . .>) to continue reading texts from a different part of the MOO system. Yet, to invite somebody to @join you in your room—or to be invited yourself to @join—is in the world of WaterMOO most often a personal gesture to make a textual encounter more intimate. In his investigation of 'queer spaces,' Randal Woodland gives a telling example of the close connection between how place descriptions and spatial metaphors inform appropriate discourse in online cultures. The event took place in a MOO where Woodland's (male) character description incorporated a gay symbol: the pink triangle taken over from the Nazi concentration camp badge for gay prisoners. Another male character (whose typist Randal assumed was a heterosexual male) noticed the symbol, and a conversation about homosexuality was initiated. This encounter took place in one of the public rooms of the MOO. While the conversation got more and more personal, Randal suggested that they could move to his private room, to be able to continue in an undisturbed fashion. His conversational partner refused the invitation. This move from a public room to a private one—let alone their purely textual existence—was experienced as too much of a threat, as something too closely tied to certain gay-culture pickup strategies.

Paging and @joining are in several ways well-regulated communicative modes and moves, where textual bodies know their proper places in relation to the type of conversation they are engaged in. Newbies usually learn these strategies quickly, even though for some it appears to take longer:

> Big-daddy [Guest] appears suddenly in a puff of thick San Francisco fog, the reassembling atoms glancing and flaring. Big-daddy [Guest] looks about wildly, stumbles, and then orients itself.
> Big-daddy [Guest] says, "hi"
> We haven't had that spirit here since 1969.
> You say, "hi there . . . what are you doing in my room? :)"

> Big-daddy [Guest] says, "iwant to chat"
> You say, "could have knocked"
> Jenny grins
> Big-daddy [Guest] says, "sorry"
> You say, "sorry, but i'm a little busy you see . . . would love to talk to u later though . . . ok?!"
> Big-daddy [Guest] says, "wew ere do you live"
> Big-daddy [Guest] says, "@join jenny"
> You say, "please"
> Big-daddy [Guest] says, "can you tel me were you live"
> Big-daddy [Guest] says, "do you live in marquette"
> Welcome to The Hotel California!
> You exclaim, "now, leave my room, i'm busy and will talk to you later!"
> Big-daddy [Guest] says, "anser"
> Big-daddy [Guest] says, "is your last name sarison"
> Big-daddy [Guest] says, "please anser"
> [. . .]
> Big-daddy [Guest] says, "are you done with work"
> Big-daddy [Guest] says, "jenny jenny"
> Big-daddy [Guest] says, "are you home"

At the beginning of this conversation, I try to politely ask this fairly annoying guest-visitor to leave my office, but it simply did not want to listen. In a textual guise saturated with typos, this guest is not only intruding, but is doing so in what appears to be a rather careless, slovenly manner ("iwant. . .," "wew ere do you live," "can you tel me. . .," etc.). Obviously, this guest mistakes me for someone else, and it does not give up its attempts to make conversation even when I try to ignore it ("are you done with work," "jenny jenny," "are you home"). In a situation like this, there are a couple of things you can do: <@eject> the character and make sure that the security is on (that the door is locked), which makes it hard for the character to re@join you:

> @eject Big-daddy
> You expel Big-daddy [Guest] from Hotel California.
> @security on
> The security is on.

<@eject> rather violently expels Big-daddy's body from the hotel, making this command act as a bouncer that displaces unwanted characters. The existence of such commands shows that there is a need in the MOO world to regulate bodies and their locations—to create and re-create architectural boundaries that inform transgressors of appropriate positions in time and space.

So far, paging has been described as private messaging from a distance, whereas @joining somebody seems to connote physical closeness. To complicate this picture, there is a textual feature called 'remote emote' that significantly breaks down physical distance between paging characters. If 'emote' makes possible nonverbal communication between characters in the same room, then 'remote emote' works in a similar way across the MOO that in a paradoxical manner makes possible touch and gesture even if the textual bodies involved are located in different places:

> You get a nice fuzzy feeling that Guinness is trying to reach you from Guinness's room.
> He pages, "JENNY! :)"
> page Guinness GUINNESS!
> doo bee doo bee doo
> Guinness walks up from behind you and wraps his arms around you and holds you close.
> You get a nice fuzzy feeling that Guinness is trying to reach you from Guinness's room.
> He pages, "how's everything? :)"
> Guinness turns you around to face him and smiles into your eyes warmly. . .

In this exchange, there is a curious tension between the usual page-mode that communicates distance ("You get a nice fuzzy feeling that Guinness is trying to reach you. . .") and the sudden closeness that comes from a textual hug ("Guinness walks up from behind you and wraps his arms. . .").[20] The interesting thing about remote emotes is how they go against the type of realism that is a recurrent theme in WaterMOO practices. Without leaving the safety of their virtual homes, remote emote realizes what almost appears to be a telepathic mediation of physicality, a communicative mode that makes textual bodies stretch out across the MOO and reach each other in a way that challenges physical metaphors. But remote emote is not only about tenderness. It might also be the means to play practical jokes:

> Piggy sneaks up behind you, dumps a load of snow down your back, then runs away before you can recover.
> Jenny blinks

In remote emotes, there is what could be seen as a 'double twist' to imagined embodiment. In these moments, not only do textual bodies come to life through imaginative acts in the 'absence' of their physical counterparts (as is the case with online textual embodiment in general), but they come to life even in their own *textual* absence, so to speak. When remote emote is used it looks exactly *as if* "Piggy sneaks up behind you," but this effect is merely illusive, since these messages are sent from a different place in the MOO. In the moment when it looks as if Piggy "dumps a load of snow down your back," the textual body of this character has not been transferred to Her Office, but is rather performing this gesture from a distance. This puts a second twist to online embodiment in the sense that it points to ways of playing and fantasizing in the midst of the already fantastic; to the possibility of playing out make-believe acts in a place that is already a make-believe universe.

ENTRANCES AND EXITS

The sense of being together in a world gets even stronger through a character's entrance and exit messages (lines of text that announce the way characters enter or leave rooms). As with page messages, these texts can be seen as extensions of the character description, as elements of prewritten textual performances that give body and movement to MOO activities through spatial displacements. Entrances, as well as exits, seem primarily to be of two kinds. One of these departs from the notion of being in a world, or more particularly in a room, with certain physicality. These examples are from the Dome:

> A door in one of the far corners of the dome suddenly opens and out comes: lafemme
> lafemme grins from ear to ear.
> [. . .]
> From a hole in the ground, Digger appears.
> [. . .]
> Nash disappears suddenly, heading for the remote regions of WaterMOO.

In the first two examples, entrances are written in a way that give the Dome a feeling of being a fairly closed space, a room that can be entered only through a conventional opening in the wall (a door), or the more unconventional opening in the ground (a hole). The second example is evidently a pun that plays with the name of this character: Digger. The third example is an exit that not as clearly constitutes the Dome as a place with clear physical limits ("disappears suddenly"), but nonetheless locates the Dome in the center of the textual world (since Nash is "heading for the remote regions of WaterMOO"). Written movements of this kind simultaneously map out and create the MOO as a place with close correspondence to commonsense notions of 'real world' geographies, where there are (culturally defined) centers as well as peripheries, and where bodies cannot traverse walls.

However, the most common mode of making entrances and exits appears to be of a different kind, which, rather than imitating physical geography, parallels the logic of hypertext structures and experiences. In hypertext fiction, as well as with hypertextually linked Web pages, the reader/user clicks on a link and instantly finds her/himself elsewhere. Moreover, the relationship between the location before and after this inter textual leap is unclear:

> Sherry appears suddenly out of nowhere.
> [...]
> Alexander teleports in.
> [...]
> Devour floats into this location.
> [...]
> Rumor materializes out of thin air.
> [...]
> Fireman emerges from a swirling mist.
> [...]
> Ilyenna grows sad, and she fades away, headed for her home.
> [...]
> Darkness dissolves into darkness, returning to his abode.
> [...]
> izha collapses into nothing, returning to her abode.
> [...]
> Devour concentrate and float home.
> [...]
> Griffin disappears suddenly for parts unknown.

These messages of mapping the MOO space, rather than reflecting a world with material limits, take advantage of the displacement and transgression of borders in Web-based culture. As with Web pages, the Dome is still a particular place to be, a site, as is the "home"/"abode" for these characters, but the relationship between these points of location cannot easily be mapped out in accordance with a three-dimensional spatial logic. They are neither far nor close to each other, only 'connected.' When a textual body "floats into" a room and later "dissolves" or "collapses into nothing," the MOO, instead of being 'walkable,' is turned into an assemblage of interlinked localities that perhaps does not lack physical distance, but where conventional measurements are highly inadequate. The distance between various localities is rather a result of the speed of modems, connections, and systems.

In his analysis of 'virtual topographies,' Mark Nunes traces two types of cyberspatial metaphors that correspond to Gilles Deleuze and Felix Guattari's notions of 'smooth' and 'striated' space. According to Deleuze and Guattari:

> In striated space, lines or trajectories tend to be subordinated to points: one goes from one point to another. In the smooth, it is the opposite: the points are subordinated to the trajectory. [. . .] There are stops and trajectories in both the smooth and the striated. But in smooth space, the stops follow from the trajectory; once again, the interval takes all, the interval is substance.[21]

In Nunes' reading, hypertext applications (like Web browsers) make possible smooth cyberspace in their capacity of letting the user travel, traverse, of being 'distributed' in a space of fluid transit and continual passage. To 'browse,' more than being an activity of moving from destination to destination, is a drifting motion where Web pages gradually unfold as points that are being passed. In contrast, Nunes puts forth that MOOs are extremely striated in being topographies that are 'fleshed out' by descriptions of characters and rooms, and that have characters literally inhabiting these rooms. A MOO is in this sense a home, a destination, and not a point of passage on a continuous journey: "The goal of the [MOO] application, then, is not to establish a nomadic flow of users and information; quite the opposite, this striating user interface aims at creating a stable, inhabitable world."[22]

It would be hard to deny that a MOO is more of a striated than a smooth space, but as Deleuze and Guattari point out: "The two spaces in fact exist only in mixture: smooth space is constantly being translated, traversed into striated space: striated space is constantly being reversed, returned to a smooth space."[23] A MOO in its very constitution is a hypertext, linking together locations in a sense that renders the system open to a reversal from striated to smooth space. Even if the MOO world is a relatively 'closed' system that needs to be entered and exited through acts of connection/disconnection, its hypertextual structure makes possible nomadic explorations within these striated limits. In carrying out a topographic analysis of WaterMOO, place-making as a stabilizing practice is a recurrent theme, but one that repeatedly gets disrupted by destabilizing spatial metaphors. In the above examples, as well as the Dome being the center of the MOO universe, it might also be mapped out as a node in a network that lacks clear limits.

SEXUAL BODIES, DISSOLVING PLACES

As has been shown, the construction of place(s) in WaterMOO has everything to do with various types of *embodied communication*. Through different communicative strategies, bodies and locations are simultaneously created and rendered meaningful. But there are instances when the notion of 'having a body' appears to get so strong as to completely overshadow, if not dissolve, the sense of 'being somewhere.' These are moments when textual presence in the same room is absolutely needed, and when a certain collaboratively typed-in physicality dissolves distances on all levels: between characters, between typists and characters, and between typists. These moments are generally referred to as 'cybersex,' which in a text-based virtual world takes on the character of collaboratively typed-in erotica where typists through <emote> commands engage their characters in sexual acts and enactments.[24]

Like all textual practices in a MOO, cybersex might be a literary event, where collectively created fantasies and textual pleasures are acted out in an imaginative space that appears to be temporarily disconnected from the physical realm. At the same time, it is not hard to see that this type of sensuous, erotic textuality significantly blurs the boundaries between textual fantasies and fleshly desires in its capacity to retroact on the bodies of the typists. It might seem superfluous to say that there are no clear boundaries between the corporeal and the imaginative, that these realms have considerable leakages that continuously make them invade each other. But in fact it seems pretty useful within the context of studies in 'cyberculture,' in between arguments of postmodern utopianism (the online world as disengaged from the physical) and realistic determinism (the online world as a copy of the 'real'), to put forth that a text-based virtual world might be an *extension* of the corporeal, as well as the physical a refiguration or perhaps rather an *incarnation* of the textual.

It is a well-known truth in (Water)MOO culture that guest characters are not always innocent newbies, but that they might also log on and use the fairly anonymous guest disguise only to have MOO-sex with willing others. Come-ons from guests (in pages) is part of everyday life in the MOO:

> You sense that Superman [Guest] is looking for you in SomersPoint.
> He pages, "hello sweety, what are you up to?"
> [. . .]
> You sense that Superman [Guest] is looking for you in SomersPoint.
> He pages, "would you like to join me?;)"

In this sense, guests are the unknown strangers of the MOO, sneaking around in dark backstreets, so to speak, looking for adventurous company. In the above example, the proposition to 'join' this male guest marks the shift from speaking from a distance to (the wish for) an encounter face-to-face, or perhaps rather body-to-body in this case. The fairly unusual spelling in "hello sweety," which happens to fall between 'sweetie' and 'sweaty,' further reinforces the seductive connotations of these pages.

The following excerpt was given to me in confidence from one participant in WaterMOO.[25] As always in dialogical excerpts, names of characters have been changed. The episode is a log from the point of view of a female character, here called kim, in a steamy encounter with a male character given the online pseudonym Wildman:

> Wildman has engaged the lock.
> Wildman smiles
> kim smiles at you
> Wildman pulls back the top sheet of the four poster bed and slips under it, looking pleased and excited.
> Wildman unzips his jeans and slides them down, revealing his erect cock. . .
> kim comes closer as she starts pulling her top over her head
> Wildman eyes your sexy body. . .
> kim lifts her arms in the air in front of you
> Wildman helps you remove your top, exposing your small, firm breasts
> Wildman says, "there, that's much better, such a shame to confine them like that :)"
> kim sits down on the bed
> kim unbuttons her pants
> kim slides her pants along with her panties down to the floor
> Wildman says, "Mmmm, nice. . ."
> Wildman looks you up and down, nodding approvingly. .
> [. . .]
> You say, "roll over, hon"
> Wildman looks surprised, but kneels on all fours before you. . .
> kim pulls out the biggest strap-on from under the bed that you have ever seen
> Wildman 's eyes widen as he sees the size of the dildo. . .
> kim quickly straps it on. . .
> kim grabs your ass with her small strong warm hands
> kim slides her hands down your thighs for a moment and then up again . . .
> [. . .]
> Wildman reaches back and squeezes your firm tits, pinching them gently. . .
> kim fucks you harder and grabs your ass to make her movements even more powerful
> Wildman rocks his ass from side to side as you fuck him, making the base of the dildo press and rub wildly against your clit. . .
> kim closes her eyes as she keeps fucking you, feeling how the rubbing against her clit lets intense sensations run thorugh her body
> Wildman pinches your nipples harder. . .
> Wildman says, "Ohh yess, Yess!!!! that's it ! fuck me!!"
> kim slams the cock into you as she feels warm waves pulsating through her body, muscles contracting
> Wildman cries out as you slam the giant cock up his ass
> Wildman says, "oh god Yesss!!!"
> kim fucks you furiously as a tremendous orgasm runs though her body, making her screeeeeeeeeeeeeeeeeeeeeeeeeeeeeeam out on the top of her lungs!!!

Mapping Cyberplace(s) 111

In an intense textual exchange like this one, saturated with sexual fantasies, the fact that these textual bodies are located in the same room makes all the difference. No matter how seductive page messages might be, the potential tension that might build in whispering voices from a distance immediately gives in to a hands-on aesthetics when it comes to cybersex. In a careful reading of the above excerpt it becomes clear that not only the distance between bodies in text are disappearing, but also the meaning of place on all levels. There are occasional references to the room in which this encounter takes place ("Wildman pulls back the top sheet of the four poster bed and slips under it," "kim slides her pants along with her panties down to the floor"), but most of the lines are rather intensely concerned with the moves and motions of the bodies involved—regardless of 'where' this is taking place. With incredible detail and precision, a tangible *thereness* is constructed linguistically in a sense that makes language-made bodies vibrate. Fusing, almost melting together through a rhythmically co-produced narrative of digital seduction, typed-in enactments are increasingly 'fleshed-out.' Words of desire are turned into embodied sensations, and sensuous inscriptions feed back into the ongoing story of textual satisfaction. These passionate textual acts might be the ultimate case study of online bodies, since in few other moments is the line between text and matter so obviously fragile. If earlier, language was used to create place, language is here rather used to *erase* place in favor of the creation of bodily closeness. In this very erasure of the online world as a place 'in itself,' the question of 'where' (as will become clear) takes on entirely different meanings. In the disappearance of place as a merely 'textual' construction, a space is opened up that points toward the embodied nature of online textuality.

"WHERE YOU MOOING FROM?"

> ElBosso (Proudly Canadian) [to Orangina]: "where you mooing from?"
> Orangina [to ElBosso]: "the library."
> Jenny chuckles
> Tom is here.
> Orangina [to ElBosso]: "the u of t library."
> ElBosso (Proudly Canadian) [to Orangina]: "I mean where in the world??"
> Orangina [to ElBosso]: "downtown TO."
> Sunnysideup floats into this location.
> Tom hugs you.
> Oxford [Guest] drops a giant beach ball.
> Sunnysideup smiles and waves Hello!
> ElBosso (Proudly Canadian) [to Orangina]: "Oh, I'm in Ottawa!"
> Orangina nods at ElBosso.

Jenny smiles at Tom
Orangina [to ElBosso]: "cold up there?"
ElBosso (Proudly Canadian) waves to Sunnysideup
Sunnysideup [to Tom]: "Hi."
Orangina [to ElBosso]: "have you seen the new american embassy yet?"
ElBosso (Proudly Canadian) [to Orangina]: "not so bad . . . around 12"
ElBosso (Proudly Canadian) [to Orangina]: "j yep. .don't like it"
Dana (when I sing, I see the world) teleports in.
Orangina [to ElBosso]: "I haven't heard anything good about it. . ."
Orangina hugs Dana.
Orangina says, "It's be er supposed to be abeautiful day tomororw."

Conversations in WaterMOO are constituted through at least two different types of references, relating to two kinds of placial geographies: those that point toward the physical world of the typists ("where you mooing from?"), and those that refer to the textual world itself ("Sunnysideup floats into this location"). In the above excerpt, utterances being 'spoken' belong to the former type of reference, whereas words used to create actions belong to the latter. The dialogue between ElBosso (Proudly Canadian) and Orangina is concerned with where in the world they are physically located. Questions like "Where are you?" or "Where do you live?", here phrased as "where you mooing from?", are posed frequently in the MOO, which seems to suggest a wish to disrupt the uncertainty of location inherent in online worlds. In other words, the relative instability of online textualities is continuously disrupted by the seemingly stabilizing construction of placial belongings. In Water-MOO, you can never know if the person you meet lives on the other side of the world, or if s/he is your next-door neighbor, which is certainly part of the magic. Nevertheless, this feeling of a fairly abstract, free-floating space is constantly challenged by WaterMOOers, who spend a considerable amount of time on the creation of geographical anchorage for unanchorable texts.

When Orangina answers the question "where you mooing from" with "the library," she seems much less eager to elaborate on the topic than ElBosso, wittingly avoiding the question altogether. But ElBosso keeps trying: "I mean where in the world??" No matter if Orangina's typist is seated in "downtown TO" (Toronto) or not, these questions and their answers constitute a sense of geographical connectedness in contrast to the often assumed 'placelessness' of cyberspace. This notion of a recognizable location is further negotiated and refined in the continuation: "have you seen the new american embassy yet?" answered with "j yep. .don't like it," suggesting a mutual architectural knowledge about the place in question.

In the above excerpt, WaterMOO is constituted simultaneously as a place 'in itself' and as a place with diverse belongings, both text *as* place and place as always materially/geographically dependent. Typed-in motions between these levels of 'placefulness' (a concept that attempts to break with the all too stable stability of commonsense understandings of 'place,' flirting with the kindred 'playful') weave together playful chains of utterances and actions that explore the limits of the keyboard in a narrow interactional context, with exchanges pointing toward the unknown. Conversational elements that take advantage of the existing situation and the comedy of textual presence ("Oxford [Guest] drops a giant beach ball") intertwine with assumptions about the textually absent ("cold up there?"). Together these two different textual modes constitute a blend of different styles, in which allusions to the physical world are constantly mixed with manifestations of the world of WaterMOO.

THE RELATIVE STABILITY OF MOO PLACES

The world of WaterMOO can be said to be characterized by a fundamental lack of stability, in the sense that digital texts at any time might be invisibly cut, pasted, deleted, transformed, altered, extended, rewritten. Besides carrying the potential of being altered, these texts are most often untraceable, non-locatable, efficiently concealing their once earthbound origins. Nevertheless, compared with other types of virtual worlds, a MOO appears to be suspiciously stable. Don Slater emphasizes the 'dynamic' character of IRC, in that nothing exists on IRC if nobody is there. IRC encounters do not leave any traces behind, but are urgently ephemeral, melting into air when the session is finished. In the same way, identity on IRC is exclusively created through a nick and a current performance, completely dependent on the presence of a typist. Participants cannot save anything for the future, not even the nick, and have to constantly reconstitute themselves in the present moment.[26]

Compared to IRC, MUD culture immediately appears strikingly material, since rooms, objects, and even characters are created and left behind, even in the absence of their creators.

There is, for example, a type of page message, a 'not there' message that substitutes for a character whose typist is not currently logged on. These messages of absence might be simple notes telling the pager that so-and-so is not in at the moment: "lennon is not currently logged in," "Marena is not here right now, but if you try to talk to her when she is she'll be happy," etc. Some characters have a more complex feature to handle their typists' absences, a so-called event log, which works like a textual answering machine:

> Your page has been logged in candle's Event Log.
> candle (asleep) is currently dreaming.

Characters, literally, fall asleep in the MOO when their typists log off and disengage themselves from their textual creations. This might even happen in the midst of a dialogue due to troublesome connections:

> mira has fallen asleep.
> Taxidriver raises his eyebrow at mira.
> mira has connected.
> mira opens her eyes and blinks a little, the clashing silver in her eyes gradually fading away.

The state of being asleep in the MOO, even dreaming, quite wonderfully works as an inversion of the 'real' and the 'textual.' If dream worlds or imaginative universes in the discussion of 'cyberspace' are usually associated with online modes of being, then the dream world of MOO characters works in the opposite direction. Deeply asleep in their textual beds, the physical world is what seems to illustrate the imaginative, a place that the inhabitants of WaterMOO can only dream about but quite never reach. In the above example of candle's event log, candle is still there (asleep) but unreachable in the absence of the typist.

When you connect to the MOO, you enter a world with its own structures, politics, and norms. You enter a place, a room, a character with a name, with friends, and maybe lovers. When you enter an IRC channel, even during an ongoing discussion, you face an empty screen. It is not difficult to see how this difference can deeply affect the ease with which you can textualize yourself and have a history and a potential future together with others. This is not to indicate that IRC participants do not develop relationships, but it does suggest that it is much harder for them to do so. In fact, IRC "lacks those processes of objectification through which cultural transmission is accomplished. While this might make for even greater freedom to experiment with identity and to marginalize the notion that any identity could be authentic, it actually militates against projects of either identity or community."[27] In a place where nothing is solid, it takes a lot from the participants, in terms of emotional investment and experience with the medium, to establish relationships and trust. The sense of not knowing who you are meeting online is in this way radicalized on IRC.

On the other hand, no matter how place-like, even corporeal, WaterMOO appears to be, it is only through the participants' textual practices that this world comes into being, or *materializes as* a place. The question that needs to be asked at this point is what type of 'reality' takes shape in place-making practices in WaterMOO. Which images of (physical) geography are reflected in online practices? What cultural positions, openly articulated as well as merely implied by significant silences, act as textual points of reference? An interrogation of this kind appears unavoidable after spending some time in the MOO, since the question of 'where' in terms of physical location is posed several times during each and every session, sometimes even from several characters almost in unison:

> You sense that Tim is looking for you in oOoO THE AQUATIC DOME oOoO.
> He pages, "where are you from irl?"
> Octopus (braindead) [to Jenny]: "so where ya from?"
> page Tim viking country
> Your message has been sent.
> Tim nods at you.
> You say, "viking country"
> stephanie [Guest] suddenly appears out of nowhere.
> Jenny grins
> stephanie [Guest] [to Tim]: "hi"
> stephanie [Guest] says, "evening all"
> Octopus (braindead) [to Jenny]: "Minnesota?"

'AMERICA' AS THE ONLINE 'REAL'

In the introduction to *Cyberspace: First Steps*, Michael Benedikt questions the "significance of geographical location at all scales." For Benedikt, "we are turned into nomads [. . .] who are always in touch" with the "spatial dynamics of the whole world collaps[ing] to those of a pinhead."[28] But, as I have been hoping to show, this assumed absence of geographical significations is seriously contested when looking at textual practices in an online world like WaterMOO. And not only are various notions of place and location written and acted upon, but this is done in a way that has everything to do with physical geography and cultural dominance. More particularly, as was hinted at in the above excerpt, this is strikingly often done in a way that constructs 'America' as the center of the (online) universe, whereas other parts of the world are left in the periphery:

> look Jayse
> A 24 year old graduate student from the south. He is 6'1 with brown eyes and short brown hair. He is sporting a goatee. He is dressed in a bleached pair of blue jeans, a white tee-shirt and a blue and green plaid flannel shirt. His feet are covered in Timberland boots. Page him and say hi.

Americanness can be said to be a silent norm, a hidden subtext that almost invisibly constitutes texts in WaterMOO. But this norm not only operates in its absence but sometimes rather is explicitly present in the making of characters. In Jayse, for example, the very first line hides an intriguing cultural implication: "A 24 year old graduate student *from the south*" (my emphasis). In the WaterMOO context, this hardly points in the direction of Skåne (the most southern of Swedish provinces), Provence, or any other 'southern' destination in the world. "From the south" is rather an expression of the underlying, constantly present US culture in the MOO, and refers most likely to the US South. Expressions such as "on the East coast" and "10.30 am, central time" are common, apparently understood in accordance with an American point of view. There are many indications of other locations and cultural references in the descriptions, but these are communicated as exceptions, in terms of deviations from the norm. For example, references to locations outside of the US are always made in terms of national belongings:

> look Arcade
> As you look at Arcade, you see a Dutch person aged 25, he's 1.86m (6'1" in length. That's the average for Dutch people by the way, they are the tallest people in the world. His hair is cut short, in sort of a tabletop. His face is friendly, although hardly ever smiling. That's the way his face is. :(
> http://www.tjohoo.nl/~tjolahopp is the place to be if you want to know more.

'Arcade' is an unmistakable example of the writing of difference. In the phrase "he's 1.86m (6'1") in length," the metric system is immediately translated into feet within parentheses, which indicates not only the deviation, but also the norm it is deviating from. Even if 'feet' is used in countries beyond the borders of the US, in the text Arcade indicates belonging to a nontypical system, which obviously needs an explanation in relation to the constantly used and seemingly all natural measurement of 'feet' in the MOO. Arcade is marked as deviant in: "As you look at Arcade, you see a Dutch person. [...] That's the average for Dutch people by the way, *they* are the tallest people in the world" (my emphasis). As opposed to the assumed nationality of most Water-MOOers, "Dutch people" are referred to as "they." They become the liminal case, the oddity on the border of the unknown.

If places outside the US are communicated as belonging to whole nations, all other texts, if containing a geographical location at all, do so in a much more precise way by mentioning American states or cities:

> look Dusk
> You see a girl who stands about 5'7 with strawberry-blonde hair and hazel eyes. She is an incoming junior at Richard Stockton College in New Jersey where she is working towards her degrees in Psychology and El. Ed. Her interestin include working out at the gym, enjoying thunderstorms, thinking the

> 101 dalmations are the absolute cutes, playing the drums and piano and being a litel silly from time to time. Well for all you that know me, I made it! I am officially living in New Jersey just 5 minutes from the love of my life! Johnny and Dusk are together at last! :) We are engaged and are planning our wedding for next June. I am an optimist who loves to smile. Always remember my motto! A smile a day keeps the grumpies away! :)

It seems as if the closer to the 'real' US the texts get in their references, the more detailed they become. "Strawberry-blonde" and hazel-eyed, the girl described in 'Dusk' is "an incoming junior at Richard Stockton College in New Jersey where she is working towards her degrees in Psychology and El. Ed." This is a very precise specification of locality, as well as activity, for everyone familiar with the location of New Jersey, what a college junior is, and what a degree in El. Ed. contains. Dusk is a brilliant example of the taken-for-grantedness related to the US as place and culture in the MOO, here in terms of geographical specificity and knowledge of the American educational system. The strong influence of American imaginary on the fantasy of WaterMOO textuality is constantly concealed, as if these texts refer to an absolutely natural reality. As with literary realism, this writing operates in a transparent mode, in which subtle processes of naturalization hide its discursive constitution. 'America' in this sense, almost unnoticed, becomes the online 'real.'

But America as the self-evident referent not only applies to the construction of WaterMOO geographies, but also brings with it a whole package of other cultural references:

> look Gilligan
> A clumsy young first mate, with a red butterfly collar shirt, a white sailor hat, blue jeans, and tennis shoes. I'm skinny and tallish, and I trip over things a lot. The Skipper hits me with his hat . . . OUCH!
> Gilligan appears awake and alert.

After looking at this character, I certainly could have done some research on my own to find out whether this was a figure that already existed in some context, but Gilligan helped me with this by referring to the creator of a TV show:

> (from Gilligan's Island) Gilligan mindspeaks, "you'll have to talk to Sherwood Schwartz about that one. . he created the show, not me"
> page gilligan i see . . . hm . . . what show exactly? :)
> Honest Skipper, it wasn't me this time!
> (from Gilligan's Island) Gilligan mindspeaks, "Gilligan's Island . . you have

never seen it?"
page gilligan noop, i'm afraid not . . . have i missed anything?
Honest Skipper, it wasn't me this time!
(from Gilligan's Island) Gilligan mindspeaks, "every American has seen the show at least once"
[. . .]
page gilligan so, is this show any good or not?
Honest Skipper, it wasn't me this time!
(from Gilligan's Island) Gilligan mindspeaks, "hmmm it's so bad it's funny . . . it first run in the 60s"
page gilligan see . . . and who's Gilligan?
Honest Skipper, it wasn't me this time!
(from Gilligan's Island) Gilligan mindspeaks, "a clumsy guy who trips over his own feet, and ruins every rescue attempt"

This exchange makes evident how readings always depart from particular cultural locations. But, as I have tried to show, such a particularity in WaterMOO is most often obscured by texts that proceed *as if* they were universal, constituted by typed-in utterances that skillfully masquerade as culturally and geographically unmarked. At the same time, drawing from the above examples, in what appears to be absences of cultural belongings, a wide range of subtle allusions to US cultures and locations are discernible. By logical implications of such allusions, images of America are written as the self-evident points of departure for WaterMOO textuality.

It seems as if the closer to the 'real' Bay Area the texts get in their references, the more specific they become. This can be seen not only as an expression of a belonging to 'American' culture, but also as a connection to a particular physical place. During the first nine months of fieldwork, I lived and worked in Berkeley. This was a strange feeling, since I actually experienced closeness, not only to the physical Bay Area, but also to WaterMOO itself. After returning to Sweden, by traveling several thousands of miles, I was suddenly far removed from life in the MOO. Overnight, the MOO was nearly empty and unpleasantly silent, because when I entered my virtual office from my computer in Sweden, I hit the MOO in the middle of the night! Almost all the characters were, literally, asleep. It is not surprising that WaterMOO, by being a textual reconstruction of the Bay Area, is thought of as somehow connected to this place. Neither would it be astonishing if people connecting to the MOO have a particular interest in the Bay Area. But what surprised me was how life in the MOO actually mirrored the way life was lived in the city of San Francisco and its surroundings. Drawn by a desire to be there, to feel the pace of California life, WaterMOOers even conform to California diurnal rhythm:

You say, "must be in the middle of the night where you are now. . ."
Evelyn says, "5 am"
You say, "tired?"
Evelyn says, "hardly"
Jenny is impressed
Evelyn says, "i'm home on sick leave. i live +/- on pacific time at the moment :)"
You say, "i see. . ."
Evelyn grins.
You say, "like that you won't be jet-lagged"
Evelyn says, "nope :)"

'Evelyn,' a self-identified Dutch WaterMOOer, was at the time of this conversation preparing to (physically) go visit an American-based MOO friend (hence, the talk about not being jet-lagged). Living 'on pacific time' here becomes a significant characteristic, a necessary investment in the most vibrating activities of place-making in WaterMOO.

A REALIZED UTOPIA

In his *Amérique*, Jean Baudrillard (1986) outlines an intriguing image of America as 'realized utopia.' This image comes into being through a double gesture, a paradox, since a utopia in its usual sense simply stops being utopian after its realization. But, according to Baudrillard, this is the surprising logic of the 'hyperreal.' He describes a place that is neither a dream nor real, but dramatically intensified in the present—a utopia that has, from the very beginning, been lived and experienced as realized. When America *as fiction* (that is, the way it dominates the world) is entered, Europe, Baudrillard's Paris, vanishes from sight, as if it were no longer there. Within this disappearance, 'America' becomes the center of the world, with New York and California as the centers of the center. These are places of pure acceleration, of high voltage, where dreams are not dreamt, but materialized, in a surface landscape of billboard images. In this sense, America is the very incarnation of simulation.

Knowing, living, and breathing hyperreal scenarios of deserts, skyscrapers, freeways, motels, and shopping malls, it is impossible simultaneously to know the language of simulation. To incorporate simulacra makes impossible an analytical approach to the simulated. Such an analysis becomes possible only from a point of view by which simulation can be denaturalized. To Baudrillard, this perspective emanates from 'the old world,' from (central) Europe, where reality is conceptualized (rather than concepts themselves being realized). In 'Europe,' 'we' have the same ideals of progress and (post)modernity, but the powerful linearity of history prevents us from making these dreams come true. If America is the 'original' version of modernity, we are the dubbed copy, hopelessly left behind in vain attempts to catch up, to imitate. We will forever lack the naiveté and the boldness that comes with a non-culture or un-culture, a cultural *absolute zero*. Along the lines of such a radical break with the past, the American 'original' version of modernity is a version that lacks origin, a version without mystical authenticity and 'truth.' Living through an experience that lacks/denies a past, a moment that misses every accumulation of time, life takes place in the eternal actuality of signs.

In contrast to an American life in the paradox of the realized utopia, there is to Baudrillard the lived negation of Europe. If the quality of the American lifestyle can be found in a pragmatic and paradoxical sense of humor, then, in Europe, we have critical thought, subtlety, and irony that come with a conceptual divide between the metaphysical and the imaginary. In America, this divide never existed, since the imaginary is always already materialized. Fiction does not equal the imaginary, but is rather what anticipates the imaginary by realizing it. This is why Europeans will never exist in a 'real' fiction, since we are bound to reside in the imaginary, in a nostalgic longing for the future.

Baudrillard speaks about contemporary America, and of California in particular, as 'a universe after the orgy.' California has become the ground for people who survived the struggles of modernity on the territories of sexuality and political violence. It has become the home for those who lived through anticapitalist fights in parallel with an accelerating passion for money, success, and new technologies. Somehow, they have all ended up here, on airy California campuses, jogging on the beaches in a decentralized, de-intensified, air-conditioned paradise of Silicon Valley soft technology. A paradise, as Baudrillard puts it, that with very little alteration can turn into hell. In a place where aesthetics and noble values disappear into pure kitsch, along with the disappearance of the 'real' into the televisual, the mythical power of California is: *"just in this mixture of extreme irreferentiality and deconnection overall, but embedded in most primeval and great-featured natural scenery of deserts and ocean and sun—nowhere else is this antagonistic climax to be found."*[29]

Even if Baudrillard's rhetoric depends heavily on cultural generalizations, efficiently erasing every similarity between 'Europe' and 'America', along with differences *within* their borders, his analysis is very persuasive. Now, my intention is not to cheaply state that Baudrillard's theory of the hyperreal appears to be written for studies in cyberculture, since life online is nothing but a *literal* simulation. To say that the Internet is the very realization, or even materialization, of a Baudrillardian hyperreality would be to miss his point altogether, since the realization is already in the image, in America *as lived fiction*. Nor am I saying that the Internet intensifies, or heightens the sense of hyperreality, but rather that an online place like WaterMOO is yet another manifestation, an imprint or perhaps a result of the mechanisms of simulation. In an analysis of WaterMOO textuality, of textual strategies used in the making of WaterMOO as place, California is certainly located in the middle of the universe. WaterMOO is a version of the American dream come true, a surface domain realized in nodes and networks that deny its very constructedness. The distinction between 'real' and 'virtual' evaporates, since when logging on to WaterMOO, you *are* in a sense entering the city of San Francisco and the Bay Area. While physically residing in this particular place, this phenomenon might be hard to discover. Only when back in 'Europe,' connecting to the MOO from this hopeless, 19th century bourgeois province (!), will the *distance* to this textual place be noticeable. A typically California 'flattened out' density is also part of WaterMOO, a textual place that simultaneously mirrors, extends, and retroacts on our images and experiences of the Bay Area. European WaterMOOers force themselves to stay up all night to get a glimpse of this density, of life as it is lived on the other side of the big ocean. And still, they seem able to only dream about the realness of its virtuality. When they (or rather, 'we') enter this place, the imaginary is being entered. To California, or 'American,' WaterMOOers, the MOO is no less real, no more fantastic than anything else in their surroundings. WaterMOO simply *is*.

EMBODIED PLACES

Through this topographic analysis of WaterMOO place-making and embodiment, several interesting features can be discerned. To briefly return to a Bachelardian 'topoanalysis,' the imaginary world of WaterMOO is far from chaotic in its organization. To Bachelard, dreams and memories appear in the shape of houses and rooms: bedrooms, attics, and cellars, clearly interlinked and limited by stairs and doorways in different directions. In his thinking, houses we have inhabited leave traces that are physically inscribed in our bodies. This puts not only 'place' but also 'body' at center stage of imagination. Dream worlds are thus not only highly 'placial' in their orientation, but also clearly 'embodied.' In this sense, body and place are inseparable; bodies are incarnations of places, they carry their dreamt and remembered imprints in ways that furnish and organize the imaginary. Along the lines of the analytical strategy of 'mapping' used in this chapter, this close relationship between body and place also works in reverse, since places can be said to be the result of physical mapping.

In WaterMOO, this intimate dialectic between body and place is exceedingly present. WaterMOO as place and imaginative universe has a clearly *inhabitable structure*. In the same way as bodies might bear the marks of those places that they have dwelled upon, rooms of WaterMOO incorporate the marks of imagined bodies of characters. Far from being a chaotic jumble of hypertextual links and networks, a MOO rather consists of the interlinkage of three-dimensional rooms—most of them belonging to the same symbolics as physical architecture. This certainly marks the limits not only for the textual world itself, but for which dreams can be dreamt and in what ways they can materialize. On the other hand, even if the placial organization of the world of WaterMOO sets limits for and shapes its embodied practices, these practices not only confirm this structure, but also challenge the borders of such construction. As has been shown in this chapter, *textual embodiment in WaterMOO simultaneously creates and exceeds online places*. Textual places are continuously written and rewritten through communicative strategies related to bodily movements within and between various locations. At the same time, these places are discursively exceeded, and thus 'opened up' in the direction of multiple elsewheres. Along the lines of Bachelard's poetics of the doorway, the notion of place in WaterMOO seems constantly displaced, or perhaps expanded, in the sense that it balances right on the border between worlds of text and matter, both creating and dissolving a place to stand.

This doubleness of (Water)MOO practices, which simultaneously realize textual immersion and critical distance, parallels in a sense the double logic of what Jay David Bolter and Richard Grusin (2000) call *remediation*. Remediation is the result of two interrelated but apparently contradictory tendencies— 'immediacy' and 'hypermediacy.' Within the paradigm of immediacy, the presence of the medium is denied. This denial strives toward putting the 'user' in the presence of the thing represented, in the very space where the objects that are being viewed are positioned. In a transposition of this term to text-based online worlds, 'immediacy' reflects moments of residing in a textual place in a sense that erases every act of mediation involved in connecting to and participating in this world from the online experience. These are moments when the question of 'where' coincides with the interface, since it is precisely this surface layer of the screen that smoothly overshadows the chain of interconnected con-texts at work in the creation and interpretation of virtual venues. As Beth Kolko puts it:

> Our interactions are with the representation of the machine rather than with the wires and circuits themselves; we meet technology at the interface. And while the technology that is the Internet brings us a cyberspace of multiple machines, multiple users, and multiple locations brought together in apparently seamless conversation, the interfaces that govern our interaction with such a cyberspace are responsible for multiple translations and accommodations.[30]

Hypermediacy, on the other hand, works in the opposite direction to discern how the creation and maintenance of this illusion of being *in* the image/text is completely dependent on multiple layers and connections within and between various media.³¹ It is these layers that are accounted for in questions concerned with the physical location of the bodies of others—since these bodies are as much part of the network as the computers they are engaging with. In discussions of the Net as a placeless medium, the paradigm of immediacy dominates that of hypermediacy. Immediacy, in its efficient ways of naturalizing the politics of the medium, is of course a perfect tool for creating romantic arguments of 'global (wireless!) connectivity,' of being connected with and to a networked world where everybody has a voice and where everybody can make a difference. The mission for the critical theorist is then to rather use the logic of hypermediacy to make visible the underlying requirements necessary to this apparently seamless globality. When digital technologies are thought of as having a built-in potential to unify the world, the fact that these technologies are nothing but immaterial and disembodied is being ignored.

In the textual interface of WaterMOO, mechanisms of immediacy are not alone, but continuously intermingle with those of hypermediacy. In this constant wavering between different but overlapping realities, falling into reveries does not contradict an alertness that simultaneously explores the material limits of these dreams. It is exactly in this in-betweenness, tying together multiple bodies and locations, that it becomes possible to lose oneself, again and again, only to find anew the importance of 'body' and 'place.' As long as some of the most common questions in online encounters are "where are you from?" and "where are you right now?"—reexamining and reintroducing borders and differences that seem to have vanished in the interface—mediation as well as geography on various levels will play an important part in stories of a networked, global world.

CHAPTER 4

CORPOREAL OBSESSION

Maybe what theoretical feminism needs now is a strap-on.[1]

    mira enters with the sound of chimes.
    Jenny waves to mira
    mira curtsies.
    mira asks, "Is there a particular thing I am supposed to discuss?"
    Jenny smiles
    Yazmine gestures to Jenny.
    mira clambers to sit on the side of the boulder nearest the fire.
    You say, "Yazmine here thought you would be a good person for me to talk to . . . i'm Jenny, as you can see, and i'm looking at the way people present themselves in text-based VR for my doctoral thesis. . ."
    mira nods.
    mira says, "ah"
    Yazmine [to mira]: "I thought she'd want to speak to you because of all the mystery you surround yourself with"
    You say, "i'm especially interested in the way gender works in spaces like this. . ."
    mira nods.
    Jenny nods
    mira says, "Gender doesn't seem to work very well at all"

In the midst of my fieldwork, Yazmine invited me to her virtual home to tell me a story about another female character in the MOO: mira. The peculiar thing about mira is that she is referred to as an 'it' by other WaterMOOers:

    You ask, "mira, you said?"

> Yazmine nods.
> Yazmine says, "I'll leave a note for it to contact you or something"
> You say, "sounds pretty womanly to me. . ."
> Yazmine nods.
> Yazmine says, "That's one of its female morphs"
> Yazmine says, "Most of its morphs are female, as well"
> You say, "that would be great. . i'll look for it too"

In this passage, Yazmine tells me that she will leave a note for *it* to contact me, which left me wondering why a female character is not referred to as a 'she' (in particular if the typist of this character chooses to let her curtsy on her entry, which is in Western culture a clear way of 'doing femininity'). Yazmine explains that the female-sounding name 'mira' is an index that this particular 'morph' happens to be female. In the excerpt that introduces this chapter, I express a wish to find out how 'gender' works online, and I get the reply from mira that: "Gender doesn't seem to work very well at all." The purpose of this chapter is to explore statements like this one, to investigate the connections between textual talk and typed bodies, in particular along the dimensions of gender and sexuality.[2] If the previous chapter was an attempt to map the relationship between 'having a body' and 'being in a place,' this chapter performs on a similar level and explores in what ways notions of sex(uality) are played out between 'the body typing' and 'the body being typed.' Toward the end of the chapter, the story of the 'death of the author' will be recounted in an attempt to situate (online) textuality in the wake of 'his' death, to move the argument from postmodern readings of textual 'surfaces' toward a theory of texts as always materially and sexually engraved.

"I'M STILL NOT SURE SHE'S A SHE"

> mira says, "Gender doesn't seem to work very well at all"
> You ask, "doesn't seem to work?"
> mira says, "That is why I never let anyone be sure of mine"
> mira shrugs.
> mira says, "People treat you differently if they think you are female or if they think you're male."
> You ask, "how long have you been doing that??"
> mira asks, "Isn't it better to make them just treat you as you?"
> mira grins.
> You say, "of course it is"
> mira says, "Well, I have been physically ambiguous for as long as I can remember."
> Yazmine [to Jenny]: "I met her, and I'm still not sure she's a she."
> mira grins.

mira says, "I do it in real life as well"
mira says, "Although of course it's easier in moos"
Jenny nods.
mira says, "It's a little funny. People on MOOs are more demanding about knowing what you are than people are in real life"
You ask, "but why did you set your gender to female then??"
mira says, "Which is rather stupid considering that it means more there"
You say, "that is very silly, i agree"
mira says, "My gender is set to female because this character is female"

In this excerpt, mira, who is @gendered female, explains that people (online) treat each other differently depending on whether or not they think the person they meet is male or female (in 'real' life), and asks: "Isn't it better to make them just treat you as you?" The wish to be treated 'as oneself' seems to parallel the ancient desire to leave the body behind and inhabit a disembodied universe. To mira, this longing for an existence in relation to which the body no longer matters is rendered accountable in terms of her physical ambiguity ("I have been physically ambiguous for as long as I can remember"). At this point, it is very difficult, if not impossible, to tell whether this physical ambiguity refers to mira's typist or the online character (or both). The uncertain distinction between 'real' and 'virtual' gets increasingly complicated throughout the excerpt, and culminates in Yazmines' line: "I met her, and I'm still not sure she's a she."

In MOO discourse, participants certainly say that they 'meet' in the MOO, no matter if these encounters are purely textual affairs. "I met her, and I'm still not sure she's a she" in this case, however, rather seems to indicate that these typists have met face-to-face, but that the additional resources available in face-to-face encounters (physical body, voice, etc.) did not clarify much. What captures my attention is the use of pronouns. mira is suddenly referred to not as an 'it,' but as a 'she,' even if the status of this 'she' remains unclear. "I'm still not sure she's a she" is of course a wonderful contradiction in terms, since it is most unlikely that one would be uncertain about a 'she' being a 'she' when a linguistic determination of sex has already been made. More importantly, this (Freudian) slip at the keyboard shows how hard it is to rest within a gender-neutral discourse in discussions of uncertain bodies. "I'm still not sure she's a she" can also, on the other hand, be a perfectly logical way in typed-in interaction to account for the multiple selves involved in MOO discourse, where the first 'she' corresponds with the female character mira, whereas the uncertainty of the second 'she' is directed toward the physical ambiguity of the typist.

Similarly to a novel, WaterMOO provides its inhabitants with a fictive world open to play and imagination. But apart from being textual in this 'literary' sense, MOO dialogues are literally technological extensions of the physical bodies of the participants, which, as mentioned earlier, make them an intimate part of a networked *social* space. Within this blend of fantasy and everyday socializing, the question of 'gender' (or rather sex) appears to be a burning one. In sympathy with Haraway's notion of the cyborg, WaterMOOers are certainly fusions of mechanical and organic parts in being both embodied typists and computerized, textual characters. But instead of embracing Haraway's hopes and desires related to uncertain and sometimes contradictory subjectivities whose significations are not determined by categorizations such as human and machine, man and woman, textual talk in WaterMOO is rather concerned with the reinscription of these categories. Following mira's lines throughout the conversation above, this text points toward a general obsession with sex and gender. At the same time, mira wants people to stop thinking about these categories and to start treating one another as (supposedly sexless) persons. A wish to liberate ourselves from the limits of sex is here repeatedly turned into discussions of these limits as inescapable.

Samantha Holland, in her work on body and gender in cyborg cinema, addresses the question of what it means to be human in an era when the boundaries between humans and machines are becoming increasingly blurred. She finds that cyborgs in films such as *The Terminator* and *Eve of Destruction* not only have bodies, but that these bodies are highly gendered. She further points out that the fears related to technology in the cyborg film are the fears of being replaced by, or actually becoming, a machine. In this becoming, which refers to a cyborg future in which bodies no longer need an organic foundation, the biologically engraved body is at risk of disappearing, and with it the notion of biologically grounded difference. In fighting this double fear—the fear of not only losing the category 'human,' but with it the category 'sex'—cyborg bodies are hyper-gendered, to ensure that sex differences remain even in a world populated by posthumans.[3] In WaterMOO, consistent constructions of virtual sex as either male or female (through the @gender command as well as the conversational use of 's/he' and 'her/him') could be understood in a similar way. In a world where you cannot be sure of whether the person you are meeting is a man or a woman (in the flesh), or even if it is a *person*, one way to deal with this insecurity is to textually reinscribe familiar categories on the level of sex and gender, to insist on a system of recognizable differences.

In the midst of the above conversation, a third character, Taxidriver, enters "A Cave":

> Taxidriver politely knocks on the entrance to A Cave. You get the impression that he would like to come in.
> A black fog rolls in from everywhere, and obscures your sight. When it finally

dissipates, you see Taxidriver standing nearby.
Yazmine says, "What a party today."
mira nods.
Jenny smiles
Taxidriver bows to all, and sundry
mira says to Taxidriver, "How do you feel about not knowing my gender?"
[. . .]
Taxidriver says, "Well, from a relational point of view, it causes a bit of difficulty, because normally people relate to people by gender among other things."
Jenny nods
Taxidriver says, "Translation to English: It bugs me and my pronouns"
Jenny thinks Taxi sounds very professional
mira . o O (that is something I tend to try to avoid)
mira laughs.
mira says to Taxidriver, "I hear that I have become "it""
Taxidriver [to mira]: "I dislike calling you an "it." But it's the only fitting pronoun I know."
Jenny chuckles
You say, "could have been worse."
Taxidriver says, "I mean, if I say "she" or "he" I could be wrong, and it's misleading to myself to fit one of them to you. Else if/when I find out the truth, I could be disappointed."
Jenny hmmms
mira hmms, as well.
Taxidriver hmms.
[. . .]
Taxidriver [to Jenny]: "Well, I know mira from powermoo. mira's character there has both female, and male morphs. So, if she had stayed to one gender or the other, I'd relate to mira as one or the other."
Jenny [to Taxidriver]: "but here—in the WaterMOO context—she's female . . . even if *it* doesn't wanna reveal its "true" gender. . ."
Taxidriver [to Jenny]: "Of course, all the intellectual stuff aside, I'm curious as he** to find out mira's true nature ;)"
Taxidriver doesn't relate to mira in the "WaterMOO" context.

In this passage, mira is returned to the position of an 'it,' even if Taxidriver eloquently articulates the dilemma this puts him in: "It bugs me and my pronouns." The paradoxical tension between mira's reputation of being an 'it' and the fact that the character mira is @gendered female is significantly explored. On one hand, the mystery surrounding mira does not seem to have much to do with the online character, but rather with the person behind the text who refuses to answer the question "are you male or female?"[4] This becomes particularly clear when Taxidriver says, "I mean, if I say 'she' or 'he' I could be wrong, and it's misleading to myself to fit one of them to you. Else if/when I find out the truth, I could be disappointed." Here, the online character mira seems to become almost transparent. What matters is the 'true' body of mira's typist, regardless of the fact that the character mira is female. But in the next moment, a few lines further down, the online body is instead saturated with meaning: "Well, I know mira from powermoo. mira's character there has both female, and male morphs. So, if she had stayed to one gender or the other, I'd relate to mira as one or the other." Here, the typist of Taxidriver goes explicitly out of character by referring to another game, "powermoo," where s/he has met the character mira. "So, if she had stayed to one gender or the other, I'd relate to mira as one or the other" indicates that a certain degree of consistency in the online performance is needed, in order for its integrity not to be questioned. As long as the character is convincingly coherent, and consistently written as either male or female, the issue of an underlying 'truth' might never be called into question.

ONLINE CROSS-DRESSING?

This raises some interesting questions related to the possibility of online 'cross-dressing.' In cybercultural research, the concept of cross-dressing has been limited to describe instances when female typists perform male characters and vice versa. Brenda Danet notes: "At least on the face of it, virtual cross-dressing should be much easier than real-life (RL) cross-dressing [. . .] [but] textual passing may be more difficult than appears at first glance."[5] In spaces where language literally substitutes for the 'real,' the notion of cross-dressing is intimately connected to not only the way bodies can be read *as* texts, but actually to the way bodies *become* text. 'Passing' is further turned into a textual practice, a matter of being able to uphold, textually, the illusion of stable gender identities.

Marjorie Garber investigates how cultural discourses of transvestites and transsexuals reveal fundamental asymmetries between definitions of male and female. She points out how transvestites (as opposed to *female* transvestites!), even though they dress up as women, paradoxically, still manifest their male subjectivity: "Their wives will address them as 'Donna' or 'Jeanne' or whatever, when they are wearing women's clothes. Yet this is clearly not 'female subjectivity,' even though it goes by women's names. It is a man's idea of what 'a woman' is: it is male subjectivity in drag."[6] In a similar fashion, characters with names like "Sexy_Babe" and "sugarpie" can easily be found in MOOs. Typically, these 'women' carry descriptions that point in the direction of 'woman,' but perhaps without convincingly reaching this destination. These texts could without much effort be read as male fantasies about women, or as male subjectivities in drag. But to do this kind of reading would be to reestablish the view of language as itself 'gendered' that I have intended to avoid. It would be to reconnect language to gender, to insist that language is grounded in and determined by gender differences.

Generally speaking, acts of cross-dressing rely on the knowledge of the underlying sex, no matter how unstable. It depends on a complex interplay between gazes and physical bodies, on the activities of looking at and being seen, on the power of the visible as well as the unspoken. According to Butler, drag has the potential to denaturalize and disrupt the notion of an 'original' gender, since the distinction between the material and the imaginary, between the physical body of the performer and the gender being performed, is put into question.[7] Parody, in this sense, has the power to unveil the constructed nature of gender, and ultimately that of sex itself. But, in a transfer of the concept cross-dressing, from physical drag to language-made online bodies, there needs to be a reorientation of the argument. If cross-dressing is understood as something that depends on the visual/visible, the discussion of online cross-dressing—rather than obsessing with a (possible) lack of correspondence between the body typing and the body being typed—would be better off investigating inter- and intratextual cross-overs. The kind of rift between the sexed body and the staged gender that Butler speaks of is openly actualized in WaterMOO as a rift between different *textual* levels. In this regard, mira and all the surrounding differently @gendered morphs is a prime example. Apparently, mira's shape shifting and @gender swapping render virtual sex-constructions unstable to the point where other participants simply run out of appropriate pronouns.

To return to the above excerpt, the difficulty of staying within a gender-neutral discourse when discussing mira, without being carried away by the inert dichotomy dividing humanity in two, is apparent in some of Taxidriver's formulations: "So, if *she* had stayed to one gender or the other, I'd relate to mira as one or the other" (my emphasis). In statements like this, mira's typist is no longer understood as positionless, but more or less consciously interpreted as a (physical) woman. In Taxidriver's concluding comment, this belief, or wish, is made even more explicit: "Of course, all the intellectual stuff aside, I'm curious as he** to find out mira's true nature ;)." In his capacity as a male character, Taxidriver here seems to express a desire to find out whether this textual female is a woman for *real*, thus actualizing what could be called a *heterotextual* male perspective. 'Heterotextuality,' obviously a fusion of heterosexuality and textuality, seems to be an always present reality in the MOO. No matter who the typists are, the relationships between these textual men and women are regulated by a heteronormative online system. The construction of WaterMOO as a heterotextual space might not be grounded in frequent, explicit references to heterosexuality (even though this occasionally occurs). Rather, silences and absences of alternatives to male/female sexual desires speak for themselves. Through their nonexistence, these voids of unformulated desires create a powerful normative framework in which WaterMOO relationships and fantasies are played out.

"SEXUAL BUT SEXLESS"

>   Jenny [to Taxidriver]: "so. . . . what's your image of mira?"
>   Jenny [to Taxidriver]: "as a 'person'. . ."
>   Taxidriver says, "Good question."
>   Jenny smiles
>   Taxidriver [to Jenny]: "Do you read Clive Barker at all?"
>   mira chuckles.
>   You say, "i'm afraid i don't. . ."
>   Taxidriver says, "Ah well."
>   You say, "would i understand this better if i did? :)"
>   Taxidriver says, "The best image I could compare mira to, would be the mystif, in Clive Barker's Imajica"
>   [. . .]
>   Taxidriver says, "The literary character is a mystif, named Pie'oh'Pah."
>   Jenny is listening carefully
>   Taxidriver says, "A mystif is a special being, rarely born, but very magical."
>   Taxidriver says, "And also a very sexual being, Although, it has no sex."
>   Jenny nods
>   You say, "interesting. . ."
>   Taxidriver says, "It's appearance differs for anyome looking at it."
>   You ask, "it has really no sex. . . . or is it just different?"
>   Taxidriver says, "Er anyone"
>   Taxidriver says, "It's all sexes, and none."
>   You say, "fascinating"
>   Taxidriver says, "It's sex depends on the person looking at it. For me, it could be a woman. For you, a man."
>   Taxidriver says, "Whatever person you would most desire, that's what it looks like."
>   Taxidriver says, "And it's appearance could change, even to you . . . because your desires could change"
>   Jenny nods
>   Taxidriver says, "I thought it quite fitting, since mira is sexual, but sexless . . . to me anyway."
>   You say, "very fitting . . . although i've never met mira before"
>   Taxidriver says, "Neither have I ;)"

In this excerpt, a distinction is made between having a sex and being 'sexual.' Taxidriver's comparison of mira with a "mystif" disconnects sexual desire from a body with a certain sex. Desire is here textualized as something constantly shifting, which appears in the shape and flavor of others' sexual longings. mira and 'its' other male and female morphs interestingly correspond to the idea of polymorphous sexuality and shape shifting. At the same time, the uneasiness related to 'plural' beings in the MOO turns this potential space for multiple desires into something safely unified and 'sex neutral,' projected onto the body of the typist. This move from multiplicity to unity makes mira "sexual, but sexless."

In all of these excerpts, the ambiguity related to the issue of 'agency' is striking. Who is talking? Where is 'it' (that is talking) located? In the above excerpt, this becomes evident when I tell Taxidriver that I have never met mira before, and he answers "Neither have I ;)," which with a hint of irony produces a difference between textual and 'fully fleshed' encounters. Lynn Cherny identifies the complexity of the relationship between the 'real' person and the character as one that contains both identification and distinction, but concludes:

> Generally, it is not a question of pretended or playful identification when a user describes something that happened to her character as something that happened to her: her character is her in the context of the virtual world, and there simply aren't enough pronouns in English to differentiate between the selves involved.[8]

This approach seems reasonable in relation to her purposes, since her primary interest is in how 'speech' in a social MUD constitutes notions of community. In analyzing MUD practices as a *register*—a particular linguistic repertoire—Cherny explores how communicative elements at a micro-level, such as turn-taking, back channels, and nonverbal expressions, create and confirm insider status. In her exposé of speech patterns in a MUD, the differences between MUD dialogues and face-to-face interactions are richly illustrated, but her discussion never quite complicates the relation between user and character. In fact, this relation has been very little explored in MUD research, but as these WaterMOO excerpts suggest, there is an intense dialectic between different levels of embodied subjectivity and the construction of textual talk.

Throughout these excerpts, it becomes clear that the relation between typist and character is a complex one, consisting of mediations between textual and physical realities. The MOO character mira is (unproblematically) @gendered female, but is also accompanied by a whole set of other textual beings (morphs), some of them male but most of them female, which belong to the same typist. This inconsistency in the online performance obviously makes room for suspicions regarding the sex of the typist, which might never have occurred if s/he had merely performed, for example, coherent and believable female characters. WaterMOO is an imaginary space, open to creative writing and textual pleasure. But when it comes to constructions of sex and gender, the demand for realism is striking. It is as if the online 'fiction' is suddenly too thin to embrace performances with uncertain or contradictory relationships to their embodied creators. At the point where textual playfulness intersects with @gender, nonrealistic aspects of an imaginative universe suddenly have to give in to a discourse based on naturalistic sex/gender incarnations. On the other hand, this means that if the online fiction is convincing enough, it might never be questioned. No matter if gender practices in online worlds typically follow 'conventional,' even exaggerated, gender codes; the demand for coherence (rather than correspondence) potentially creates space for a more subtle textual drag not immediately visible on the written surface. Or rather, this would be an example of online 'passing,' since the sex/gender fiction would pass unnoticed. But, then again, since it passes unnoticed it will lack subversive potential. The act of textual passing might be subversive for the individual typist, but it will have a very limited power over the demand for gender realism and heterotextuality in the MOO.

SURFING TALES AND ONLINE BETRAYALS

Textual passing might also have catastrophic consequences. One well-known surfing tale is the story of an American male psychiatrist who, out of curiosity of how it felt to 'be a woman,' created an incredibly lively and persuasive female online persona. In Sandy Stone's telling of this story, the woman is given the online pseudonym 'Julie':

> Julie first signed on in 1982. She described herself as a New York neuropsychologist who, within the last few years, had been involved in a serious automobile accident caused by a drunken driver. Her boyfriend had been killed, and she had suffered severe neurological damage to her head and spine [. . .] She was now mute and paraplegic. In addition, her face had been severely disfigured, to the extent that plastic surgery was unable to restore her appearance. Consequently she never saw anyone in person. She [. . .] [was] seriously planning suicide, when a friend gave her a small computer and modem and she discovered CompuServe.[9]

The setup seemed perfect. Julie's wheelchair-bound condition in combination with her extraordinary personality and willingness to help others soon gave her a lot of friends online. Many of these were women who experienced a rare sense of closeness and intimacy with her. But with time, too many contradictions entered the scene; Julie met a man, got married, and even began traveling to conferences all over the country. The problem was that nobody had ever met her. After a series of complications, Julie's friends started to get suspicious and her typist realized that he had to tell her friends that she didn't exist—that she was nothing but a figment of his imagination. The emotional response online was overwhelming. Most people were openly mourning Julie, but some women expressed feelings of being deeply emotionally violated, one of them even conveyed feelings of being sexually assaulted.

This tale is part of a relatively early era of Internet culture, when people were unfamiliar with this particular mode of (sometimes very intimate) communication where the physical bodies of others are hidden. The assumption is that cyberspace has since grown into a place where unexpected compositions of the 'cross-dressed' or 'transgendered' body are the norm. The 'unnatural,' problematic position of the 'real' transgendered body is in Stone's view turned into a 'natural' starting point online through the ever-present possibility of gender performances and play. In her thinking, the fact that online texts always have ambiguous origins turns the virtual world into a breeding ground of unrestrained gender play with subversive connotations. It is this surface layer of interface textuality that can seduce the naive user, who will then feel betrayed if there proves to be a discrepancy between textual and physical bodies.

Stone's vision of the online world as a paradise for transgressive gender performances is certainly a feminist dream come true, but one that still seems to be far from a widespread online reality. But the reason for this is not that the inhabitants of WaterMOO would be unfamiliar with online communication. Many of them could rather be labeled 'computer virtuosos,' but with a quite different understanding of what it means to be online compared with those inhabiting Stone's transgender utopia. This difference becomes particularly obvious in one WaterMOO tale of intimate friendship and bodily betrayals (which at first sight seems to carry a deceptive likeness with the Julie story), here told by a character given the online pseudonym Walter:

> Walter says, "I started mooing 3 years ago. A friend of mine spent most of her nights online on LambdaMOO and introduced me to it."
> Jenny nods
> Walter says, "At the beginning I was guesting and could think of more interesting places to hang out. But I had to stay online while at work and I got soon attached to the virtual world and the nice folks you can meet here"
> Jenny thinks she has heard stories like this before. . .
> Jenny smiles
> Walter says, "after 3 months I requested a char and I had to wait a long time to get it finally. 3 years ago there was a run to all the virtual places. it has become less, because there are too many out there on the net."

Already at the beginning of this story, the reader/listener is given an image of how online landscapes have rapidly changing terrains ("3 years ago there was a run to all the virtual places," etc.). At this point in MOO history, there was a long wait to get a character, which appears to insert a hint of nostalgia in this typing of a past where online places were rare and exclusive phenomena.

> Walter says, "I didn't take all the virtual places seriously, even though I could watch how my friend kept regularily falling in love with people online and soon afterwards was meeting them for real."
> Jenny nods
> You say, "did it work out well for her. . .?"
> Walter says, "she has had 4 virtual relationships and all have ended in a real meeting, but none of them had a happy ending."
> You say, "yes, that's the way it might turn out"
> Walter nods.
> Jenny sighs a little and smiles

In this passage, it is interesting to notice how concepts like 'virtual' and 'real' are introduced and used. 'Virtual' seems to stand for 'computer-mediated' ("she has had 4 virtual relationships"), as a way to point out the type of medium involved in these encounters. This is also the increasingly prevalent commonsense understanding of 'virtual' in the era of the Internet.[10] 'Real,' on the other hand, appears to involve physical bodies in a more direct sense ("all [relationships] have ended in a real meeting"). But this seemingly unproblematic division gets increasingly complicated throughout the story:

> You say, "how about you?"
> Walter says, "I am a very emotional being and I have been spending lots of time online. I couldn't avoid heartaches and falling in love online."
> Walter says, "I created a few morphs for role play games and after some time I have spent most of my time as the female morph. As I said I hadn't taken virtuality seriously."
> Walter says, "I lived my virtual life as a female for a longer time and made lots of friends online, who only knew me as a female."
> You say, "sounds very familiar"
> Walter says, "around xmas 96 I met a girl online who seemed very depressed and I talked to her for some time. We became friends during the next months and it was a good and close friendship. But during the summer we were spending too much time together and unfortunately our emotions became too strong for each other."
> You say, "did you do that as a female char?"
> Walter nods.
> Walter says, "when I realized how much I felt for her I knew that I would have to tell her about my real self."
> Jenny nods
> Walter says, "It wasn't an easy decision, because I also knew that it would end

the virtual life of my female char. And I knew that it would also hurt and disappoint other friends of mine."

If Stone's argument moves on from the naive user who feels betrayed when online texts turn out to be nothing but dislocated fictions to the experienced user who instead takes advantage of the disconnectedness of online fictionality, then Walter's story moves almost in the opposite direction. It starts with a user who playfully tries out different @genders but then learns that 'going virtual' involves both feelings and corporeality ("I am a very emotional being [. . .] I couldn't avoid heartaches and falling in love online"). When Walter's (self-identified male) typist had been textually passing as a female character for quite some time, he finally felt the need to let go of the cover, since the relationship to a character that he assumed was maneuvered by a woman ("I met a girl online") had reached such a critical level of intimacy.[11]

"As I said I hadn't taken virtuality seriously" stands out as one of the key lines in this passage. This formulation points toward a troubling of the real/virtual dichotomy as defined initially in the sense that it is no longer clear how the two domains of 'the computerized' and 'the corporeal' can be separated. "When I realized how much I felt for her I knew that I would have to tell her about my real self" is where the physical body has to enter the 'text.' This moment of discursive exposure of a sexually specific physical body both disrupts the act of textual passing and, by necessity, destroys the online body ("I [. . .] knew that it would end the virtual life of my female char"). Once a 'sexual difference' between text and matter is revealed, there seems to be no easy way back to a more innocent phase of interface pleasures. In the moment when the body of the typist leaves textual marks that point in unexpected directions, the spell of the online world is, at least temporarily, broken:

> Walter says, "She freaked out. "
> You say, "i'm sorry"
> Walter says, "She @gagged me right away and refused to talk to me."
> Walter says, "It took me 6 weeks before I could talk to her in a direct online conversation"
> Jenny nods
> Walter says, "that was 11 month ago"
> You say, "aha . . . and now?"
> Walter says, "we're still talking together and spending lots of time together. It's a weird relationship."
> Walter says, "There have been so many ups and downs. We have spent almost every day talking together for the past 2 years. There haven't been bigger breaks. Though we're both very unstable in our emotions. That what happened is still between us like a wall. Walter says, "she isn't ready for a real life meet-

ing yet. She is very interested in my life and what's going on, but she is still full of fears. She doesn't want to see me or a picture of me."
Walter says, "I have often offered to visit her, but . . . I have also invited her to Europe (paying the flight and the hotel)"
You say, "i see . . . very complicated, intense, interesting, frustrating, fascinating. . ."
Walter nods.
Walter says, "It's the most intense experience of emotions I've ever had."

Within the disappearance of the online body of the female morph, Walter's male body is introduced, and along with it a different type of 'virtuality.' If earlier, the relationship between the two took place in an online world experienced as an interface landscape, constituted through a series of playfully interlinked screen images, then this second phase of encounters is characterized by an almost painfully clear physicality. After the virtual sex-change, Walter says that she "@gagged me right away and refused to talk to me," which means that she made it technically impossible for him to textually talk to her. "She doesn't want to see me or a picture of me" further points toward a wish to return to the place where they were before, to clear the screen from all its suddenly revealed references to overlapping and interdependent materialities. This second stage of their friendship is distinctively different from the first stage in its sudden unveiling of *how (sexually specific) physical bodies are never opposed to virtuality, but are rather an intimate and integrated part of its very constitution*. This is not to say that the knowledge of the sex of the typist (which in online contexts most often is an ambiguous matter) provides a fruitful analytical point of departure, nor that the typist's sex can be traced and securely defined through the text. This analysis rather suggests that (all) texts always bear witness to the material processes of their making, and that, perhaps, this 'material testimony' is taken to a higher degree—that it becomes particularly obvious—in online textuality.

THE HETEROTEXTUAL MATRIX

Far from being disembodied and non-sensuous, the pleasure politics of cyberspace are an intricate issue with potentially far-reaching, yet to be explored consequences. If the relationship between Walter and his 'girl' was halfway disrupted by a sudden exposure of how textual talk is always dependent on embodied typists, the physical engagement in sexual textual talk is of a different kind. In the previous chapter, a sexual encounter between a female and a male character was briefly discussed as being a moment where the interplay between typed bodies is on the verge of dissolving the meaning of 'place' online. If initially the fact that these textual bodies were in the same room was highly significant in relation to the fantasies that could be acted out, the ongoing construction of this room (through references to doors, walls, furniture, etc.) soon gave in to a textual obsession with intertwined bodies to the point where every trace of the surroundings disappeared. In a rereading of this excerpt (this time the uncut version!) with sensitivity to the ongoing construction of heterotextuality in the MOO, the analytical focus will shift from an interrogation of body and place toward an engagement with textuality and desire; how sexually specific bodies are typed into being through a co-produced enactment of a particular (male) fantasy:

> Wildman has engaged the lock.
> Wildman smiles
> kim smiles at you
> Wildman pulls back the top sheet of the four poster bed and slips under it, looking pleased and excited.
> Wildman unzips his jeans and slides them down, revealing his erect cock. . .
> kim comes closer as she starts pulling her top over her head
> Wildman eyes your sexy body. . .
> kim lifts her arms in the air in front of you
> Wildman helps you remove your top, exposing your small, firm breasts
> Wildman says, "there, that's much better, such a shame to confine them like that :)"
> kim sits down on the bed
> kim unbuttons her pants
> kim slides her pants along with her panties down to the floor
> Wildman says, "Mmmm, nice. . ."
> Wildman looks you up and down, nodding approvingly. .

The opening lines of this excerpt indicate a fairly 'traditional' encounter, heterotextually speaking. Wildman reveals "his erect cock," "eyes [kim's] sexy body," exposes her breasts, and watches her undress while "nodding approvingly." He is the one who acts and initiates action; he engages the lock, shows off his excitement, and starts the undressing. She is rather the object of his desire; she lets him undress her with eyes and hands and does nothing but be there for his approval and appreciation.

In *Masculinities*, R. W. Connell (1995) discusses the gendered character of sexual desire: "The practices that shape and realize desire are [. . .] an aspect of the gender order,"[12] which acknowledges that sexuality cannot be understood regardless of 'gender,' or, more specifically, of those power structures that render different bodies meaningful. Heterosexual practices, relationships, and institutions are not given by nature, even though they are consistently and tirelessly portrayed as such. All those mechanisms that in almost invisible ways make heterosexual desire appear as natural and privileged

Corporeal Obsession 139

constitute what is commonly referred to as the system of 'compulsory heterosexuality,' or, perhaps even better in reference to the Net, the 'heterosexual matrix.'[13] Within the hetero*textual* matrix of WaterMOO, kim and Wildman are in this opening section mutually performing gender and sexuality in a way that neatly corresponds to cultural expectations in accordance with their @gendered bodies and a stereotypical active/passive patriarchal paradigm. The inscription of stable gender identities naturalizes the normative fiction of heterosexual coherence. But in the next moment, this fabrication is notably challenged:

> You say, "roll over, hon"
> Wildman looks surprised, but kneels on all fours before you. . .
> kim pulls out the biggest strap-on from under the bed that you have ever seen
> Wildman 's eyes widen as he sees the size of the dildo. . .
> kim quickly straps it on. . .
> kim grabs your ass with her small strong warm hands
> kim slides her hands down your thighs for a moment and then up again . . . where they follow your ass crack
> Wildman moans softly, trying to relax. . .
> kim explores the crack, finds immediately your hole . . . and suddenly slides in a couple of fingers
> Wildman says, "mmmmm. . ."
> Wildman feels your fingers stretching him, preparing him. . .
> kim slides in two more fingers. . .
> Wildman's ass relaxes as you slide in more fingers. . .
> kim slowly comes closer and lets you get a taste of the size of the head of hm, her cock kim slides the head into your ass, gently, slowly
> Wildman gasps aloud as the thick head penetrates his tight ass, stretching it. . . .
> Wildman clenches the sheets as you thrust into him. . .
> kim holds it there for a moment, to let you get used to the size
> Wildman says, "Oh God, that IS big!"
> kim pushes in a couple of more inches into your tight ass
> Wildman moans loudly as you ease in deeper. . .
> kim pushes some more as she slides her hands down to your balls
> kim smiles at your shivering back
> kim squeezes your balls as she sinks deeper into you
> Wildman says, "Oh God Oh God!!!"
> kim lets go of the last few inches and penetrates you all the way down to the root
> Wildman cries out "Oh God you're so fucking BIG!"
> kim slowly slides out . . . and then, all the way in again
> Wildman moans loudly, grunting as you thrust into him. . . .
> Wildman says, "I never knew a woman could feel so powerful!!"

> kim lets her hips meet the back of your thighs for a second . . . and then starts moving them back and forth
> Wildman clenches the sheets as the fucking begins in earnest. . .
> kim wraps her arms around your belly to come real close as she dives into your ass, again and again
> Wildman 's cock stand out like asteel shaft, it swells each time you pump into his ass. . .
> kim now fucks you as if she was born a man, as if the part of her penetrating you was part of herself

When kim suddenly gives Wildman the order to "roll over, hon" and "pulls out the biggest strap-on from under the bed that you have ever seen," there is a sudden shift in the line of action. "You say, 'roll over, hon'" is the only thing kim actually *says* throughout the whole encounter, which is why these words come through with certain weight.

The log of this session is from kim's point of view, so this is the only instance when the phrase "you say" appears. As was mentioned earlier, there is a grammatical difference between <say> and <emote> in the sense that <say> appears as 'you say' to the textual talker, but as 'kim says' (in this case) to other participants. When <emote> is used, this produces lines in the third-person singular to everybody involved.

Sexual textual talk is almost entirely constructed through <emote> commands (due to the focus on nonverbal actions). The peculiar thing with these moves and movements in third person is that they are constantly disrupted by the use of 'you' and 'your' in approaches of the body of the other, which makes the perspective change back and forth between the act of touching and the experience of being touched ("Wildman feels *your* fingers," "kim grabs *your* ass," etc.). This leads to a textual mode that reflects the experiences of two bodies, a *double-ended narrative* that entangles two stories in one. An alternative way of co-typing these passionate stories would have been to stay within the world of third-person constructions, to let these characters meet on their own terms ("Wildman feels kim's fingers," etc.). The consistent use of 'you' suggests otherwise. When "kim slides her hands down your thighs," this motion not only touches thighs in text, but seems to stretch out and simultaneously caress the thighs of the typist, if only imaginatively. In this moment, the difference between textual and physical thighs is merely illusory, the text being an extension of the body possible to reach through typing. As if the distance between the physical body and the body in text in the obligatory third-person construction is too pronounced in relation to the intensity of these encounters, it is constantly bridged by textual turns that do not distinguish—as clearly—between text and matter.

A 'LESBIAN' PHALLUS?

At first sight, the shift marked by "roll over, hon" in the above excerpt appears to indicate a complete reversal along the active/passive axis. kim is turned into the dominating character 'on top' in both metaphorical and actual terms; she not only takes charge of the line of events, but literally takes hold of the 'phallus.' In her work on the 'lesbian phallus,' Butler (1993) suggests that the phallus is an imaginary effect—an 'idealization'—that might also operate through symbolizing other body parts (than the male penis):

> The simultaneous acts of depriviliging the phallus and removing it from the normative heterosexual form of exchange, and recirculating and repriviliging it between women deploys the phallus to break the signifying chain in which it conventionally operates. If a lesbian 'has' it, it is also clear that she does not 'have' it in the traditional sense; her activity furthers a crisis in the sense of what it means to 'have' one at all.[14]

Along this argument, the phallus is deprived of its position of being the privileged signifier of the symbolic order, dislocated from its location of 'origin' of signification. Butler argues that if the phallus signifies, then, it is also in a process of *being* signified, which in turn renders it open to a chain of reiteration and resignification. It is no longer the beginning of signification, but rather a continuous *becoming*. On the other hand, the lesbian phallus can never be completely disconnected from figurations of masculine power and authority, nor can it function independently of physical points of contact. It is rather paradoxically tied to a simultaneous displacement and evocation of masculinity in its intersection with lesbian desire—an intersection that both expands and reinscribes the phallic territory. The point is that if the phallus can be an object of 'citation' in relation to a range of different corporealities, then "the lesbian phallus offers the occasion (a set of occasions) for the phallus to signify differently, and in so signifying, to resignify, unwittingly, its own masculinist and heterosexist privilege."[15] As when the male body in drag reveals the constructedness of the sexed and gendered body, lesbian appropriation of the phallus similarly exposes the constructed nature of (hetero)sexuality. It is exactly these points of tension between the assumed natural and the more obviously fabricated that opens up for a possible site of subversive desire, but one that is never fully freed from the heteronormative conditions that make this site imaginable.

When "kim slowly comes closer and lets you get a taste of the size of the head of hm, her cock," this plays with corporeal contours of sexually specific bodies and suggests that when these contours are altered, the meaning of these bodies are altered as well. The use of the dildo does not turn kim's body into a male body, but rather playfully adds a body part to her own that inserts a shift in meaning right where kim's skin and the fabric of the dildo come together. This shift is clearly present in the slight hesitation ("hm,") that precedes "her cock," as if the border separating the organic from the inorganic also linguistically separates these words. The parodic element of this sexual act is clearly spelled out further down: "kim now fucks you *as if* she was born a man, *as if* the part of her penetrating you was part of herself," marking out a 'politics' of make-believe, of displacements and rearrangements of bodies and meanings.

In her discussion of 'lesbian fetishism,' Elizabeth Grosz (1995) expresses considerable doubts in relation to the strategic value of notions like the 'lesbian phallus.'[16] Even though she admits that 'lesbian dildos' have a transgressive effect in relation to the naturalization of heterosexuality, that they call into question their seemingly natural connection to a masculine body shape, she also points out how "they do so only by attempting to appropriate what has been denied to women and to that extent remain tied (as we all are) to heterocentric and masculine privilege."[17] In this sense, female appropriation of the phallus can be only compensatory. But this is not a bad compensation, as it seems. If nobody escapes the regulations of the matrix, it is not clear that lesbian sexual arrangements that exceed every phallic allusion formulate a more radical critique of heteronormative regulations (than do those that playfully disconnect and repetitiously reinsert the phallus in the heart of their practices), as Grosz seems to imply.

The question is whether and how the critical potential of the lesbian phallus can be transferred into the encounter between kim and Wildman. Strictly speaking, the notion of the *lesbian* phallus can have only limited relevance in relation to this case. It might be possible to use this concept as a parallel figure in relation to kim's appropriation of the 'phallus,' but it stops being applicable (in this narrow sense of the term) at the moment when the head of the dildo touches the body of Wildman. The reason for this is that this action is far removed from the field of lesbian desire and sexuality. The fact that the body being penetrated is a male body makes all the difference. This might seem like a trivial observation, but as will become clear, one that deserves full attention. In an attempt to approach the same scene from the other end of homoerotic desire, to read it as a male fantasy of being penetrated by another man, there will be a similar set of problems. Even if the dildo here is used *as if* it were a penis, and even if it does good work in masquerading as one in a sense that on the surface possibly mirrors a sexual act between men, the fact that it is attached to a woman's body makes this interpretation problematic. Connell discusses the significance of corporeal materiality in analyses of sexuality:

> Bodies cannot be understood as a neutral medium of social practice. Their materiality matters. They will do certain things and not others. [...] Some bodies

are more recalcitrant, they disrupt and subvert the social arrangements into which they are invited. Homosexual desire [. . .] is not the product of a different kind of body. But it is certainly a bodily fact, and one that disrupts hegemonic masculinity.[18]

To argue that bodies cannot be understood as a neutral medium is not the same as saying that there are meanings attached to bodies that precede sexual practices. Rather, it is a way to take into account how the materiality of bodies matters for the kind of activities that are possible, and how these possibilities are always impregnated with meaning. It is a way of showing how bodies are never innocent, blank slates open to unbounded signification, but always caught up in discourses such as those spelled out by the heterosexual matrix. In speaking of 'recalcitrant' bodies, Connell does not refer to different types of bodies, but bodies that in and through various practices give rise to 'bodily facts' that criticize the matrix from within. One such bodily fact is homosexual desire that in Connell's words disturbs 'hegemonic masculinity'—a concept that stands for the dominating, most powerful form of masculinity at a given historical moment.[19] But, there are other bodily facts than homoerotic desires that might disturb and shake heterosexual coherence. Heterosexuality can never be a singularity, but is rather an umbrella term for a variety of desires and practices, some of which take place in the outskirts of what is thought of as 'normal' heterosexuality. In similarity to the powerful denial/pathologization of homosexualities, these alternative formulations and sexual enactments seem to be almost as efficiently silenced, or else labeled as 'perversions.' The existence of these variations implicates slippages or inconsistencies between norms as prescribed by the matrix and those activities played out in the name of heterosexuality.

ONLINE MASOCHISM

The encounter between kim and Wildman can be read from, at least, two different but doubtlessly overlapping perspectives: as a male fantasy of being dominated/penetrated by a woman, and as a bodily fact that links a 'phallic woman' to the rarely acknowledged penetrable, heterosexual male body. The scene between the two is certainly a display of female domination, but one that appears to be a common heterosexual male fantasy.[20] There are several indications throughout the encounter between kim and Wildman that this performance is fundamentally *his* fantasy *mise-en-scène*, reducing her to a mere instrument of his own desire. Even if she is the one who initiates the shift marked by "roll over, hon," as well as defining the size of the dildo ("kim pulls out the biggest strap-on from under the bed that you have ever seen"), he is in control of the whole situation in the sense that he both verbally and nonverbally expresses, creates, and comments on his own experience and pleasure in a sense that she does not ("Wildman clenches the sheets as you thrust into him...," "Wildman says 'Oh God, that IS big!,'" "Wildman's cock stand out like a steel shaft, it swells each time you pump into his ass...," etc.). Even if he literally puts himself in her hands, this does not seem to be an answer to her needs or desires, but rather an expression of his own wish to be dominated in ways he has himself directed. If this, partly, is a reading 'between the lines,' every thread of doubt regarding its accuracy vanishes if the following excerpt of textual talk (in pages) preceding the sexual act is taken into account:

> You sense that Wildman is looking for you in TheBedRoom.
> He pages, "hiya sexy :)"
> page Wildman hi:)
> You page Wildman.
> You sense that Wildman is looking for you in TheBedRoom.
> He pages, "wanna have some fun?"
> page Wildman i do
> You page Wildman.
> He pages, "have you ever used a strap-on before?"
> page Wildman yes
> You page Wildman.
> You sense that Wildman is looking for you in TheBedRoom.
> He pages, "ever thought about strapping one on and fucking a guy with it? :)"
> You sense that Wildman is looking for you in TheBedRoom.
> He pages, "sound like fun?"
> page Wildman maybe...
> You page Wildman.
> You sense that Wildman is looking for you in TheBedRoom.
> He pages, "care to join me?"
> page Wildman sure.
> You page Wildman.
> @join Wildman
> You join Wildman.

In this passage, it becomes clear that the entire performance to come is a staging of Wildman's fantasies. At this point, kim ('you') even expresses a slight hesitation toward his proposal in answering the question "sound like fun?" with "maybe..." One obvious source of inspiration in relation to this conscious staging of the desire to be dominated is cultural images of masochism, and in particular as these are narratively constructed in the writing of the German novelist Leopold von Sacher-Masoch.[21] In his essay "Coldness and Cruelty," Gilles Deleuze (1967/1991) makes an intriguing argument regarding the *lack of* symmetry between masochism and sadism, departing from the originary figures of these 'genres': Masoch and Sade. Deleuze's main argument is that there is no such thing as a sadomasochistic entity, that one cannot assume that the strategies, fantasies, or 'symptoms' expressed in Sade only have to go through a reversal to be turned into Masoch. Deleuze shows instead how these two sexual domains belong to two different aesthetics that radically question the idea of s/m complementarity—how their different languages and dynamics disrupt the notion of these positions as mutually dependent opposites.

If in Sade the language is primarily 'demonstrative' (in the sense that it demonstrates to the victim that reasoning and calculation is a form of violence), then, in Masoch, it is tied to persuasion and even 'education.' If sadism is monological, demonstrative reason, then masochism, rather than being the negation of this monologue, takes the shape of dialogue, or of what Deleuze calls 'dialectical imagination.' The masochist's torturer is not herself initiating the act of torture (as would have the sadist), but must be talked into a commitment to the task. It is, thus, a contractual relation in which "the woman, although persuaded, is still basically doubting, as though she were afraid: she is forced to commit herself to a role which she may prove inadequate, either by overplaying or by falling short of expectations."[22] It is exactly this kind of doubt that kim gives voice to when asked by Wildman: "sound like fun?"—and that leaves traces throughout the scene through the relative absence of comments on and inscriptions of her own pleasure. This encounter also seems to be one of her own learning experiences, where every move is enthusiastically supported by Wildman's joyous acclamations ("I never knew a woman could feel so powerful!!" etc.). Even if it appears as if the torturous woman molds and shapes the masochist with words and fetishes, it is basically "he who forms her, dresses her for the part. [. . .] It is the victim who speaks through the mouth of his torturer, without sparing himself."[23] Even though kim is a relatively gentle torturess (there are of course degrees also in masochism. . .), she is the 'medium' through which Wildman's desires are actualized; she is the prosthetic realization of the kind of actions he wishes himself to be exposed to.

In the final excerpt from this encounter, there is a shift in focus toward more of a mutually shared intensity:

> Wildman reaches back and squeezes your firm tits, pinching them gently. . .
> kim fucks you harder and grabs your ass to make her movements even more powerful
> Wildman rocks his ass from side to side as you fuck him, making the base of the dildo press and rub wildly against your clit. . .
> kim closes her eyes as she keeps fucking you, feeling how the rubbing against her clit lets intense sensations run thorugh her body

> Wildman pinches your nipples harder. . .
> Wildman says, "Ohh yess, Yess!!!! that's it ! fuck me!!"
> kim slams the cock into you as she feels warm waves pulsating through her body, muscles contracting
> Wildman cries out as you slam the giant cock up his ass
> Wildman says, "oh god Yesss!!!"
> kim fucks you furiously as a tremendous orgasm runs though her body, making her screeeeeeeeeeeeeeeeeeeeeeeeeeeeeeeeam out on the top of her lungs!!!

In these culminating lines, where orgasms with great precision are typed-in simultaneously, references to kim's pleasure (initiated by Wildman) are introduced ("Wildman reaches back and squeezes your firm tits [. . .] making the base of the dildo press and rub wildly against your clit. . ."). In the moment bordering on climax, right before kim experiences "warm waves pulsating through her body," Wildman gives voice to the 'penetrative reversal' of this encounter: "Ohh yess, Yess!!!! that's it ! fuck me!!" Along the lines of the heterosexual matrix, men cannot, in a fundamental sense, 'be fucked.' The intimate heterosexual entanglement of the oppositions 'to fuck'/'to be fucked,' generated from an anatomical imaginary of the male sex as hard and persistent and the female sex as soft and accommodating, is seriously disturbed by an explicit male desire that loudly calls for a reversal of these positions.

THE CYBERNETIC BEDROOM

In her article "Destruction: Boundary Erotics and Refigurations of the Heterosexual Male Body," Catherine Waldby (1995) shows how the phallic male body has a powerful resistance toward receptive anal eroticism:

> Anal eroticism carries disturbingly feminizing connotations. Part of the significance of intercourse understood in its ideological aspect is its assertion not just of the woman's penetrability but of the man's *im*penetrability, the exclusive designation of his body by its seamless, phallic mastery. Intercourse can count as a demonstration of the idea that women's bodies lack the means to penetrate another body, and that male bodies are impenetrable. [. . .] In a sense then, anal eroticism is the sexual pleasure which conformation to a phallic imago most profoundly opposes.[24]

Against the contours of this impenetrability of the straight, male body, the *actual possibility* of entering this body from behind, of accessing its soft, sensitive, internal space, poses a serious threat to the maintenance of phallic imagery. Waldby traces opportunities for such a 'dephallicizing' of the straight male body in a noticeable increase in circulation of images of the 'phallic woman' in popular culture, as well as within an expanding periphery of sexual practices. Among other things, she refers to the considerable trade in sex toys, and the invasion of dominatrix imagery in mainstream pornography. A more liberal rereading of the 'lesbian phallus,' with an emphasis on the phallus as mobile property, as citational machinery in relation to differently sexed bodies and body parts, could very well relate it to this eroticization of the phallic woman. Fantasies and images of the phallic woman not only disrupt the masculine privilege to 'have' the phallus and in that sense rewrite the boundary of the female body, but also shed light on sexual encounters involving male and female bodies and could thus "be taken to indicate a realization of the masculine erotic potential for pleasure in passivity, a desire to be fucked, to be taken."[25]

However, Waldby is careful to ascribe to instances of instability in the binary logic of heterosexuality any effect on feminist politics of sexual difference, as long as these instabilities are not incorporated in social practice. Her point is that when men, for example, play out fantasies of female domination with women prostitutes, this has "a 'theme park' effect, in that it allows the client to experience the thrill of subjective danger when no real danger exists."[26] From this follows that not until this danger gets 'real' (i.e., when it gets embedded in practices of continuous relationships) will there be a transformative opportunity. Although the point is well taken in the sense that phenomena on cultural margins will remain fairly marginal if they do not get more broadly assimilated, I would not be so sure that there is no 'real' danger in the 'theme park.' Instead, I agree with Sadie Plant in stating that 'cybersex' is "a merging which throws the one-time individual into a pulsing network of switches which is neither climactic, clean, nor secure."[27] I am not so sure that there are such clear boundaries between the corporealization of fantasies in particular venues on one hand, and those bodily facts created through everyday sexual practices on the other. Nor am I certain that a perspective that speaks of centers and peripheries is particularly useful in understanding (sexual) culture, since it tends to depart from (as well as return to) the kind of heterocentrism it sets out to investigate and criticize. (Textual) fantasies, rather than being a safely isolated phenomena that never come to touch 'reality,' must be understood as always already part of those social practices to which they refer. Once the permeability of imaginative universes is acknowledged, domains such as fiction and imagination can no longer naively be conceived of as harmless, or lacking in political potential. Why were books turned into bonfires if they were not, in any sense, experienced as a 'real' danger?

In a slightly different approach, which does not assume that the 'theme park' is as clearly separated from the 'real,' there can never be any entirely safe havens. Sexual encounters in a text-based online world might appear, at least on the face of it, to be the ultimate act of safe sex on all levels in the sense that it does not involve 'unmediated' physical access to the body of the other. Again, I would argue that there cannot be such a thing as an unmediated access to the body of the other, nor to the body of one's own. Even if the typist never gets to touch this other body—to feel the warmth of the skin, taste the saltiness of its surface—the heated stories told in these encounters can be seen as yet another version of those narratives that shape and mold sensuous experiences 'in the flesh.' Textual sexuality is a delimited instantiation of the loop of mediation that always inserts itself in communicative acts—between 'I' and 'you' as well as between 'I' and 'myself.' And once these stories are told, they inevitably become part of a 'field' of sexual experiences, inscribed in the flesh of the typists, trickling themselves into scripts of desires yet to be played out.

A ride with a (textual) dildo can, thus, never be innocent. A textual construction of a phallic woman and a penetrable/penetrated male body will not be kept safely in the 'theme park,' since it already in the moment of its own making transgresses the world of the text. This means that a "masculine erotic potential for pleasure in passivity" might already be part of a *cybernetic bedroom culture*, where bedrooms (digital as well as analogous!) become components in cybernetic systems of circulating fantasies and desires. A scene played out in one part of the system will, inevitably, have an effect on other parts, thus making (textual) imagination an intrinsic part of a feminist politics of sexual difference. An online world is certainly a place for experimenting and role-playing, a place for immersion in textual pleasures, for the staging of dreams, wishes, fantasies, and desires. But it is simultaneously a site where characters, bodies, and body parts, no matter how textually entangled, repeatedly point toward the corresponding bodies of typists (most noticeably through the use of 'you' which again and again interrupts a more distancing story in third person). This entangling movement between erogenous zones and bodily sensations is a matter not only of textual couplings, but of intense machinic negotiations that bring text and matter together in literary circuits of typed-in erotica.

SEXUAL TEXTUALITY

One question that remains to be explored is how these cybernetic circuits of bodies, texts, and machines tie into contemporary literary theory, and in particular how the both divided and intimate linkage between typists and characters in textual talk relates to the story of 'the death of the author' that still seems to dominate discussions of texts and textuality.

More than twenty years have passed since Roland Barthes proclaimed the 'death of the author' and Michel Foucault wrote his famous text about the 'author-function.' To briefly summarize these articles, their core argument is that the meaning of a text can never be found in its authorial 'origin,' in the biographical, psychological reality of its predecessor; that one cannot, in fact, even speak of a person who in any sense precedes the text. To read a text with the belief that it has a straightforward connection with the author's intentions, wishes, hopes, and dreams is therefore nothing but an endeavor to secure and oppress its inherent ambiguity and multiplicity of meaning. Foucault emphasizes that instead "we must locate the space left empty by the author's disappearance, follow the distribution of gaps and breaches, and watch for the openings that this disappearance uncovers."[28] When released from its 'founding figure,' the meaning of the text needs to be sought and found, again and again, in the space opened up by 'his' vanishing. In regarding the text, in Barthes' words, as something that "is made of multiple writings, drawn from many cultures and entering into mutual relations of dialogue, parody, contestation," the act of reading is not about 'decoding' the text, but about following and confronting its ambivalent destinations, to trace in its surface, endlessly, new meanings.[29] The notion of the text as parody points to the way texts are never, fundamentally, written for the first time, but always parody each other, directly or indirectly, through chains of intertextual allusions. Barthes describes texts as shifting webs of meaning, where 'depth' coalesces with the textual surface, and 'writing' becomes yet another instance of 'reading':

> In the multiplicity of writing, everything is to be disentangled, nothing deciphered; the structure can be followed, 'run' (like the thread of a stocking) at every point and at every level, but there is nothing beneath: the space of writing is to be ranged over, not pierced; writing ceaselessly posits meaning ceaselessly to evaporate it, carrying out a systematic exemption of meaning.[30]

This shift in perspective—from the idea of texts with 'roots' to the notion of texts as networks of quotation marks—is symptomatic of a bigger picture where not only the author, but the subject itself is called into question. Since the Age of Enlightenment, the idea of the subject as an exceedingly free, autonomous, and rational being, in whom reason conquers both tradition and passion, has been a dominant figure. This sovereign subject is imagined to exist *before* 'his' deeds, independent of the symbolic order that he uses, deliberately, to reach his own ends. In sharp contrast, the postmodern subject is born simultaneously with language and is in no sense able to precede or surpass what Foucault names 'discourse,' but s/he is rather constructed, unendingly, in the very moment of enunciation. To Foucault, this shift "is a matter of depriving the subject (or its substitute) of its role as originator, and of analyzing the subject as a variable and complex function of discourse."[31]

In being constituted in and through 'texts,' broadly speaking, the 'scriptor' (as Barthes calls the post-author subject to emphasize its dependence on continuous acts of 'inscriptions') is written to life along with a framework sensitive to how various discursive power relations are intrinsic to this process of becoming. This understanding of subjectivity is incredibly persuasive by stressing the view of the subject as an open-ended process, but one that can never operate independently of dominating discourses (in a given historical moment). On the other hand, this subject never seems to leave the textual 'surface.' In opposition to Barthes, who claims that writing "is that neutral, composite, oblique space where our subject slips away, the negative where all identity is lost, starting with the very identity of the body writing,"[32] I would instead argue for a perspective on writing—or, in this case more specifically, on *typing*—where "the body writing" is a fundamental part of the process. This approach to the relationship between text and matter can be seen not as a break with the discussion emerging from the death of the author, but as a continuation and 'corporealization' of its central ideas. One fruitful consequence of the author's disappearance is how this very absence introduces a clear distinction between the textual 'I' and the 'I' producing the text, that these subjectivities can never be assumed to be one and the same. In line with the idea of the subject as a continuous, citational construction, as opposed to the idea of the subject as having an inner core that can be accessed and expressed, the 'I' writing cannot straightforwardly be connected to the 'I' written about—an argument that equally applies to the relationship between typist and character.

It seems as if once the text is de-psychologized, when it is released from the illusion of being the key to the heart and soul of its creator, ways of looking at text production as a *material* process are opened up. In her thought-provoking essay "Sexual Signatures: Feminism After the Death of the Author," Elizabeth Grosz (1995) discusses the divide between the writer and the written and points out: "These two terms cannot be definitively separated, for the processes of the production of the utterance are always inscribed in the utterance itself,"[33] meaning that even if the author can never control the text, no conclusions can be drawn about the author from the text (or vice versa); the material practice by which the text is brought into being is always engraved in the text itself, as a mark of its own becoming. To put forth the paradoxical and divided relationship between 'text' and 'body' in (online) textuality is thus not to reawaken or reintroduce the Author into the picture, but to attempt to take part in a feminist discussion that followed in the wake of 'his' death. To speak of 'typists' is not to create yet another category in which the author can be reinscribed, but to highlight the material side of writing; to emphasize that every act of inscription is always a material manipulation of signs and symbols, with its own technical devices, protocols, and regulation that most intimately involve technologies as well as bodies.

In his more recent work on autobiography and signatures, Derrida (1976/1984, 1984/1986) has also come to acknowledge this complicated line between author and text, life and work, as one that is far from clear-cut and stable. He speaks of the crosscutting of corpora—of the fluid boundary between the 'body' of work and the body of the writer, and puts forth: "This divisible borderline traverses two different 'bodies,' the corpus and the body, in accordance with laws we are only beginning to catch sight of."[34] Since then, it seems as if 'we' have come closer to an understanding of the logics of text production as a material and not least corporeal process—even if very little has been said about the *political* implications of this process. Derrida, most invaluably, speaks of the paradox of separation and intimacy in the relation between the body of writing and the body writing, but he never discusses the *types* of bodies involved. In a feminist extension and complication of this perspective, I am, along with Grosz, intrigued by "the ways in which the author's corporeality, an always sexually specific corporeality—not the author's interiority, psyche, consciousness, concepts, or ideas—intrudes into or is productive of the text."[35]

This notion of embodiment, as simultaneously *intruding into and being productive of* the text, is closely related to my understanding of the complicated dance between typist and character in textual talk. It points to a double gesture that is significant to an understanding of online textual embodiment. This doubleness is constituted through continuous divergences and convergences between the embodied self and the textual 'I.' Conversational journeys within and between these 'locations' invite both playfulness and anxiety. But, as the excerpts in this chapter have shown, anxiety, or at least a fairly demanding curiosity, dominates textual talk about (online) bodies. The insecurity tied to the state of not knowing how character and typist are related in terms of sex and gender creates conversational strategies to counter maybe not the absence, but the *invisible presence* of physical bodies in online encounters. The body of the other is still there, on the far side of the screen, but it cannot be reached, looked at, or touched—other than through typing.

CHAPTER 5

THE EMBODIED COMPUTER CODE

Many of the engineers currently debating the form and nature of cyberspace are the young turks of computer engineering, men in their late teens and twenties, and they are preoccupied with the things with which postpubescent men have always been preoccupied.[1]

Seduced by the beauty of the interface, too many thinkers in 'cyberspace' have described online textualities as disengaged from the physical reality of the medium, as well as from that of material bodies. Countless are their stories about the ease with which 'virtual' bodies are written and altered, the lightness with which they travel, morph, move, and dance—as if these performances had nothing to do with the medium in which they take place, or with the cultural context of which they are part. No matter how tempting the narrative of cyberspace as a haven for bodily transformations might be, it lacks all those intertwined story lines that speak of how interfaces are never as neutral or innocent as they might appear at first sight. Even when facing a 'blank' Word document, or an 'empty' chat room, there are certain things that might be done (but not others) that quite clearly and concretely set the limits for the activities of textual production. A MUD interface (everything that appears on the screen when someone connects to and engages with the MUD world) is the textual point of contact not only between participants, but also between participants and the underlying technology—a mediating textual surface between sociality and computer logics. It is exactly this techno-social intersection that calls attention to the political dimensions of interfaces. If the 'interface politics' of a Word document contain notions that concern fonts and formats, spelling and grammar, the issues embedded in the creation of a MUD system are of a different kind. To write the code for a text-based, social online world includes a series of intricate design choices that inevitably implies assumptions about, for example, interaction and embodiment—choices that through their consequences might even favor certain bodies and discriminate against others.

This chapter could be described as a reflection on this inter-linkage of textuality, embodiment, and programming in WaterMOO.[2] It is an attempt to challenge the notion of boundless creativity in online contexts, along with the idea of technology as a completely neutral tool in the hands of the typist. The activity of writing (and reading) in a MUD is to a large extent based on, and guided by, techno-cultural restrictions. These restrictions set the limits not only for what you can do, but ultimately for whom you can be. In the two previous chapters, it became clear that, for example, the <page> command gives the MOO a 'placial' orientation, and the <emote> command makes possible a somewhat peculiar corporeality that fluctuates between third-person narrativization and a more direct second-person address. But if these chapters were primarily concerned with how online embodiment depends on material implications of place, gender, and sexuality, this chapter takes this argument one step further and investigates the techno-cultural limits of the system itself in which these online bodies are created. It expands the focus from how online bodies are permeated with the politics of location and sexual difference to an analysis that incorporates how the 'typing in' of these bodies is always dependent on coded constraints, themselves cultural products open to critical readings.

The investigation of this intersection between writing and programming in the creation of online embodiment will be performed in three different parts. First, I will briefly discuss the notion of 'online textuality,' starting with key arguments in (American) hypertext theory, and then turn to the increasing emphasis on the materiality of the virtual. If, initially, online textuality was seen as the ultimate realization of postmodern literary theory, the discussion has come to include an awareness of how acts of reading are always confronted with the viscosity of mediation—how every medium leaves marks in processes of textual production. Secondly, letting this shift in perspective serve as a background, the discussion will focus on the practical construction of online bodies in WaterMOO by taking a close look at the <@gender> command. Again, @gender gives the textual body a 'sex' (what I have called 'virtual sex'), and is as such an ideal site for an analysis of intersections of online bodies and machine code. What possibilities/limitations does the @gender command have in relation to the creation of online bodies? How are various @gender positions interpreted and used by the participants? As a second step in this line of argument, I will also look at cultural/political meanings of the most basic level of encoded body-logics: the relationship between zeros and ones. Finally, I will revisit the introductory approach to materiality, having it reworked in the light of this MOO excursion.

HYPERTEXT AND POSTMODERNISM

During the last decade, there has been an exciting development of new literary modes in the intersection of computer technology and literature. If earlier the computer was primarily associated with internal logic and ice-cold aesthetics, the growth of virtual worlds, multimedia networks, and digital storytelling has turned the attention from logics to poetics—but with a maintained sensibility to the interplay between code and creativity. Along with this change of focus, there is a growing discussion of ways in which texts are written differently in the presence of invisible cuts and seamless stitches, when words, paragraphs, and pages can be instantly effaced or released, transferred, and inserted into new (con)texts. The image of the computer as an advanced calculator has gradually been transformed into an image of the computer as a theater, as a stage for a series of performances where contemporary narratives are being collectively created and played out in 'real time.' When text-based domains in cyberspace are seen as performance spaces, a literary format indissolubly intertwined with the electronic environment is created.

One question that is constantly being actualized in discussions of textual technologies is in what way the digital text is different from other text types, and how this difference can be described. It should be evident that there is no such thing as a single, homogeneous 'cyberspace textuality' or 'electronic literature,' but many.[3] In the hypertextually spatialized world of a MUD, for example, there is an interplay between a relatively stable textual architecture on one hand and ephemeral dialogues on the other, between the creation of pre-written textual bodies and instantaneous physical movements within and between online locations.

Nevertheless, homogenizing concepts, such as 'digital/online/electronic textuality,' are making their way through the Net, or rather, through cultural and literary theory. Ironically, these all-embracing concepts have, primarily, been concerned with a specific type of electronic textuality, namely *hypertext*. And not even hypertext is a singularity, but rather the underlying principle for very different things such as the linkage of Web pages, multimedia networks, and hypertext fiction (in which readers may or may not be able to make changes in the already existing text). Stories written in hypertext are maybe best thought of in George Landow's term 'lexias,' which he borrowed from Roland Barthes to describe reading units.[4] Where pages of paper in a book are bound together in a determinate sequence, blocks of text on a screen become lexias by the possibility to both connect them to each other and follow them in a myriad of ways. Stories written in hypertext have often more than one point of entry, a lot of internal connections, and no clear ending. These stories might unfold differently each time, depending on which of all potential routes is being actualized.

Hypertext in (early) hypertext theory is assumed to have the potential to construct nonlinear textual modes, as Sadie Plant puts it, through "webs of footnotes without central points, organizing principles, hierarchies."[5] Hypertext theorists have argued that the digitalization of the text has entailed radical changes within the domains of reading and textual production, where the positions of authors and readers are assumed to become more and more vague and unstable.[6] Not surprisingly, in relation to this view of hypertext, postmodern literary theory has come to hold a unique position. For hypertext theorists, its ideas about 'the open text,' the text as a web of intertextual references, the liberation of the reader from authorial intentions, the active interpretation, etc., seem to be realized quite literally through the digital text. Hypertext fiction writer and literary theorist Stuart Moulthrop states:

> Seen from the viewpoint of textual theory, hypertext systems appear as the practical implementation of a conceptual movement that [. . .] rejects authoritarian, 'logocentric' (i.e., truth-affirming) hierarchies of language, whose modes of operation are linear and deductive, and seeks instead systems of discourse that admit plurality of meanings where the operative modes are hypothesis and interpretive play.[7]

There are good reasons to be skeptical in relation to such confusions of textual theory and digital textuality. First of all, there is a confusion of at least two levels: one technological/material and the other ideological/conceptual. If hypertext is seen as the very fulfillment or realization of postmodern theory, there seems to be a curious slippage between these levels. When hypertext, for example, is assumed to have the potential to liberate the reader from the author, it is far from clear how the ability to move through the text in a nonsequential fashion 'in itself' can liberate the reader from its creator. Neither is it clear why hypertext somehow would be better equipped to divorce the author-god than would the narratives of the Codex book. It is, in fact, even hard to see how the reader of hypertext fiction could be truly imaginative and creative, since s/he usually does not have any other choice than to 'click' his/her way through immense and incalculable textual landscapes, completely in the hands of the creator of texts and links.[8] Instead of being given a sense of freedom, the reader might instead experience frustration in not knowing the (hypothetical) outcome of paths *not* taken, and in not being able to get an overview of the work before starting—which, paradoxically, might lead to a sense of being *more* controlled than in the case of a narrative bound to book pages easy to flip through.

Moreover, even if a bound book seems better suited for a linear narrative to be followed from the beginning to the end, in the same way that hypertext appears to be tailored for discontinuous jumps between lexias in any order desired, these structures are not inherent to the medium itself. Creativity is a matter not only of exploiting easily accessible built-in features, but of pushing the limits, to resist or transform the obvious. The hypertext reader hardly exists in an ideological vacuum. Neither is s/he freed from the material constraint of the machine. Nonetheless s/he is 'liberated' time and again within hypertext theory by arguments that confuse theoretical perspectives with interface qualities, where the liberating potential is tied to the hypertextual structure itself—and not to our ideas of what a text is and what can be done with it.

The critical task seems to be to disentangle the influences of postmodern ideas of textuality and subjectivity from the 'technophoria' of certain computing cultures. The odd twist in the transposition from postmodern conceptualization to technological incorporation is that the postmodern dissolution of the subject suddenly appears to be moving in reverse—toward a renewed degree of autonomy and homogeneity. In the call for empowerment and liberation of the user, the boundaries of the subject are far from put into question, but rather accentuated and fortified. If the authoritarian author-subject is (still) being erased, the qualities of this subject are not dismantled through a critical discussion of their constructedness, but are rather transferred onto the newborn authoritarian reader-subject free to perform 'his' potentiality regardless of those socially or culturally oppressive mechanisms that would hold 'him' back. The discourse of (computer-mediated) liberation thus cuts only one way, releasing the reader/user in a deconstructive dance that, miraculously, is never close to deconstructing the place from which 'he' 'himself' is typing.[9]

Secondly, one easily gets the impression that hypertext fiction is something that was brought into being along with the birth of the computer. This indicates a lack of historical context in hypertext theory. Hypertext is, of course, nothing new. Obviously, even printed literary works are hypertextual in their allusions, through their intertextual references to one another, and through the linkage of footnotes. On a more explicit level, there are pre-electronic print examples of hypertext with a built-in structure of a multiplicity of textual routes. One example is George Perec's *La Vie mode d'emploi* (1978). This novel is more a building than a narrative, a text that gradually constructs life staged in a Parisian apartment building. Besides many clever textual strategies, its extensive register encourages the reader to trace certain characters or themes in the text. These readings replace the sequential narrative with interlinked textual fragments.

THE MATERIALITY OF DIGITAL TEXTUALITY

The discussion of hypertext as the ultimate realization of postmodern literary theory stands far from unchallenged. Espen Aarseth is equally skeptical of the extensive procuring that has combined (pre-electronic) literary theory and digital textuality. He states that the attempts to reuse these models of thought can be seen as a colonial strategy, where the enthusiastic application of one's favorite theories to a new field makes the theorist blind to other options. Aarseth suggests instead that one should, as far as possible, develop new perspectives for new media.[10]

In his influential work *Cybertext: Perspectives on Ergodic Literature*, he outlines a perspective of what he calls a 'textual machine.' The concept 'cybertext,' derived from 'cybernetics,' points to organic and inorganic (literary) systems that contain an information feedback loop. Aarseth argues that a feedback loop is part of all texts, but that there is a considerable difference between metaphorical and mechanical processes. In every encounter between a text and a reader, the text carries the potential to generate new or different meanings compared with earlier readings. Through the act of interpretation, itself context specific—historically, culturally, and socially situated—a text can be said to (metaphorically) start moving in the sense that its meanings are never singular, nor fixed. If the text is experienced as something possible to enter and explore, as something that would not even exist before this entrance, 'texts' and 'readings' can no longer be clearly separated. This marks the partiality and situatedness of textual experiences, how texts are mute and meaningless on the 'outside' of interpretative practices.

In relation to this understanding of 'feedback loops' as interpretation, Aarseth clarifies his perspective: "The different ways in which the reader is invited to 'complete' a text—and the texts' various self-manipulating devices—are what the concept of cybertext is about."[11] 'Completion' in this context is no longer metaphorical but rather taken to be literal, which constructs cybertext as an agent. In other words, this approach is not primarily about the making of textual meanings, but rather about the (mechanical) organization and (re)production of texts: "The text is seen as a machine—not metaphorically but as a mechanical device for the production and consumption of verbal signs. [. . .] The machine, of course, is not complete without a third party, the (human) operator, and it is within this triad that the text takes place."[12] The boundaries between the three components (verbal sign, medium, and operator) of Aarseths' textual machine are fluid, where each part cannot stand alone, but needs to be defined in relation to the other two. This intimate interchange moves beyond the level of texts and interpretation that most models of textuality are concerned with, toward a higher sensitivity to the material specificity of the medium and the performative dimension of textuality.

This discussion, which has partly followed in the footsteps of, and partly radically separated itself from, its forerunners in (American) hypertext theory, is successful in placing the discussion about new textualities in a historical context in which the division between electronic and pre-electronic texts is far from clear-cut. Nevertheless, even if the particularities of hypertext are not, in themselves, emancipating, they do make certain textual qualities that might be found in any text particularly obvious. Marie-Laure Ryan eloquently points out: "What the marriage of postmodernism and electronic technology has produced is not the virtual text itself, but the elevation of its built-in virtuality to a higher power."[13] All texts are thus virtual objects in their capacity to generate potential worlds, interpretations, uses, and experiences, but electronic texts clearly and quite literally take this virtuality-as-potential to a higher level. Avant-garde literary theory might perhaps be a point of departure for a critical theory of online texts, but it is simply not enough to account for the complex interplay between bodies, computer technologies, and labyrinth-like textual nodes and networks involved in the making and reading of these texts. When texts move from written pages to screened performances, we need to take into account the change of medium and the change of *matter*.

These inter-linkages between text, body, and machine are of course always present in acts of writing/reading, but they are becoming distinctively intimate when texts are being digitalized. In text-based online worlds, this intimacy is crucially exaggerated, since these spaces are constituted through simultaneous physical presence, collaborative writing, and collective access to code and formulation of narrative structures. If the distance between author and reader of hypertext fiction is significant, it has rather disappeared in a MOO, since the (singular) author has abdicated and been replaced by as many typists as there are inhabitants. A MOO might first and foremost be an entertaining networked sociality to its participants, but the fact that these worlds are constructed in and through pure text poses new challenges for cybertextual studies.

<HELP @GENDER>

In chapter 2, "Reading Online Bodies," I discussed the politics/poetics of character writing in WaterMOO. After many close readings-in-context of WaterMOO character descriptions, I learned that no matter how 'fluid' and 'transgressive' online gender has been in the dreams of some online gender theorists, the online *reality* is very different and often fairly mundane and conventional. One way of understanding this is to put forth that online practices in no sense are separated from a world that is culturally based on two sexes. It suggests that WaterMOOers have difficulty imagining encounters in which @gender—conceived of as a literal mapping of bodily contours onto language—would not be relevant. A different approach, curiously neglected in cybercultural studies, is to investigate how the writing of character descriptions relates to the *encoding* of virtual sex, to possibilities and limitations of the @gender command.

The Embodied Computer Code   159

Following the path outlined by Aarseth's textual machine, it seems necessary in an analysis of online embodiment not only to perform readings of what online texts are speaking about, but to simultaneously take into account the material specificity of this textual production. Writing in a MUD has certainly lots of room for (individual and collective) imagination and textual playfulness, but this 'writing space' is nonetheless intertwined with, indeed permeated by, its coded origins of existence. It might be useful to point out that I do not intend to do 'readings' of the actual computer code. To be able to understand how the MUD program in various ways shapes and delimits the activities of participants, it is uncertain whether it is fruitful to search for the answers in the code itself. Rather, what appears to be needed is a heightened attention to the ways in which the program sets the limits for online performances; what kind of bodies are made possible, and, in reverse, if there are any mechanisms of exclusion that make impossible certain incorporations.

In WaterMOO, there are, again, ten different @gender positions available. Interestingly, these ten ways of creating a sexed ground for textual characterization are not equally valued by the MUD program. This becomes obvious in relation to the use of pronouns inherent in the program, since there are apparently some (grammatical) bugs connected to 'unusual' constructions of virtual sex. The following can be found in the help texts:

help @gender
———

Syntax: @gender <gender>

The first form, with an argument, defines your player to have the gender <gender>. If <gender> is one of the standard genders (e.g., 'male', 'female', 'neuter', . . .), your various pronouns will also be set appropriately, making exits and certain other objects behave more pleasantly for you.

The second form tells you the current definition of your player's gender, your current pronouns, and the complete list of standard genders. It should be noted that some of the 'genders' on the standard gender list need verb conjugation in order to work properly and much of the MOO isn't set up for this (. . . yet). For example, you should expect to see `they is' a fair amount if you @gender yourself `plural'.

The first paragraph shows how the @gender command is used. The participant is told that if a standard gender is chosen, pronouns will work smoothly. ("Standard genders" in the MOO context refer to any of the ten @gender positions available.) Ironically, the first paragraph seems to indicate that participants are free to name and create any @gender position they want, only that a self-created virtual sex will not work as pleasantly with the program as any of the preprogrammed ones. This statement is somewhat vague, since a self-created @gender, in fact, does not affect the use of pronouns by the MUD program. If I, for example, have a character @gendered female and want to call this @gender position something I have come up with myself, let us say 'bitch,' this maneuver has no effect on the grammatically gendered structures set up by the program. On the other hand, ten ready-made @gender positions are not a bad offer!

Already in the second paragraph, this 'freedom' to pick and choose is severely circumscribed. Clearly, the choice of a virtual sex other than male, female, or neuter is not encouraged ("For example, you should expect to see 'they is' a fair amount if you @gender yourself 'plural'"). The reason for this is that third-person constructions in singular are the foundation of the program, from which other compositions by necessity deviate. Thus, performances of characters @gendered something else than male, female, or neuter will most likely be filled with grammatical imperfections in terms of incorrect use of verbs. The above help text shows how these errors are regarded as not yet resolved problems, seemingly resulting from a view of unconventional @gender positions as being less important to work smoothly compared with more conventional ones.

In an attempt to investigate possibilities, uses, and interpretations of various @gender positions, one way would have been to start with the most unusual @genders, and then gradually move the discussion toward the more common ones. This would have been an option, if only I'd had logs from sessions with characters @gendered something else than male, female, and neuter (itself telling evidence of their striking rareness in the MOO!). In looking at character descriptions alone, of those thirteen characters @gendered 'other' in my collection, only five are something else than neuter. And the fact that none of these characters are present in any of my session-logs of textual talk might result from what appears to be a reluctance by the participants to use unusually @gendered characters in typed-in interactions. As previously mentioned, it is not unusual for typists to have several 'morphs' to shift between, but usually only one that they treat as a 'serious' incarnation. These main characters are very often @gendered male or female, and sometimes (even though rarely) neuter. What then appears to be a more productive outline for investigation is to closely scrutinize this @gendered triad—to look at the meanings and matter of the male/female binary, but also at the part played by the neuter in this picture.

A VIRTUAL @GENDER ORDER?

In a critical reading of this @gender order, in which male, female, and neuter are coded as 'conventional' positions, it is tempting to conclude that these three virtual sex constructions give participants the potential means for creative, and maybe even transgressive, writing. Against the background of 'real life' physical embodiment, where everyday reality for most people is structured around the male/female duality, the third position in the MOO appears to represent something truly subversive. As with Donna Haraway's cyborg, this third location could envision an alternative world beyond 'gender' as we know it. Haraway has argued for a positive reading of the cyborg mythos in a world that has blurred distinctions between these oppositions, in a "border war" in the territories of production, reproduction, and imagination. Her ambition is "to build an ironic political myth faithful to feminism, socialism and materialism."[14] It is a cyborg interpretation with no commitment to an absolute grounding for knowledge, but with an emphasis on 'situated' and 'partial' knowledges, uncertain and sometimes contradictory subjectivities and identities whose significations are not determined by the categorizations of human/animal/machine.

But, on second thought, it becomes obvious that such a vision is very far from the WaterMOO reality. Besides the fact that 'neuter' is a position rarely chosen by the participants (which, of course, is highly significant), *it precedes rather than transgresses a male/female dichotomy*. All characters, guests as well as regulars, are @gendered neuter in the 'raw'; they inhabit a sexless position awaiting a more specific cultural determination. The following excerpt shows an encounter with a neuter, where the typist obviously was unaware of the @gender of his/her character:

> You sense that Red is looking for you in Green.
> It pages, "I'm a neuter?"
> You sense that Red is looking for you in Green.
> It pages, "News to me. I suppose I forgot to set my gender."
> page Red hmm, well, aren't you??
> Your message has been sent.
> You sense that Red is looking for you in Green.
> It pages, "Yeah, guess I am."

The position that a character @gendered neuter occupies is interpreted as a negation—as a positionless 'non-location' defined through the very absence of activity: "I suppose I forgot to set my gender." This does not position the character outside of or beyond a system with a male/female polarization, but rather reveals what this @gender-system is built on. I would not go so far as to say that the MUD program in itself constitutes an @gender order in which creations of male and female bodies are encouraged, while the writing of other-gendered characters is discouraged, but this tendency is certainly there.

162   *Material Virtualities*

Neuters never need to be actively created. They are rather an intrinsic part of the beginning of the coded origin of MOO bodies:

> surfer has arrived.
> Jenny waves to surfer
>
> look surfer
> You see a player who should type '@describe me as . . .'.
> It is awake and looks alert.
>
> surfer says, "hello"
> Driver [to surfer]: "g'day stranger, welcome to watermoo"
> [. . .]
> surfer says, "im off to get a room"
> surfer leaves for elsewhere.
> Driver waves.
> Driver shrugs his shoulders.
> You say, "is it checking in now?"
> Driver says, "lemme see"
> Driver says, "aha, he has a room"
> You say, "already?"
> You say, "he???"
> Driver nods.
> You say, "it was a minute old!"
> Driver says, "and it can't even set a gender, i wonder if it's got it's priorities straight"
> Webmaster emerges from a swirling mist.
> You say, "still . . . neuter is a gender, isn't it?"
> Webmaster. o O (neuter is a gender to my dog. . .)

In this excerpt, a new character, surfer (probably in the process of description writing and @gendering), is entering the world of WaterMOO. Driver welcomes it. After a short conversation (which I left out in the excerpt), it leaves to get itself a hypertextual hotel room. I am amazed at how this character, only a minute old, already has a room of its own. Driver's amazement is rather related to the fact that it got a room before using the @gender command: "and it can't even set a gender, i wonder if it's got it's priorities straight." This shows how 'neuter,' as a point of departure in the creation of MOO characters, is not regarded as a valid state of being, only a neutral foundation awaiting a more appropriate determination. I admit that I'm pushing this question a bit in saying: "still . . . neuter is a gender, isn't it?" only to be met by the thoughts of Webmaster who just arrived: ". o O (neuter is a gender to my dog. . .)." Moreover, when asking Driver if surfer is getting itself a room ("is it checking in now?"), he takes a look in the hotel bookings and answers automatically: "aha, he has a room," which through a curious Freudian slip at the keyboard shows how neuters might be perceived as being closer to male than to female (characters). In a motion that parallels analyses revealing how seemingly neutral subjects in mainstream philosophy are efficient disguises of, or have been interpreted as *male* subjects, WaterMOO bodies in their most original and machinelike state are in a similar manner often assigned cultural implications of male bodies. Far from being illustrations of one-time episodes, these excerpts are telling examples of how 'neuter' is commonly interpreted in the MOO.

No matter how complex, detailed, and persuasive an online world like WaterMOO might be, among participants there is (not surprisingly) a never-yielding awareness of the necessary (wo)man/machine parts involved in the making and interpretation of this world. This awareness of the ongoing intense interplay between typists, computer technologies, and online texts seems to make even temporary disconnections (metaphorically speaking) of these texts from their material groundings very hard for the participants, since what they encounter is not only text and technology, but *people*. Therefore, it might not surprise that online bodies, at large, reflect contemporary masculinities and femininities, while not only being part of the same symbolics, but also related to the materiality of human bodies. What may seem more surprising is that a similar gender logic can be found already on the level of the MUD program, revealing how supposedly neutral computer technologies actually have body politics.

ENGENDERED PRONOUNS

Grammar is politics by other means.[15]

Language-made online bodies certainly have an intricate and complicated relationship with those strings of machine code that bring them into existence as well as govern their movements and interactions. One important part of this relationship is how the encoding of these bodies is intertwined with linguistic structures, which in a place like WaterMOO leads to a particular type of embodiment. Even if computer languages in a sense are languages in their own right, the outcome of their operations in a place like WaterMOO are continuously entwined with typed-in enactments of textual talk. This entanglement of language and code is obvious in the construction of the @gender command, since every @gender position is accompanied by a set of pronouns. (Virtual) sex is communicated via pronouns in the sense that they replace a character's name when presenting, for example, exit messages ("Ilyenna grows sad, and *she* fades away, headed for *her* home"), page messages ("You sense that Jayse is looking for you in Hard Hat Area. *He* pages, 'where are you from?'"), and in third-person narrativization of the <emote> command ("Dana blindfolds Orangina and spins *her* around 3 times"), perhaps most obvious in sexual textual talk. Beth Kolko (2000) mentions that in an e-mail exchange with James Aspnes, the creator of TinyMUD, Aspnes "says he added @gender 'in a fairly late version' of his world TinyMUD 'because users were complaining about not being able to have grammatical gender in descriptions of actions.'"[16] Before the insertion of the @gender function, everybody was referred to as 'it.' The interesting thing with this piece of MOO history is that it shows how it was not the programmers of the MOO-engine that initiated the @gender command. Quite the contrary, it was a way to meet the desire of the participants to have the option to take on a virtual sex different from 'neuter.'

This intimate connection between the sexed body and (MOO) discourse not only points to how bodies, always sexually specific, are *present* in language, but how they in a sense come into being through language as such. In her work on hate speech, Judith Butler (1997) draws upon the idea of how one comes to exist, how one becomes, not only recognized, but *recognizable* as a subject through address:

> Language sustains the body not by bringing it into being or feeding it in a literal way; rather, it is by being interpellated within the terms of language that a certain social existence of the body first becomes possible. To understand this, one must imagine an impossible scene, that of a body that has not yet been given a social definition, a body that is, strictly speaking, not accessible to us, that nevertheless becomes accessible on the occasion of an address, a call, an interpellation that does not 'discover' this body, but constitutes it fundamentally.[17]

Following her earlier work on the discursive process through which bodies are materialized, Butler points out that it is only through address that the body is brought into existence, a gesture without which this body would be inaccessible, meaningless, and ultimately unthinkable. In an emphasis on language and the act of naming, she shows how interpellation not only calls attention to a certain body, but more fundamentally *creates a body possible to interpellate*. In a MUD, bodies are quite literally brought into being through language. The most obvious reason why gender, or rather, sex, is a much debated issue and a recurrent theme in WaterMOO textuality (as opposed to, for example, race, class, and sexuality) is the fact that sex is linguistically determined when characters interact.[18] While constantly being present in language, in and through the use of pronouns, the sexed nature of MOO interaction cannot be ignored. Rather, this continuous enunciation of virtual sex creates a type of online embodiment that overshadows other ways in which bodies are marked. Discursively fleshed out, called into existence through a networked, social space, these bodies cannot exist prior to their positioning as addressed.

"To understand this, one must imagine an impossible scene," Butler says. She refers to a thought experiment where one needs to imagine an impossible body, "a body that has not yet been given a social definition," and how this body becomes thinkable—or is in fact fundamentally constituted—through address.[19] One example of this scene that comes to mind is that of an unborn child not yet given a sexed definition. The answer to the question "Is it a boy or a girl?" assigns the child an identity as male or female through which s/he becomes recognized as a subject. In this sense, it is impossible for human subjects to escape being socially constituted as such through the act of naming. And if this naming not only turns a 'nonsubject' into a subject, but through that very gesture constitutes this subject as sexually specific, this shows how hard it is to think of a subject *as* a subject at all if it belongs to the 'unthinkable' domain of sexless creatures.

Interestingly, with the help of new technologies (such as sonography), it is possible to know the sex of a child even before birth, which makes the process of subject creation coincide with that of pregnancy. If earlier, the unborn child inhabited a position open to imagination—the position of the sexless nonsubject—it might now be turned into a *person* who is either a boy or a girl. Some parents' hesitation when facing the possibility of getting to know the sex of their unborn child can be seen as a wish to linger a while longer in the borderland of imagination, to postpone the discursive process through which the child becomes sexually specific and enters the realm known as social reality.

The same kind of thought experiment could also be transposed onto body dialectics online. The body of the typist can be seen as Butler's 'impossible' body—a body that is not possible to reach, yet possible to fantasize about. If one then imagines that this body is being interpellated through the question "Are you male or female?" (not directed toward the character, but to an unreachable location behind or beyond the text), the answer to this question both defines and constitutes this body as a material point of reference. Once called into question, and therefore created, there seems to be no way back to an earlier, innocent phase where the body of the typist existed only as a figment of the imagination. Moreover, the fact that this corporeal becoming simultaneously is a sexed determination partly explains why the question of 'sex' is discussed so tirelessly in relation to online body practices. To be human is most often a matter of being either man or woman, which is why in the same moment as the typist is recognized as human, the question of sex is being evoked. Sexual specificity can thus be said to precede every other way in which bodies are marked.

On the other hand, Butler is careful to point out that this does not prevent contestations or transformations of the names through which one comes into being as a subject.[20] In WaterMOO, such possibilities exist in terms of those @gender positions other than male or female. An @gender like, for example, Spivak is certainly capable of calling a *textual* subject into being differently, but it does not seem to manage to bridge the gap between such a subject in text and the assumed less fantastically sexed body of the typist. As long as these 'otherly' @gendered bodies do not convincingly capture this doubleness of online corporeality, it seems hard for such bodies to become anything but rare exceptions.

SEXUALLY ENCODED

Perhaps the tendencies of a gender system found at the level of the @gender command, reinforced by an imaginary linkage to an unambiguously sexed body of the typist, have considerable connections with the logic of the zeros and ones of computer code itself. The binary that constitutes the foundation in computing culture knows only the mechanism of on or off, presence or absence, positive or negative, which forms an absolute divide that makes impossible a 'third' position, an alternative elsewhere that troubles and transgresses this opposition. The language with which online worlds are built is in this sense a high-tech incarnation of ancient Western metaphysics that structures even the 'virtual' in terms of being and nonbeing, a figuration that inserts an uncompromising rupture that violently excludes every nuance of the 'in-between' in the heart of the MOO-engine. The question that craves an answer at this point is what zeros and ones have to do with sexual difference. (How) does this numeric binary relate to cultural categorizations of man/woman, masculine/feminine, etc.? In a brief examination of the sexual significance of zeros and ones in contemporary philosophy, one important point of interrogation is the work of Luce Irigaray (1977/1993), who performs a familiar mathematical operation considering the relationship between man and woman based on the contrast between the one and the *not* one:

> The *one* of form, of the individual, of the (male) sex organ, of the proper name, of the proper meaning ... supplants, while separating and dividing, that contact of *at least two* (lips) which keeps woman in touch with herself [...] *She is neither one nor two.* Rigorously speaking, she cannot be identified as one person, or as two. She resists all adequate definition. Further, she has no 'proper' name. And her sexual organ, which is not *one* organ, is counted as *none*. The negative, the underside, the reverse of the only visible and morphologically designatable organ (even if the passage from erection to detumescense does pose some problems): the penis.[21]

Irigaray points out that there is no access to a woman's imaginary, including her sexuality, which is not mediated by phallocentric, masculine discourse.[22] This discourse of 'sameness,' she says, has never been able to represent woman as anything but a reflection of man, a 'phallic feminine,' conceptualized on the basis of masculine terms. Every difference between men and women (and between women, for that matter) is thus erased to secure the status of the masculine subject. In her reading of Freud, Irigaray puts forth that he does not see two sexes, either actually or symbolically. "The 'feminine' is always described in terms of deficiency or atrophy, as the other side of the sex that alone holds a monopoly on value: the male sex. Hence the all too well-known 'penis envy.'"[23] Following this argument, female sexuality becomes unthinkable. Where woman does not reflect man, she cannot exist. In comparison with the singularity the male organ implies, the female organ, which in Irigaray's words "is not one," cannot be counted at all. To counter this unaccountability, she emphasizes the *multiplicity* the female organs imply, how the female sex(uality) is not one but "at least two. [. . .] Indeed, she has many more. Her sexuality, always at least double, goes even further: it is *plural*."[24] In what appears to be a contradiction in terms, Irigaray thus simultaneously expresses a belief in the transformative potential of female sexuality *and* a conviction that the masculine order makes every escape attempt futile. These lines of thought show how difficult it is to articulate alternatives that are not fully produced or captured by dominant discourses—how impossible it seems to make a 'negative' signify.[25]

In Irigaray's footsteps, Sadie Plant (1997) conveniently transposes this sexual logic onto the operations of computer code:

> The zeros and ones of machine code seem to offer themselves as perfect symbols of the orders of Western reality, the ancient logical codes which make the difference between on and off, right and left, light and dark, form and matter, mind and body [. . .]. And they made a lovely couple when it came to sex. Man and woman, male and female, masculine and feminine: one and zero looked just right, made for each other: 1, the definite, upright line; and 0, the diagram of nothing at all: penis and vagina, thing and hole [. . .]. It takes two to make a binary, but all these pairs are two of a kind, and the kind is always kind of one. 1 and 0 makes another 1. Male and female add up to man. There is no female equivalent. No universal woman at his side.[26]

Departing from a reading of zeros and ones as a gendered relationship where 1 signifies male dominance and 0 marks the female absence, Plant suggests that there is an intimate and maybe even subversive element between women and machines. She argues that women in the shadows of the male culture have been the ones who did the groundbreaking work, from the very first computer program to the latest incarnation of virtual reality. In a nontraditional, 'hypertextual' manner she examines these female absences through a fascinating, somewhat disruptive historical framework of stories about the contributions women have made to the progress of computing. Plant argues that when it comes to typing as well as telecommunicating, women have, aside from doing the actual work, through their bodies provided the male world with a living interface to the machines. Her idea is that women have always been the 'machine parts' in a male culture by reproducing both the species and communication. Through this notion of the female capability of translation, she fills the previous absence in the history of the machinery by inscribing women's activities, bodies, and emotions in a very close, if not symbiotic, relationship to machines. When machines get more autonomous, women go the same way, and between them an alliance is being developed.

Even if the relationship between zeros and ones in Plant's thinking carries a certain likeness to Irigaray's argument, the outcome of her analysis is very different. If in Irigaray's work there is an intricate tension between a phallic order that nobody escapes and lines of flight related to female sexuality (among other things), Plant sidesteps patriarchy altogether. In describing the Net as a quintessentially female technology, everything from its organization in terms of nonhierarchical, nonlinear structures to the parallel, processed nurturing life in virtual communities is clearly tied to and expressed as female values. It is not quite clear how she gets from 'woman as absence' to the realization of an online, feminist utopia, but she seems to suggest that this process of 'feminization' is "not happening because people are trying to make it happen—or even because feminist politics are driving these changes (although that is a part of it), but changes are occurring almost as an automatic process."[27] In this perspective, women do not even have to fight for their cyberspaces—they are in fact already there, perfectly formed for their female inhabitants, who themselves are 'naturally' suited to live, breathe, and act in a constantly shifting, chaotic landscape. All those things that earlier served the white male—capitalism, machines, women—are now going their own way, forming alliances, and it is all "beautifully effortless."

Plant's contribution to a different historiography that radically inscribes women and their close relationships to machines in the field of computing and telecommunications, presumed from a male perspective to be a genderless territory, is important. However, it is far from clear how her cyberwomen are able to *effortlessly* escape the dilemma of being the 'negatives' of a pair where only the 'positives' signify. Considering the amount of hard work that during several decades feminists have devoted to the difficult but important task of writing women into existence, to articulate the unspeakable—either by turning woman-as-absence into a multiplicity of presences or by transgressing woman-as-category altogether in an attempt to overcome binary thinking—it is quite clear that this process is far from "automatic." In his investigation of how gender is inscribed in software design, Sean Zdenek notices that the 'gender' variable in chatterbots (programs that interact with Internet users in ways that can be mistaken for human) follows a logic where 1 stands for male and 0 for female. In the part of the program (written in the computer language known as C) that handles one of two gender assignments, male is constructed in the 'if' section—which leaves female with the option 'else': "it is [. . .] true that the 'female' chatterbot is unmarked (assigned a 0 value), the default other or 'else,' what's left over after the 'male' *if* clause fails to return a true value."[28] Male is, thus, clearly inserted as the norm, the self-evident case that even on the level of code treats everything else—in this case the option 'female'—as the exception.

In an attempt to reach beyond the most obvious interpretations of an @gender order in WaterMOO, where very few participants perform characters that are something other than male or female, a discussion of the sexual significance of zeros and ones seems necessary. In accordance with the grammar of computer languages, there can never be a 'third course,' a neither/nor that realizes a mind-bending performance of the in-between. Computer code knows nothing about threshold experiences. Add to this the difficulty that several generations of thinkers have experienced in making the 'second sex' signify (to begin with!). If woman as the other of man can only with great difficulty be thought of as something other than part of those structures that tie her to patriarchy through negation, how can we then even start thinking of a *third* sex? If to think the second sex into being (as something different than the other side of the 'first sex') is bordering on the unfeasible, no wonder it is hard to imagine an alternative position. If, further, the architecture of Western thought and that of computer code is one and the same, in which the ones are those who appear to be the backbone of the system(s), a MOO character @gendered something other than male or female has very little (techno-)cultural space to take possession of.

At the same time, it is interesting to observe that the @gender command in WaterMOO is not coded in a sense that elevates male at the cost of female. In contrast to Zdenek's chatterbots, female is not the default 'other' that inhabits the 'else' clause in WaterMOO. As discussed previously, this position is occupied by neuter. This is a significant difference, since instead of being yet another reflection of an order in which 'woman' is the other, the @gender command creates an online system where male and female are equally valued. The fact that neuter is the unmarked @gender potentially unleashes 'woman' from her conventional reduction to the negative side of the 'one.' The @gender command thus provides the participants with a more open and liberating foundation for the creation of sexually specific online bodies (than does the encoding of the chatterbot). But this more 'equal' structure does not seem to solve the dilemma of how significant bodies will keep gaining their significance in contrast to insignificant nonbodies. And if bodies @gendered female are freed from their dwelling in this state of the nonexistent, this oppositional interplay is obviously only being transferred into another corporeal domain: that of the 'third' sex.

WIRED INCORPORATION

Where is the subject in MUD practices? There certainly is a subject in text; living, speaking, moving, and breathing. But where does it end? When not activated by their typists, WaterMOO characters are merely lifeless replicas of their once connected vividness. The fact that they are automatically put to sleep when their typists have logged off points to the online interpretation of reality and virtuality, turning the 'real' into nothing but a dream for virtual beings. The ritual of connecting and disconnecting does not point to the entrance or exit of the character in the virtual world (since the character is there the whole time), but to the (dis)connection of the typist from text and machine. Therefore, the limits of MUD subjects can be neither only textual nor only mechanical or material, but are constantly being drawn and redrawn in between these domains.

In an attempt to take into account this complex interplay between sexed bodies, texts, and machines, Aarseth's 'textual machine' needs sensitivity to various forms of embodiment along with a politics of 'sexual difference'—since bodily differences (in flesh as well as in text) apparently matter in online encounters. In Aarseth's approach, the importance of the 'human operator' in the making of ergodic signs is certainly not underestimated, but this (sexless) creature never leaves the realm of the neutral, disinterested, and abstract. The term 'human operator' itself is quite revealing in terms of its strikingly instrumental connotations. In contrast, Hayles clearly and consequently introduces the body as an important element in text production. One starting point for a widened perspective that embodies the human operator is her useful triangulation of *inscription, incorporation*, and *technological materiality*.[29] Hayles's pairing of inscription/incorporation builds on the more common distinction between 'body' and 'embodiment' (where body is understood as a universal cultural construct, and embodiment is seen as particular, situated embodied practices). Similar to the relationship between body and embodiment, inscription is conceptual abstraction, whereas incorporation deals with instantiated materiality that can never be separated from its embodied medium:

> Like the body, inscription is normalized and abstract, in the sense that it is usually considered as a system of signs operating independently of any particular

manifestation. [...] In contrast to inscription is incorporation. An incorporating practice such as a good-bye wave cannot be separated from its embodied medium, for it exists as such only when instantiated in a particular hand making a particular kind of gesture.[30]

Inscription thus naturalizes and universalizes the specificity of incorporation, as when computer interfaces wipe out not only the dependence on physical bodies but also the very materiality of 'information' itself. Take as an example of inscription a printed interview appearing in a newspaper. No matter if this text originally was a conversation between an interviewer and an interviewee, captured with a tape recorder, further transcribed into a written text within a word processor, edited and partly rewritten, to finally appear in a different typeface in the narrow columns of a newspaper. It is still commonly experienced as 'being' the interview. Even if the editing process is taken into consideration (like an awareness of the fact that people are rarely as coherent and eloquent in speech as they appear to be in the print version of the conversation), other transitions and transformations are rarely thought of as being part of the picture. The logic of inscription thus wipes out the specificity of texts; it deletes the fact that texts have themselves 'bodies' that might take various shapes. Inscription concentrates on what a text speaks about—not on those ways in which the meanings of this textual 'content' is always permeated by the medium in which this act of 'speaking' occurs; where, when, and by what kind of technologies a particular inscription is made.

Incorporation, on the other hand, works in the opposite direction and underscores how each medium has specific material properties, with its own historical background and narrative capacities. As with the interplay between the body and embodiment, there is an intense dialectic between inscription and incorporation—between texts that effortlessly travel in time and space and texts that cannot be separated from their mechanisms of production.[31] As soon as an embodied activity is transferred from one medium to another, incorporation is turned into inscription in the sense that embodiment becomes a sign that can travel and morph between different material shapes. Take the moves and movements of online textual bodies as an example of incorporating practices. These bodies are entirely dependent on the medium in which they take shape, as well as on the co-presence of their typists. When the lives and adventures of these embodied characters are then captured in log files by me as a researcher, and further transferred to various Word documents and printed out on paper pages, they immediately move from incorporation to several levels of inscription. They are transformed from being a series of embodied gestures (no matter if their 'embodiedness' happens to be purely textual) to signs that represent these gestures in different media.

Hayles argues that in order to understand mechanisms of change, looking at the level of the body (or inscription) is not enough. Embodiment (as well as incorporation) on the other hand "links a changing technological landscape with the instantiated enactments that create feedback loops between materiality and discourse."[32] In relation to the domain of online textual embodiment, an analysis of inscription alone would concentrate on the writing and reading of online bodies as cultural signs and symbols in general—it would stay on the level of text as itself a surface, without looking at the relation between the body as sign and the means by which this inscription is being performed. An analysis that on the contrary features the logic of incorporation instead speaks of online bodies as being on a never-ending voyage between text and texture, sign and matter.

As mentioned earlier, online bodies are certainly bodies that are being written, but they are simultaneously bodies to write *on*. Put differently, online bodies come together through an interplay between 'writing' on at least two levels: One of these levels consists of character descriptions and textual talk, whereas the other level consists of the writing of computer code. The writing and meaning of messages appearing in character descriptions and interactions, what I have called virtual gender, is intimately related to the specificity of *virtual sex* constituted through the @gender command. Online bodies are not created in a vacuum. Just as bodily materiality makes a difference in the meaning of inscribed messages, *the materiality of the virtual* makes a difference in processes of online intextuation. Coded either as 'natural' nor as entirely 'textual' or 'discursive,' the material existence of machine code creates a tension in relation to textual inscriptions. Without being viewed as 'essence,' the materiality of body and code can provide embodied subjects with a potential site of (online) resistance. I have tried to show that, as opposed to the flesh-and-bone materiality of the physical body, online bodies are materially grounded in computer code. Therefore, system developers and programmers have the power to set limits for the type of bodies that can be created. Quite logically, this also implies possibilities for subversive virtual surgery—depending on the ways in which the code is (re)written.

CHAPTER 6

MATERIAL VIRTUALITIES

The story of this book took off from the online home and workspace "Her Office": a hypertext hotel room of WaterMOO that for two years provided Jenny (and me) with a most exciting research site. To fully take advantage of the narrative structure of a Codex book—in which story lines perform all sorts of curlicues to finally come to an end and a sense of closure—this particular venue is also the place where the story ends. Or rather, its ending has to do with the (involuntary) erasure of this room, as well as of Jenny herself. To say that my stay in WaterMOO lasted for two years is a way of framing the period when my engagement with the field was the most intense. There certainly was a particular moment when the field was 'entered' (as described in the first chapter), but, as opposed to the anthropological ritual of 'leaving the field'—tangibly marked by the fact that the researcher leaves, physically, to go home—the end of the WaterMOO study was less abrupt. Even though I left in the sense that I ended what I think of as the 'formal' part of the study, I kept coming back, occasionally, to see how people were doing. With time, these 'post-ethnographic' visits got more and more sporadic, and one day more than six months passed since my last visit—a time limit that proved to be crucial in relation to the life of online bodies:

> connect Jenny ********
> Either that player does not exist, or has a different password.
> connect Jenny ********
> Either that player does not exist, or has a different password.
> help
> - - - - - - - - - - - - - -
> WaterMOO General Help
> - - - - - - - - - - - - - -

174   *Material Virtualities*

Help is available on the following commands:
connect
create
theme
uptime
version
@who
Type `help <command>' to see the help on that topic.
help connect
- - - - - - - - - - - - - -
Syntax: connect <player> <password>
- - - - - - - - - - - - - -
This command connects you to an already existing character providing you enter the correct password. If you wish to connect to the MOO, but you do not already have a character, type `connect guest'.
connect guest

*** Welcome to WaterMOO! ***

You have connected as a Guest to WaterMOO. We want our guests to feel welcome here. As a guest, you may create up to 2 objects. You are about to be asked to give yourself a name and description. . .
[. . .]
[Please type the name you wish to be known as.]
Jenny
You typed: 'Jenny'. Is this what you want? [Enter `yes' or `no']
yes
Please type in a brief description of yourself. Example: A tall skinny man with a perpetual grin on his face. He wears a worn suitjacket and jeans, and has his hair tied up in a ponytail.
[Please enter a brief description of yourself.]
This guest looks a bit sad since it appears to have forgotten password to main char
Description and name set.

When trying to wake Jenny up this particular morning, to connect 'me' to 'her' in the exact same manner as I had done hundreds of times before, something strange happened. Instead of entering Her Office, with all its bookshelves and the (dusty?) French writing desk, I was met by the message "Either that player does not exist, or has a different password." I tried again, only to have the same both annoying and frightening message repeated. I did no longer exist? Jenny was gone? I consulted the help text on the command <connect>. Nothing. The only way to find out what had happened to me, or Jenny, was to log on as a guest and ask some friendly soul in the MOO for advice. I created a guest character carrying the description "This guest looks a bit sad since it appears to have forgotten password to main char." The fact that it was possible to name this guest 'Jenny' was already a fairly clear indication of what had happened to the real virtual Jenny:

> page mussel do you have a sec? :)
> Off it goes!
> (from JustAroundtheCorner) mussel mindspeaks, "sure. what's your question?"
> page mussel do you know what to do if you have forgotten the password to your char. . .? Off it goes!
> mussel grins at you from across the MOO. . .
> (from JustAroundtheCorner) mussel mindspeaks, "what was your character's name?"
> page mussel Jenny
> Off it goes!
> page mussel it's been a while. . .
> Off it goes!
> (from JustAroundtheCorner) mussel mindspeaks, "i remember you! . . . hmmmmm, well if it's been longer than 6 months your character was recycled . . . since you could logon using the name jenny that's very likely"
> (from JustAroundtheCorner) mussel mindspeaks, "you can @request a new one"
> page mussel i'm recycled?
> Off it goes!
> (from JustAroundtheCorner) mussel comforts you

As easy as pushing a delete button—bodies in cyberspace might disappear. As more than six months had passed since my last visit, Jenny had fallen victim to the automatic process of 'recycling' in the MOO. Technically, this means that those strings of code and text that held her together had been erased. The help text on the command <@recycle> reads:

> Syntax: @recycle <object-name-or-number>
> Destroys the indicated object utterly and irretrievably

Trying to recover from the sad news and the kind of emptiness Jenny's disappearance left behind, I did <@request> a new character even though I sensed that it could never be quite the same. The recycling of Jenny's body, along with her online home, definitively let the WaterMOO study come to a full stop. But the story of this ending is more than a rhetorical trick; it is a way to, again, be reminded of the intricate interdependence as well as the relative autonomy between text, body, and machine in the making of online textual bodies. The story clearly shows how an online body not only needs a body writing and a body *of* writing, but that these typed-in enactments are always entwined with the 'writing machine' in which they take place. If Jenny needed me to stay alive, she also faced the other end of this logic where the machine let her life come to an end. But instead of being another incarnation of a heroine who, by necessity, must die in the end of the tale, her cyborgian features let her easily become reincarnated in almost the exact same guise. As easily as online bodies are terminated—they might also be resurrected. They might seem slightly different (in terms of, for example, object number and age), but they will doubtlessly be recognizable.

The story of WaterMOO, of which Jenny's plotline is a small part, is certainly a (poststructuralist) story of how bodies are fundamentally engraved with language, or, perhaps better, 'textualized' both metaphorically and actually; they are both *in* and *of* language. But it is also a story about how this textualization has everything to do with the materiality of physical bodies and their geographical in-placements, as well as that of computer technologies, which induces a significant twist to the argument of the (embodied) subject as a product of discourse. This closing chapter is an attempt to—against the background of the WaterMOO study—map out some of the arguments that have followed in the disappearance of the author/subject that are particularly relevant to online textual embodiment. If the subject is indistinguishable from discourse, how is it then possible to talk about different but interrelated *levels* of subjectivity/discursivity? How can, for example, the difference between 'text' and 'body' be accounted for? If the body is essentially an 'effect' of discourse, does this make points of resistance unthinkable?

TO SIGNIFY OR NOT TO SIGNIFY

In *Bodies that Matter*, with the telling subtitle *On the Discursive Limits of "Sex,"* Judith Butler asks: "Can language simply refer to materiality, or is language also the very condition under which materiality may be said to appear?"[1] The answer to these questions, which in various figurations runs through her work, consists of different but closely interlinked parts. First of all, language is viewed as material in itself (in the sense that signs are always mediated by material means, orally or visually), which "implies that there can be no reference to a pure materiality except via materiality."[2] Secondly, language is, indeed, viewed as the prerequisite for materiality. As mentioned previously, Butler has been criticized for disregarding the 'material reality' of bodies, for excluding the body in pain, by claiming that bodies are merely 'discursive.' But such a (mis)reading ignores the ways in which 'discourse' is itself material. It also overlooks how materiality is tied to processes of signification from the beginning. In pointing out that (corporeal) materiality can be reached only by passing through materiality, Butler appears to distinguish between two different but interrelated types of materiality. To reach the materiality of the body can only be done by a discursive detour in and through the materiality of language. Far from saying that physical pain is 'only' a discursive construction in a sense that has no impact on the body, this argument clearly points out that linguistic categories are essential to the (experience of having a) body:

> The linguistic categories that are understood to 'denote' the materiality of the body are themselves troubled by a referent that is never fully or permanently resolved or contained by any given signified. Indeed, that referent persists only as a kind of absence or loss, that which language does not capture, but, instead, that which impels language repeatedly to attempt that capture, that circumscription—and to fail. This loss takes its place in language as an insistent call or demand that, while *in* language, is never fully *of* language.[3]

To speak of an 'absent' referent of language, a loss that will always escape attempts to be thought into being, this passage indicates a slippage between the materiality of language and that of bodies in the sense that the former will never fully or completely be able to imprison the latter. On the other hand, this does not indicate that there are instances or areas of materiality that are placed outside of language, unhampered by processes of signification, but rather that the body "while *in* language, is never fully *of* language." How do we then account for bodies that can never fully hide from the process by which they are signified, but that simultaneously appear to inhabit a domain of what Butler calls 'radical alterity,' which in a sense actually *does* escape signification ("that which impels language repeatedly to attempt that capture [. . .] and to fail")?

Butler works primarily in a Foucauldian register of power in which 'unthinkable' bodies are essential to the formation of bodies residing on the 'safe' side of the regulatory fiction of heterosexuality; a perspective in which bodily normalization is completely dependent on repeated and repeatable acts of violent exclusions of bodies that do not (yet) fit in. The question is whether the dynamic of such delimitation can be viewed differently; if the idea of a radical alterity of the body might be productive in exploring what could be called a *de-disciplining* of bodies. Would it be possible to use the field of corporeal materiality as a site of resistance against how far bodies might be 'textualized' (even if there can be no shortcut to this materiality other than through language)? And if so, how could this be visualized?

One feature of online textual embodiment that was increasingly salient in the WaterMOO study was that there seemed to be an utmost limit of the body—a viscosity of the material (of whatever kind)—that put up a certain resistance in reference to the kind of meanings that can be inscribed. Put differently, the materiality of the virtual body, constituted through intense cybernetic negotiations between the body of the typist and that in text, makes a difference in relation to processes of signification. Without implying that the materiality of online bodies is in any sense natural, or innocent, it seems both fruitful and necessary to depart from this insight in a search for the formation of an embodied subject in online practices. In her discussion of the relationship between body and embodiment, Katherine Hayles uses the notion of embodiment as a possible site of opposition in relation to discourses of the body:

> Embodiment differs from the concept of the body in that the body is always normative relative to some set of criteria. [. . .] In contrast to the body, embodiment is contextual, enmeshed within the specifics of place, time, physiology, and culture, which together compose enactment. Embodiment never coincides exactly with 'the body', however that normalized concept is understood. Whereas the body is an idealized form that gestures toward a Platonic reality, embodiment is the specific instantiation generated from the noise of difference. Relative to the body, embodiment is other and elsewhere, at once excessive and deficient in its infinite variations, particularities, and abnormalities.[4]

Even if "embodiment never coincides exactly with 'the body,'" Hayles is careful to point out that embodied experiences are in constant interaction with constructions of the body. The ways in which bodies are discursively constructed in, for example, medical discourses, are foundational to the way people view their bodies and make their bodily experiences meaningful: "Experiences of embodiment, far from existing apart from culture, are always already imbricated within it."[5] This suggests that a focus on embodiment does not necessarily need to result in a romantic picture of 'lived experience' as something that would precede discursive mediations. On the other hand, not only do discourses of the body constitute embodied experiences, but these experiences may provide certain variations in relation to dominating cultural norms. Without saying that there is an 'outside' of culturally inscriptive practices, a focus on embodiment (as opposed to a focus on 'the body') makes room for a possible emphasis on the situatedness, partiality, and particularity of inscribed meanings. Hayles puts forth that since embodiment is individually articulated, there is a possible discrepancy between embodied experiences and hegemonic cultural constructs: "Embodiment is thus destabilizing with respect to the body, for at any time this tension can widen into a perceived disparity."[6] With a focus on the continual dialectic between images, representations, and discourses of 'the body' on one hand, and situated physical enactments of (and responses to) these discourses on the other, not only are practices of *inscription* unveiled, but also instances of *incorporation*, to use Hayles's terminology.

To sum up, the common understanding of bodies as textualized—or discursively inscribed—is only one narrative thread in the story of WaterMOO. Another strand, which persistently twists and twirls around the first one, is that of the text as always material and, indeed, embodied, which lets particular texts do certain things and not others. But to argue that bodies are not only textual in the sense that they can be read as cultural signs, but that textual signs themselves are material in ways that encourage certain readings and discourage others, is not the same as claiming that there can be no distinction made between text on one hand and body on the other. No matter how intense their twisting and twirling, text and body never fully collapse into one another and become redundant. In a discussion that focuses on the complex relation between body and writing, Elizabeth Grosz usefully points out that "bodies and discourse produce and transform each other" but that there is "*always a mismatch between representation and corporeality.*"[7] Playing with Derrida's notion of the signature, Grosz puts forth that although it is never possible to ensure a correspondence between the 'I' writing and the 'I' written about, texts are nonetheless marked by their own processes of inscription. The signature performs in this discussion as a borderline mark that simultaneously divides and binds together the embodied subject and the text. On one hand, a signature is a proper name, the means by which a particular individual 'signs on' to a text to testify to, if possible, its authenticity. On the other hand, as Derrida makes clear:

> In order to function, that is, in order to be legible, a signature must have a repeatable, iterable, imitable form; it must be able to detach itself from the present and singular of its production. It is its sameness which, in altering its identity and singularity, divides the seal.[8]

In being not only a sign of individuality, a signature is by necessity also a mark of repetition; it is an iteration of a name that easily disconnects itself from the writing subject and slips into the 'content' of the text as a noun. It is transformed from corporeal instantiation that marks the border of the text to a sign of inscription that, instead, textualizes the body writing:

> The signature not only signs the text by a mark of authorial propriety, but also signs the subject as the product of writing itself, of textuality; it functions as a double mark, a hinge, folding together (or separating) the author/reader or producer and the text or product. The signature cannot authenticate, it cannot

prove, it cannot make present the personage of the author; but it is a remnant, a reminder of and a testimony to both a living past and a set of irreducible and ineliminable corporeal traces.[9]

In a similar way, bodies in WaterMOO are 'signatures' in the sense that they inhabit a borderland that at once separates and joins together the body writing and the body of the written. On one hand, their machine text features make them intrinsically repeatable. The responses from the MUD program are series of reiterations, always returning the same value to each specific variable. As signs of writing with mechanical features, online bodies appear at interface level to be part of the same text, seemingly disengaged from the singularity and individuality of their typists. On the other hand, they are incessantly (re)connected to the bodies of their typists, technologically as well as symbolically; they are "a reminder of and a testimony to [. . .] a set of irreducible and ineliminable corporeal traces." As has been shown, online bodies in text operate as reminders of the crucial physical presence of typists, the fact that they need the body typing in order to stay awake (or even *alive*). This material dependency, in turn, raises questions about the *specificity* of the body typing—always present, but never visible. In constantly being evoked through the use of pronouns in textual talk, as well as being an indissoluble part of subject formations, the most prominent feature of this corporeal specificity is *sex*. Far from smoothly inscribing itself in the widespread myths of 'cyberspace' as disembodied, placeless, and immaterial, the WaterMOO study shows that online textuality is rather saturated with *the politics of the sexually specific, situated, and mediated body*. How could these politics be conceptualized?

CYBORGFEMINIST CONFIGURATIONS

The conception of text and matter in online textual practices as closely related, but never identical, makes room for a contribution to the ongoing cyberfeminist discussion of a possible reinstatement of a (female) subject. The term 'cyberfeminism' has been cruising the Net in different forms for several years, avoiding any final definition of its inner content and purpose. Despite this fluidity, it is possible to find at least two partly contradictory tendencies. One of these operates on a rather theoretical level of feminism and technoscience, whereas the other formation is more openly connected to a political movement, searching to integrate different women's uses of communication technology. The tension between the two is very much a high-tech version of the classical feminist paradox between the striving for a breakdown of 'woman' as a category in order to minimize the meaning of sex(ual) difference, and the need to keep the category as a foundation for identity and political action.

Where a woman interacts with and integrates new communication technologies into her life, she is, as Dawn Dietrich frames it "situated between a gendered, material body and an ethereal, cyberspatial identity; between patriarchal culture and feminist community; between 'inside' and 'outside' [. . .]. [She] must embrace ambiguity and conflict in order to appropriate a cultural space for feminist discourse."[10] It is probably exactly these contrasts between earthliness and virtuality, the material and the textual, that can generate the energy to reconstitute a feminist subject after its dissolution by postmodernism. At the point where the feminist concept of the cyborg provides a radically different way of seeing and being in the world built on dissolved dichotomies, this eliminates at the same time the position from which a woman might speak as a (feminist) woman. It is nevertheless possible to use the cyborg metaphor in a different way, in which women do not necessarily *become* cyborgs but are rather *compared to* these creatures. As Zoë Sofia formulates the reason for a feminist fascination with cyborgs and technobodies: "If these artificial second selves can be loved and accepted as powerful, resistant, speaking subjects, so too might women, long acclaimed as monstrous to conventional categories of self and other."[11] In this sense, instead of being erased from a feminist position in cyberspace, female subjectivity might act as a point of critical departure.

Nonetheless, and in parallel to the previous discussion of the tendency in cybercultural studies to fortify the sex/gender dichotomy (by relating 'sex' to the material body of the typist, whereas the online world appears to be freed from the messiness of matter), there is a similar inclination within cyberfeminist discourse(s)–but one that has slightly different consequences. It seems as if the divide between the striving for a decomposition of 'woman' on one hand and the need to preserve this category as a political foundation on the other translates into the cyberspatial realm in a way that creates yet another divide: that between 'real' and 'virtual,' and perhaps even between the 'political' and the 'imaginary.'

Within this unfortunate division, the act of deconstructing 'woman' is easily logged onto the Net, in a textual universe where the invisibility of physical bodies provides an electronic landscape where genderlessness can be imagined. According to Sadie Plant:

> Of all the media and machines to have emerged in the late twentieth century, the Net has been taken to epitomize the shape of this new distributed nonlinear world. With no limit to the number of names which can be used, *one individual can become a population explosion on the Net: many sexes, many species* [. . .] there's no limit to the games which can be played in cyberspace. Access to a terminal is also access to resources which were once restricted to those with the right face, accent, race, sex, none of which now need to be declared.[12]

Such virtual bodies of "many sexes, many species" move freely and imaginatively through virtual space, in a constantly ongoing performance of various (non)gender positions. At the same time, on the far side of the screen, the 'real' body is seated. If the dissolution of 'woman' fits right into an online world of gender ambiguity, then the activity of holding 'woman' together as a political foundation is as easily aligned with the material groundings of the 'real.' In a discussion of the limits of the cyborg metaphor, Susan Hawthorne puts forth: "The problem with this reification of cyborg identity is that the writers appear to forget the real body inside or outside the cyborg,"[13] that the cyborg may not be liberating since it is not embodied and localized. Although I agree with Hawthorne that the all-inclusiveness of the cyborg figure might be puzzling, that it loses critical impact if suddenly "we are all cyborgs," this reading of the cyborg seems to be as problematic as the interpretation of cyberspace as a postmodern feminist dream come true.

If narratives of cyberspace as a genderless utopia sometimes lack all those intertwined story lines salient in the WaterMOO study of how online worlds are always already gendered and far from immaterial and disembodied—how late modern patriarchal capitalism not only infiltrates these spaces but acts as their founder—then the story of the 'real' body within or beyond the cyborg incorporates a lack in the opposite direction. One easily gets the impression in some cyberfeminist statements that computer technologies, more than being viewed as potentially subversive extensions, are experienced as a threat to the 'real.' To Hawthorne and Klein: "Critical is a resistance to total immersion in the technology which results in detachment from the world, rather than an engagement with it."[14] This perspective seriously overlooks how cyberfeminist online actions and activities are as political as any protest march, how engaging with technology is a serious engagement with 'the world,' since this technology can hardly be seen as anything but an integrated part of this world. To dismiss cyborg politics by arguing that the 'real' body is being forgotten is to undervalue how embodiment includes the virtual in the shape of imaginative projections and phantasmic bodies of dreams, how the imaginary has a capacity to retroact on the physical that significantly blurs the boundaries between the corporeal and the imaginative.

Without denying the existence and meaning of matter, it seems almost impossible to talk about the 'real' body in this sense, as if there were such a thing as a body unmarked and unmediated by technologies. This notion of an 'untouched' body along with authentic, locally grounded encounters and communities are hardly products of our own time, but are rather rooted in ancient distinctions; like those between orality and literacy, or between nonmediation and mediation. Among the multitude of discussions arising from these pairings, a romanticization of the spoken word in face-to-face encounters—under the illusion of immediacy—has proved to be a die-hard theme. Richard Coyne traces this tendency in contemporary technoculture to Rousseau's romanticism, where aural culture beyond the terror of print was seen as the site of true relationships.[15] The difference this time is that it is hardly the printed word that causes the threat, but the digital.

A POLITICS OF SEXUAL SPECIFICITY

As has been discussed previously, it is urgent that online research stop making sharp divisions between sex and gender. In contrast to a simplified translation of the sex/gender dichotomy onto virtual worlds, I have argued that sex, as well as gender, is being written online. But rather than the flesh-and-bone materiality of the physical body, online bodies are rather transgressive machine texts with a multitude of corporeal connections and material implications. As a point of departure in the WaterMOO study, I was not only working with the notion of 'virtual gender,' but also with that of 'virtual sex,' as a way of showing that online bodies are, indeed, material and messy, even though there are differences in the type of matter that bodies might be made of.

Nonetheless, toward the end of this online journey, things do seem different than they did in the beginning (one would hope!). To work with the multi-layered differentiation of (virtual) sex/(virtual) gender was very useful as a departure in relation to what was going on in WaterMOO, as well as in relation to common arguments in online research. But the question at this point is rather: Where does the WaterMOO story end? Every investigation of a field is, evidently, a process of one's own learning, and the observant reader might have noticed a gradual conceptual displacement throughout the book that slowly transforms the discussion: from a concern with sexed *and* gendered bodies to an argument that instead invests in the politics of sexual specificity. This is no coincidence. The alteration of the sex/gender distinction, in which the notion of gender slowly vanishes out of sight, is parallel with yet another dislocation; namely that which gradually shifts the focus from readings of textual bodies as signs of online cultures to discussions that more obviously feature the materiality of the virtual.

Without doubt, gender has been useful in contemporary feminist thought in pointing out, for example, how 'masculinity' and 'femininity' are cultural and historical formations (that, logically, might be subject to change). Butler is one of those who have moved the discussion of gender several steps further, perhaps to the point where it is no longer useful to maintain the category as a critical strategy in feminist and queer theory. As discussed previously, gender is in Butler's thinking not only the cultural signifier of sex (which is itself understood to be as constructed as gender), but also the means by which sex as a prediscursive given is *mise-en-scène*. Gender is the performative apparatus through which the illusionary image of a clear differentiation between sex and gender is sustained. Butler argues (to reuse a previous quote) "If the immutable character of sex is contested, perhaps this construct called 'sex' is as culturally constructed as gender; indeed, perhaps it was always already gender, with the consequence that *the distinction between sex and gender turns out to be no distinction at all.*"[16] But if sex is always already gender, and the distinction between the two in the end is proved to be a chimera, what is the point then in using the concept of gender? (One could, of course, also turn this question on its head and ask what use the notion of 'sex' plays in the dissolution of the sex/gender dichotomy. But that is a different story altogether, and one that has limited relevance in relation to my attempt to 'materialize' online research).

For Butler, gender seems to be a way of distinguishing between different levels of corporeal performativity, in relation to which the body in drag becomes one example of how (more or less radical) gender performances—through the very discrepancy between the material body of the performer and the gender that is being performed—manages to uncover the constructedness of the body itself. The category of gender works as a strategy to highlight the fact that gender does not necessarily need to smoothly follow a certain sex—that gender, in fact, does not 'follow' sex at all. Even so, I agree with Grosz in questioning the usefulness of gender in Butler's thinking:

> all the force and effect of her [Butler's] powerful arguments could, I believe, be strengthened, not through the play generated by a term somehow beyond the dimensions of sex, in the order of gender, but within the very instabilities of the category sex itself, of bodies themselves. Isn't it even more threatening to show, not that gender can be at variance with sex [. . .], but that there is an instability at the very heart of sex and bodies, the fact that the body is what it is capable of doing, and what any body is capable of doing is well beyond the tolerance of any given culture?[17]

Even though this critique loses some of its edge in the light of Butler's work following *Gender Trouble* (after which she seems to orient her argument away from gender, in favor of a focus on the complex relations between language and corporeal matter), the point is well taken. What do we do with a concept that for a period of time has been very useful in pointing out that the body, always sexually specific, is anything but stable, unambiguous, and predictable—but that in the process of pointing this out gradually makes itself redundant?

The answer given in this book to this (rhetorical) question is that a discussion of the sex/gender distinction in online research is essential as a starting point to make clear that every simple division that aligns sex with 'real' and gender with 'virtual' is doomed to failure. But once the category of gender has displayed that the sexed body itself is utterly unstable—and when the category of sex, in reverse, has showed that 'unstable' does not equal unreal or immaterial—gender as a strategic concept for thinking about the constructedness of (online) embodiment might as well be abolished. In the wake of this disappearance, it is possible to develop a perspective of online textual embodiment that rather investigates the dissonances and tensions *within* the sexually specific, cybernetic body. Put differently, there is an escalating need in online research to make room for a serious engagement with online embodiment that does not base its epistemology on an inversion of the dichotomies it sets out to criticize. It is crucial to make room for a continuous discussion of online bodies as *material virtualities*.

THE (RE)TURN OF THE SHE-CYBORG

Haraway's cyborg has certainly done a fine job in this borderland by pointing out how different realms of what we think of as our world, such as 'reality' and 'fiction,' 'organism' and 'machine,' 'culture' and 'nature,' have considerable leakages that continuously make them invade each other. It is very useful in mapping out a politics of location, of situatedness, since cyberspace, far from being a global whole, is constituted through innumerable, networked localities. Through its inexhaustible telling of alternative narratives of our capacity for political change, the main mission of the cyborg is to provide its 'readers' with possible ways of thinking about how the world could be ordered. This change, which inevitably has material consequences, derives from the way the body can be regarded as a site for political struggle and strategies of resistance. Cyborgs also evoke origin stories of how computer technology is, fundamentally, a military progeny—a war machine with a certain destiny that leaves noticeable traces in its most basic protocols. But, despite its connections with socialist feminism and cultural materialism, the question of the sex(uality) of the cyborg remains unclear: "The cyborg is a creature in a post-gender world."[18]

What my stay in WaterMOO has laid the ground for is a cyborg *with* a gender—or rather, a *sex*—a *she*-cyborg who brings a politics of 'sexual difference' into the online world without losing her otherwise disorganizing and troubling borderland status. She would still be able to show how female typists and their virtual 'body doubles' in no sense are separated from each other, but are rather intertwined in ways that give women of all kinds an imaginary space for dreams and desires, but that this space, simultaneously, is permeated with feminist politics rooted in collectivities of difference. A feminist politics of difference calls for a perspective that speaks of embodiment not only in terms of sexual specificity, but that simultaneously develops an awareness of *racial* specificity.[19] As discussed in the chapter "Reading Online Bodies," the racial dimension of online embodiment in WaterMOO is rarely evoked in character descriptions or typed-in interactions, which suggests obedience to a silent norm of virtual whiteness. Through recurring subtle allusions to, for example, blonde hair and blue eyes, the WaterMOO population is efficiently constructed as virtually white in a sense that marks or even excludes deviant bodies. In sketching out a politics of the she-cyborg, the mechanisms of how such exclusion is being done needs to be further scrutinized.[20]

To say that cyberfeminism—or, more fittingly for my purposes, *cyborg*feminism—needs a she-cyborg is further an attempt to discuss the relationship between what has sometimes been labeled 'gender theory,' on one hand, and 'sexual difference theory,' on the other.[21] This is not the place for a thorough account of the historical formations, developments, and variations in these two major strands in feminist thought; it is rather an opportunity to indicate in what ways cyborgfeminism benefits from transgressing rather than maintaining the divide between these two traditions. If, for example, Butler is usually aligned with gender theory (even though she seems to be moving away from, or radicalizing, the limits of this field), thinkers like Grosz and Braidotti are rather continuing a tradition of sexual difference theory with roots in 'French' feminism. In using the term 'sexual difference,' I am following a path outlined by Braidotti (1994), who proposes a reinvented theory of sexual difference for the 90s and beyond. Braidotti speaks of an emerging trend in feminist discourse based on the vision of the subject as a continuous process along the lines of multiplicity, but one that is at the same time radically 'materialistic.' In emphasizing that the formation of subjectivity is both a material and a semiotic process, this theoretical tendency stresses "the situated, specific, embodied nature of the feminist subject, while rejecting biological or psychic essentialism. *This is a new kind of female embodied materialism.*"[22] But, this view of the subject is everything but freed from inner tensions and contradictions:

> I would say that at the beginning of the feminist 1990s a paradox has emerged: the paradox of a theory that is based on the very notions of 'gender' and 'sexual difference', which it is historically bound to criticize on the basis of the new vision of subjectivity as process. Feminist thought rests on a concept that calls for deconstruction and de-essentialization in all of its aspects. More specifically, I think that the central question in feminist theory has become: how [do we] reassemble a vision of female subjectivity after the certainties of gender dualism have collapsed?[23]

This is the dilemma that the she-cyborg is facing, and to which she might provide a possible, if only a temporary, answer. The question is how to—simultaneously—argue for a disappearance of the classical paradigm of the enlightened, phallocentric subject and an *appearance* of a perspective that deals with a sexually specific, alternative subject. Braidotti argues: "Feminists have the double task of stressing the need for a new vision of subjectivity at large, and of a sex-specific vision of female subjectivity in particular."[24] This double task is what this book—based on insights gained in WaterMOO—has been attempting to work its way through; it has from various angles discussed how the poststructurally deconstructed subject is more than text, or rather, that text itself needs to be rethought as a variety of corporeal and material mediations. But, in both challenging and creating the subject anew, the she-cyborg does not primarily move us in the direction of a world beyond gender (as appeared to be the case with Haraway's cyborg on its first arrival in the Manifesto). She is rather utterly aware that the most cybernetic embodied subjects cannot escape the fact that having a body is also a matter of being *sexed* in one way or another.

In retrospect, Haraway seems to have reconsidered the question of gender in relation to her cyborg. In an interview with Constance Penley and Andrew Ross on the question of whether her cyborg was female, Haraway answered:

> Yeah, it is a polychromatic girl . . . the cyborg is a bad girl, she is really not a boy. Maybe she is not so much bad as she is a shape-changer, whose dislocations are never free. She is a girl who's trying not to become Woman, but remain responsible to women of many colors and positions, and who hasn't really figured out a politics that makes the necessary articulations with the boys who are your allies. It's undone work.[25]

This quote marks two significant shifts. First, the phrase "it is a polychromatic girl" turns the it-cyborg into a she, a girl of many colors. Secondly, this girl is "trying not to become Woman," which signifies a distance from woman-as-image and woman-as-Other, but also a distance in relation to feminist collectivity based on sameness. Haraway's girl-cyborg, in *not* being woman, can be understood as a figuration of the unfinished, of continuous *becoming*. This is a path well worth exploring.[26] Haraway's distance from the reading of the cyborg as 'post-gender' is even more obvious in a recent interview with Randi Markussen, Finn Olesen, and Nina Lykke:

Donna Haraway: [. . .] I have no patience with the term 'post-gender'. I have never liked it.

But you used it in the manifesto. . .

Donna Haraway: Yes, I did. But I had no idea that it would become this 'ism'!

(Laughter) You know, I have never used it since! Because post-gender ends up meaning a very strange array of things.[27]

Haraway further puts forth that the way she thinks about the *Cyborg Manifesto* today is a reading that attaches meanings to the cyborg retrospectively, and how she in reading interpretations by others of her Manifesto finds herself to be one of the readers and not the writer. The she-cyborg is obviously part of these rereadings and might as such be thought of as an extension, or perhaps a way of making explicit hidden and partly unspoken potentials in Haraway's text. My main point in arguing for a she-cyborg is to form a feminist perspective sensitive to bodies, texts, and materialities in various cyberspaces. Instead of claiming that online worlds are dislocated utopias where everything is possible, or that the use of technologies has little to do with local communities of 'real' women, I argue for a cyborgfeminist perspective that problematizes every separation of the imaginary from the political, and does so in a sense that does not erase the material of the virtual. The she-cyborg is an articulation of various transitory couplings between the different parts of her coming together as a *she-cyb-org*, which connects *women*—to the *cyb*ernetic—to the *org*anic. Without ever fully fusing together, these domains are rather linked and re-linked to each other in an open, changeable fashion.

If somebody still doubts the usefulness of making the sexed cyborg a she-cyborg—and not, for example, along the lines of contemporary theories of masculinity, a *he*-cyborg—let her then appear as a reminder of the rare occurrence of female machines in Western cultural imaginary (that are still alive in the end of the story). In her capacity as an intersection of human and machine, her borderland body becomes a site upon which to project the question of what it means to be human—and with it the question of what it means to be sexed. A she-cyborg takes responsibility for her own pleasures, fantasies, and longings, and even though she occasionally might bring a he-of-some-kind into the picture, one of the main points in her very constitution is that *she is not obliged to do so*. Born as she is in a world of (tele)dildonics and biotechnology, there is little need for the 'real' thing. Especially since she, by nature, has a hard time distinguishing the 'real' from the artificial, the original from the copy. In her article "Dildonics, Dykes and the Detachable Masculine," Jeanne E. Hamming suggests that there might be a way to recode the dildo as a pleasure-giving apparatus that is not, at the same time, a phallic extension.[28] By means of a 'post-lesbian' cyborg, she moves the dildo away from the psychoanalytic order of (phallic) presence and (castrated) absence, to a cybernetic paradigm of mutating information patterns:

> The dildo acts as a post-gender prosthetic and the lesbian, then, acts a cyborg, post-human, and therefore not male, nor castrated. [. . .] In this sense, the dildo

acts as a disembodied prosthetic, not as a supplement to a woman's lacking penis, a reproductive representation of the male body, but as a productive mutation of the dildonic body as altogether different.[29]

The she-cyborg is, doubtlessly, a close relative of this dildonic posthuman woman/machine figure, even though she is uncertain of how to relate to the term 'post-lesbian.' According to Hayles, the posthuman subject, mediated by a technology that makes visible the constructedness of identity categories (such as human and machine, male and female), marks a significant shift in relation to the subject of the Enlightenment. At the same time, Hayles is careful to point out that the transformation of the human into the posthuman has never been complete. Rather, the changes that brought forth such a shift (cybernetics, informatics, VR technologies, etc.) have simultaneously rearticulated traditional ideas and understandings related to the liberal subject.[30] The question is, then, whether a use of the term "post-lesbian"—which by means of prosthetic technologies attempts to detach lesbian sexuality from its dependence on the heterosexual matrix—is the most fruitful strategy in fighting phallocentrism. It does not seem as if Hamming wishes to abandon or render unstable the lesbian as a category, which is why striving for post-lesbianism appears to be a curious move. Although less precise in meaning, the she-cyborg would instead suggest a concept like *post-phallic* (or post-heterosexual, for that matter) to describe a similar break with masculine privilege. A post-phallic she-cyborg does not as clearly team up with a single, well-defined sexual identity (which would not go well with her basic, transgressive features), but encourages rather a wider range of desires and sexualities that all have joyful and rebellious couplings between women and machines at their heart.[31]

If the cyborg of the *Cyborg Manifesto* was partly about a possible future and partly a commentary on the current situation, utopian myth and social reality, the she-cyborg is more tightly coupled with the here and now. She certainly looks for possible futures (every feminist does) as well as for the creation and maintenance of cyber-sites of resistance, but her main work in this book has been to perform an analysis of the meaning and matter of highly contemporary online bodies—who, most concretely, inhabit a world in which sexual specificity is still one of the most fundamental aspects that structure online practices. The challenge for her has been to formulate an approach to online textual embodiment in which the body while *in* text is never fully *of* text—to realize a politics of sexual specificity within intense exchanges between bodies, texts, and machines. This is hard work. Even for a she-cyborg.

Jenny looks at her alarm clock in her pocket (since she has no ordinary watch) and realizes that she has to go back to work

Jenny sighs
You say, "really nice being here with you for a while though:)"
Jenny hugs you all warmly
Jenny waves bye-bye
@go home
You stand up.

Her Office
You find yourself in the middle of a cozy messiness. The walls are covered with bookcases, filled with books and piles of papers, embracing what seems to be an awful lot of knowledge. The room is surprisingly airy, for being a hotel room, and a window reveals one of the most amazing views that you've ever seen. Next to the window, there is an old French writing desk with lots of small drawers, and probably even some secret ones behind the movable panel. The desk is covered with books, journals and notebooks, and in the middle of all this you see an open PowerBook. In the pale blue flicker you capture a glimpse of a direct connection to . . . WaterMOO on the screen. In front of the desk, there is what seems to be a very comfortable chair. And if you were to lay your hand on the seat, you would notice that it was warm . . . as if someone a moment ago had been sitting there.
Obvious exits: Hall to Eighth Floor

Your Event Log has six new entries.
Ten of your pals are online.

   @quit

*** Disconnected ***

NOTES

Introduction

1. WaterMOO is not its actual name. For further discussion on the change of names and locations in online fieldwork, see chapter 1, "Writing a Written Culture," in the section "Rethinking ethics."
2. During the last couple of decades, work on the body within a wide range of disciplines has grown considerably. Despite differences in approach, these attempts are united through their strivings to break down binaries that associate body with nature and consciousness with culture. In a collective effort to recapture what was lost in the wake of Descartes and the alignment of philosophy with reason (to which the body was a danger), this corporeal turn attempts to make the body not only visible to, but an integrated part of intellectual thought (see, for example, Featherstone, Hepworth and Turner, 1991; Weiss and Fern Haber, 1999). In contrast to scientific discourses of biology and medicine constituting the body as natural, prediscursive, unchangeable, and passive, scholars within the humanities and the social sciences have turned these discourses on their head to show how (the presumed naturalness of) the body is a social, cultural, and historical construction. Lately, this argument has developed into a discussion of embodiment, which implies a feminist critique of the concept of 'the body' itself. As if there were such a thing as an abstract, disinterested, nongendered, and nonracial entity that could be called 'the body'—as if there were no differences whatsoever between bodies and bodily contexts—'the body' performs effortlessly in a lot of social and cultural theory. This stance becomes clear in statements like: "Issues at stake in debates about the impact of cyberculture on the body—especially the gendered one—are further problematized. . . ." (Cavallaro, 2000, p. 126, my emphasis). The work on embodiment leaves this realm of the illusory universal to engage with the specificity of bodies and with situated bodily practices (see, for example, Braidotti, 1994; Conboy, Medina and Stanbury, 1997; Grosz, 1994, 1995; and Thapan, 1997).
3. For a discussion of the concept of cyberspace, see, for example, Benedikt (1991); Featherstone and Burrows (1995); Kitchin (1998); Fernback (1997); and Strate, Jacobson, and Gibson (1996).
4. Stone (1995), p. 34.
5. Bukatman (1993), p. 208. Emphasis in this passage is in the original. From now on, I will mention that emphasis is added in quotes only when emphasis has been added by

me. Consequently, when emphasis in quotes is not commented upon, this means that it exists already in the texts quoted.

6. See, for example, Moravec (1988), who states that in a not too distant future it will be possible to transfer brain functions to computer software. See also Lanier and Biocca (1992), who argue that virtual reality frees the 'mind' from corporeal encumbrances and weaknesses.
7. Cf. Coyne (1999).
8. Balsamo (1996), pp. 116–132; Hayles (1996, 1999); and Stone (1991).
9. Braidotti (1996); Hawthorne and Klein (1999); Paterson (1996); and Seidler (1998).
10. For a discussion of the mind/body split in the history of philosophy from a feminist point of view, see, for example, Lloyd (2001); Tuana (1992, 1994).
11. See Clynes and Kline (1960).
12. On the close connection between masculinity and science and technology, see, for example, Cockburn (1983, 1985); Mellström (1995); Oldenziel (1999); and Wajcman (1994, 1995).
13. Interview with Mark Dery, in Dery (1994), p. 217.
14. Cf. Marsden (1996), p. 8.
15. Huyssen (1981).
16. See, for example, Haraway (1991) on the notion of 'nature' as something invented, produced, and reproduced (rather than discovered), and as such lacking every 'natural' alliance with women and between women: "There is nothing about being 'female' that naturally binds women. There is not even such a state as 'being' female, itself a highly complex category constructed in contested sexual scientific discourses and other social practices" (p. 155).
17. Norbert Wiener (1948), professor in mathematics at the MIT (Massachusetts Institute of Technology), in Boston, coined the term cybernetics from the Greek word for steersman. According to Wiener, cybernetics would refer to "the entire field of control and communication theory, whether in the machine or in the animal" (p. 19). This field of inquiry focuses on how messages circulate in information systems of humans and machines containing "feedback loops" that, gradually, alter the behavior in all components.
18. See Turing (1950).
19. Hayles (1999), p. xii.
20. Hayles (1999), p. xiii. Cf. Halberstam (1991/1998), who in a similar way points out that Turing fails to address "the obvious connection between gender and computer intelligence: both are in fact imitative systems, and the boundaries between female and male [...] are as unclear and as unstable as the boundary between human and machine intelligence" (p. 471).
21. Barthes (1979), pp. 74–75.
22. On the other hand, to fully separate text from work in this sense might be problematic, not least since the work is (perhaps even more clearly than the text) a material result of a work process. If Barthes's argument is pushed to its extreme, the text becomes merely a fetish, an autonomous object that has nothing to do with its context, including that of its production. But, as will become clear shortly, to speak of texts in a Barthian manner is only the first step in creating a productive approach to online textuality.
23. Barthes (1979), p. 79.
24. Braidotti (1996), under "The politics of the parody."
25. Ricoeur (1976).

26. Balsamo (1996), pp. 14-15.
27. Balsamo (1996), p. 125.
28. Fornäs (1998), p. 35.
29. Foucault (1979), p. 160.
30. Haraway (1997), p. 102. Cf. also Lykke (1997).
31. The notion of a "culture of no culture" is borrowed from Donna Haraway (1997). She argues, "No one exists in a culture of no culture, including the critics and prophets as well as the technicians. We might profitably learn to doubt our fears and certainties of disasters as much as our dreams of progress. We might learn to live without the bracing discourses of salvation history. We exist in a sea of powerful stories: They are the condition of finite rationality and personal and collective life histories. There is no way out of stories; but [. . .] there are many possible structures, not to mention contents, of narration. Changing the stories, in both material and semiotic senses, is a modest intervention worth making" (p. 23). Even if women and other marginalized groups might go to great lengths in their attempts to erase themselves, to temporarily be accepted as a part of "the culture of no culture," this will only serve those whose power is dependent on a maintenance of the illusion of transparency. Haraway shows how this striving constructs a notion of 'objectivity' that stands in the way of a more self-critical position committed to partial and situated knowledges.
32. Ito (1997), p. 101.
33. Cf. Silver (2000) for a discussion of "critical cyberculture studies."

Chapter One

1. Clifford (1986), p. 2.
2. Pratt (1986), p. 32.
3. See Clifford and Marcus (1986); Geertz (1988); and Van Maanen (1988).
4. Cf. Fornäs (2000).
5. Haraway (1997), pp. 190-191, my emphasis. For this type of ethnographic approach in cybercultural studies, see also Escobar (1994).
6. See also Bryld and Lykke (2000) for their discussion of feminist cultural studies. "Epistemologically, we share with many researchers within feminist cultural studies a disbelief in the traditional dichotomies between theory and empirical objects of study, between knowing subjects and objects of knowledge. We believe in accountable storytelling and theoretically informed articulations by embodied and localized subjects in dialogue with other human and non-human subjects" (p. 25). Such a dialogue becomes particularly relevant in relation to feminist cybercultural studies, since interlinkages of human as well as nonhuman subjects are the very foundation upon which cybernetic communication rests.
7. Cf. Miller and Slater (2000) for a discussion of a 'traditional' use of ethnography in their study of the impact of the Internet in Trinidad. They argue, "We are both relatively conservative in our defence of traditional canons of ethnographic enquiry. This seems particularly important at present time, when the term 'ethnography' has become somewhat fashionable in many disciplines. In some fields, such as cultural studies, it has come to signify simply a move away from purely textual analysis. In other cases, the idea of an Internet ethnography has come to mean almost entirely the study of online 'community' and relationships" (p. 20). On one hand, I would not deny that

the WaterMOO study might be an example of such critical 'expansion' of textual analysis. On the other hand, it is also a careful, long-term investigation of a particular online place where a remodeling of concepts that originate in an anthropological tradition hopefully is productive.

8. Cf. Ito (1997).
9. MOO stands for MUD Object Oriented, which refers to the somewhat simplified version of the (object oriented) programming language known as C++ that structures a MOO. See Curtis (1992) for one of the first introductions to the MOO phenomenon and to MUDding in general.
10. Bartle (1990).
11. For good introductions to MUDs and MUDding, as well as helpful historical overviews, see Bruckman (1992a), Cherny (1999), Pargman (2000), Reid (1994), Schaap (2000), and Turkle (1995).
12. Bruckman (1992a).
13. For pioneering work on the computer as a theater, see Laurel (1991). For more recent work on the performative and playful dimensions of online narratives, see, for example, Danet (1998, 2001); Danet, Ruedenberg and Rosenbaum-Tamari (1998); Murray (1997); and Sveningsson (2001).
14. Curtis (1992).
15. Turkle (1995), p. 181.
17. See the section "Rethinking ethics" for a discussion of these choices.
18. Aarseth (1997), p. 118.
19. Aarseth (1997), p. 134.
20. Cherny (1999), p. 41.
21. Nakamura (1995/2000), p. 713.
22. Reid (1995), p. 179.
23. The cultural implications of this phenomenon will be discussed further in chapter 5, "The Embodied Computer Code."
24. Haraway (1997).
25. Ryan (1999a), p. 11.
26. Austin (1962/1975), pp. 6–7.
27. Butler (1993), for example, pp. 1–23.
28. Thomsen, Straubhaar and Bolyard (1998), under "Epistemological Validity and Authority."
29. By 'active' participants, I mean those who on a fairly regular basis take part in the activities of WaterMOO, who are known to other participants (as opposed to temporary visitors and experimenters).
30. Suler (1996), under "AsKi the Newbie."
31. Suler (1996), Ibid.
32. In a MUD FAQ (list of frequently asked questions) for the newsgroup rec.games.mud, the following can be found on what a wizard on a TinyMUD (for example a MOO) is: "Wizards [. . .] are the people who own the database. They can do whatever they want to whomever they want whenever they want. A more appropriate name for them would be 'Janitor,' since they have to put up with responsibilities and difficulties (for free) that nobody else would be expected to handle. Remember they're human beings on the other side of the wire. Respect them for their generosity."
33. "*wiz" is an internal MOOmail address to all wizards in the MOO.
34. Hammersley and Atkinson (1983), p. 65.

35. Christina Allen's dissertation (1996) Virtual Identities: The Social Construction of Cybered Selves is one example of what might happen if people's identities are not properly protected. Allen used the real MOO names of interview subjects in her dissertation, and changed only the names of people her interviewees referred to. This, combined with events, made it easy for others to identify the people with changed names, none of whom had agreed to have the details of their lives spread all over the Net. Many people in the MOO in question got very angry about it. As a result, Allen ended up pulling her dissertation from any publicly available www or ftp site.
36. Paccagnella (1997).
37. Paccagnella (1997), under "Ethics of research." See also Frankel and Siang (1999).
38. See Bassett (1997).
39. Cf. O'Riordan (2002), who argues for a discussion of Internet research ethics that besides considering the spatial metaphors commonly used to discuss online activity (in terms of public/private spaces etc.), also considers the Internet as the cultural production of texts.
40. For reflections on the impact of geography on various levels in online fieldwork, see chapter 3, "Mapping Cyberplace(s)."
41. Paccagnella (1997), under "A proposal for comparative analysis in virtual communities."
42. Friedman (1995), p. 73.
43. Jones (1995), p. 11.
44. Cherny (1995, 1999); Kendall (1998); and Reid (1994, 1995).
45. Reid (1995), p. 171.
46. Aarseth (1997), p. 13.
47. Cf. Derrida (1976) and his critique of logocentrism. Logocentrism—an elevation of logos, of the spoken word—can be traced to Rousseau's romanticism. Walter J. Ong (1982) is one contemporary voice of this tradition. To Ong, oral culture is locally anchored and vividly expressive. Then, there is the entrance of the written word, in which language stiffens on an impersonal, dead surface. Ong follows the word in a motion from aural culture, over the invention of the printing press, and into the computer age. His main point is that these stages, one by one, have made the word increasingly technologized—which has carried the 'real' thought away from people, at the same time as people are carried away from each other. Writing breaks open the intimacy of speech and takes the relationships of the private sphere up to a global level. The collective spirit of the spoken word is exchanged for the fragments and individualization of print culture.
48. Aarseth (1997), pp. 148–149.
49. See Ricoeur (1991).
50. McHoul (1987); Mulkay (1985, 1986).
51. McHoul (1987), pp. 87–88. For a similar argument, see also Mooij (1993) and his discussion of speech act theory and fictional discourse.
52. Hayles (1999), p. 210.
53. Derrida (1976), pp. 141–164.
54. I will return to and develop these thoughts on online textuality and hypertext rhetoric in chapter 5, "The Embodied Computer Code."
55. Hine (1998), under "Discussion." Cf. Hine (2000).
56. In everyday usage, the word 'virtual' stands for something that appears to be, but that is not, the 'real thing'—even if it is able to produce the same effects. Webster's Dictionary

(1996) gives three definitions: The first one is closest to the everyday use of the word: "being such in power, force, or effect, though not actually or expressly such." The second meaning has to do with optics: "noting an image formed by the apparent convergence of rays geometrically, but not actually, prolonged, as the image formed by a mirror (opposed to real)." The third definition makes its way into the computer age: "temporarily simulated or extended by computer software." Ryan (2001), in an etymological tracing back of the term, points out that 'virtual' in scholastic Latin, virtualis, does not designate lack but potential: "The meaning of virtual stretches along an axis delimited by two poles. At one end is the optical sense, which carries the negative connotations of double and illusion [. . .], at the other is the scholastic sense, which suggests productivity, openness, and diversity" (p. 27). Ryan productively places the connections between the virtual and computer technologies of today somewhere in the middle of this axis.

57. For a use of the term 'cyberethnography,' see, for example, Paccagnella (1997) and Hakken (1999).
58. See, for example, Baym (1998, 2000); Correll (1995); Kendall (1999); Markham (1998); Paccagnella (1997); and Reid (1994).
59. Haraway (1997), p. 52. For 'cyborg anthropology,' see also Downey, Dumit and Williams (1995).
60. For example, Plant (1997), Reid (1994).
61. See Bruckman (1992b), on 'gender swapping.'
62. Reid (1994), under "Identity and the Cyborg Body."
63. Hall (1996), Herring (1993, 1996), Kramarae and Taylor (1993).
64. Hall (1996), p. 154. Cf. also Wakeford (1997), who in contrast to the image of woman-as-victim online puts forth that far from all women experience themselves as victims in online spaces. In her analysis of Web pages created by and for women, she points out how "[they] actively confront the 'harassed female' stereotype by creating networks of explicitly women-centered or feminist projects as alternative spaces in computing culture" (p. 53).
65. Grosz (1994), p. x.
66. Grosz (1994), p. 58.
67. Grosz (1994), p. 156.
68. Cf. O'Farrell and Vallone (1999), on the notion of 'virtual gender.'
69. Butler (1990), p. 7.
70. Butler (1993), p. 2.
71. See, for example, Moi (1999).
72. In her discussion of 'agency,' Butler (1990) argues that the subject is constituted in and through discourse and that there is no outside of this construction. Following Nietzsche, she further states that "there need not be a 'doer behind the deed,' but that the 'doer' is variably constructed in and through the deed" (p. 142). To be constituted by discourse does not, automatically, mean to be determined by discourse, where this determination stands in opposition to agency. Neither is a prediscursive 'I' that establishes a point of departure for a certain amount of reflexivity and independence a necessity. To be constituted by discourse means for Butler that the subject is a consequence, an effect, of certain rule-bound discourses, but this signification is "not a founding act, but rather a regulated process of repetition [. . .]; 'agency,' then, is to be located within the possibility of a variation on that repetition" (p. 145).

Chapter Two

1. Pearce (1997), pp. 17-18.
2. Stone (1995), pp. 180-181.
3. Characters might have their names followed by something called an @mood whenever they are 'in action.' In this case, 'Kramer'-most likely alluding to the character Kramer in the TV series Seinfeld—is followed by the @mood "(((show me)))." The standard model of @mood is constructed within single parentheses (i.e., "Swordman (Scabbard)"), but in letting no less than three parentheses surround the "show me" on each side, this particular @mood ideographically mimes the extraordinary sweeping arm gestures of the TV character Kramer.
4. Kendall (1998), p. 134.
5. See Sundén (2002a) for an earlier version of this chapter.
6. Clifford (1988), p. 49.
7. Clifford (1988), p. 53.
8. Murray (1997), p. 98.
9. Scott Sørensen (1999), p. 48. For an intriguing discussion of the Gothic body in literature and science, see Hurley (1996). Hurley uses the supernaturalist author William Hope Hodgsons' term 'abhuman' in reference to the destruction of 'the human' in Gothic literature: "The abhuman is a not-quite-human subject, characterized by its morphic variability, continually in danger of becoming not-itself, becoming other. The prefix 'ab-' signals a movement away from a site or condition, and thus a loss. But a movement away from is also a movement towards—towards a site or condition as yet unspecified—and thus entails both a threat and a promise" (pp. 3-4). This notion of the 'abhuman' is interesting in relation to technoscientific MOO bodies (written with Gothic/vampiric connotations), since these are "not-quite-human" not only in terms of their textual thematics, but also in their way of being fusions of human and machine—a state of being that is certainly both threatening and promising. For a parallel reading of cyberpunk and the Gothic, see Cavallaro (2000), pp. 164-203.
10. Stone (1995) uses the vampire as a (cyber)feminist figuration of thought, which achieves its strength from the way it challenges and threatens cultural boundaries: "Cyborgs are boundary creatures, not only human/machine but creatures of cultural interstice as well; and Lestat inhabits the boundaries between death and life, temporality and eternity, French and English, gay and straight, man and woman, good and evil. He nicely exemplifies a style of cyborg existence, capturing the pain and complexity of attempting to adapt to a society, a lifestyle, a language, a culture, an epistemology, even in Lestat's case a species, that is not one's own. Lestat is a vampire for our seasons, struggling with the swiftly changing meanings of what it is to be human or, for that matter, unhuman" (p. 178). The Vampire Lestat is borrowed from the novelist Anne Rice, but in Stone's work he is assigned a PhD in anthropology. He embodies a special way of seeing, a vampiric gaze both part of and outside the world of the mortals, and is bewitched by beings who are able to die. He himself exists partly beyond the life of humans but at the same time is deeply entangled within it: "He will continue through time, forever tasting but never fully locked into the world of sensuous experience and sensory adventure" (p. 179). The vampire gaze sees humans captured in time and subject positions, and turns this closeness into a fluidity of possibilities, a life on the borders between subjectivities.
11. Haraway (1997), p. 80.

12. McRae (1996), p. 257.
13. Haraway (1991). For a discussion of cyborg imagery in (cyber)feminism, see Lykke (1996), Paterson (1996), Sofia (1992), and Sundén (2001a).
14. Stone (1995), p. 181.
15. Castle (1986), pp. 4-5.
16. See, for example, Lupton (1995), Land (1995), and Sobchack (1995).
17. Balsamo (1996), p. 128.
18. Turkle (1995), p. 12.
19. Slater (1998), p. 93. IRC stands for Internet Relay Chat. IRC is a medium for 'real time' chatting with other people connected to the IRC network. After choosing a nickname, or 'nick,' participants can communicate with each other, either publicly or privately.
20. Raymond (1991), p. 20.
21. Boumelha (1988), p. 81.
22. Fiske (1987), p. 36.
23. See, for example, Fiske and Hartley (1978), Fiske (1987), and Boumelha (1988).
24. Fiske and Hartley (1978), p. 163.
25. Stone (1995), p. 181.
26. For Internet demographics, see, for example, <http://www.geog.ucl.ac.uk/casa/martin/geography_of_cyberspace.html> and <http://cyberatlas.internet.com/>. The problem with these, and similar sites, is that it often remains unclear how the results were achieved. Considering that the Internet covers immense territories that are extremely hard to grasp, these statistical figures cannot be regarded as anything other than estimates. Nevertheless, after having checked many sites (not only those mentioned above), all results I have come across are in accordance with what I present in this text.
27. When discussing Internet demographics, it is important not only to look at percentages of participation, but also to take into consideration that these figures might say very little about in which ways people are participating. Josie Arnold (1996) puts forward the metaphor of aerial mapping as she examines cyberspace as a newly discovered electronic terrain that is currently being colonized. Even if it is now commonly estimated that 50 percent, or more, of all Internet users are women, this does not mean that women are 'colonizing' cyberspace in the same percentage: "Cyberspace is being colonised now and the colonisers are taking their own backgrounds with them. This means that cyberspace is not being opened up as a new and non-marginalising endless place for textual play. Perhaps it never can be. The feminist politics of cyberspace may not be able to transcend the space from which they come" (under "Cyberspace as text"). This does not mean that it is impossible to find cyberspaces where women set the limits for the discussion, but it does suggest that the Internet is a space profoundly branded by gender politics.
28. Bassett (1997), p. 547.
29. Paterson (1996).
30. For an interesting discussion on gender and computer games, see Jenkins and Cassell (1998).
31. For discussions of gender online as exaggeration, see, for example, Bassett (1997), Kendall (1996, 1998), Kramarae (1995), O'Brien (1999), Rheingold (1994), Slater (1998), and Stone (1992).
32. Wakeford (1996) p. 102.
33. See Nakamura (1995/2000) for a similar observation in her study of identity tourism and racial passing on LambdaMOO.
34. Kolko, Nakamura and Rodman (2000) p. 1.

35. See Sundén (2002, forthcoming) for a more detailed analysis of WaterMOO characters in the guise of literary and lyrical quotes.
36. Pearce (1997), p. 20.
37. Pearce (1997), p. 6.
38. Fornäs (1995), pp. 175–180.
39. Ricoeur (1991), pp. 20 ff.
40. Ricoeur (1969/1974), pp. 262 ff.
41. Castle (1986), p. 38.
42. Castle (1986), p. 35.

Chapter Three

1. Bachelard (1958/1994), p. 221.
2. See Sundén (2001b) for an earlier version of this chapter (presented at "Global Networks: The Internet as a Medium of Cultural Globalization," March 30–31, 2001, University of Copenhagen, Denmark. I am grateful to the organizers Claus Bruhn Jensen and Gitte Stald, as well as other participants at this gathering for useful comments on my work).
3. For discussions on 'the global village,' see, for example, Ess and Sudweeks (2001), McLuhan and Powers (1989), and Wellman (1999).
4. Stone (1991).
5. Cf. Meyrowitz (1985).
6. Foucault (1986), p. 24.
7. Smith and Katz (1993), p. 70.
8. Miller (1995), pp. 3–4.
9. Miller (1995), p. 4 (my emphasis).
10. This understanding of 'place' is almost the opposite of the conceptualization made by Michel de Certeau (1984), referred to in online research (see, for example, Fuller and Jenkins, 1995). In his distinction between 'place' and 'space,' place "is the order (of whatever kind) in accord with which elements are distributed in relationships of coexistence. [...] A place is thus an instantaneous configuration of positions. It implies an indication of stability." A space, on the other hand, "occurs as the effect produced by the operations that orient it, situate it, temporalize it, and make it function in a polyvalent unity of conflictual programs and contractual proximities. On this view, in relation to place, space is like the word when it is spoken [...] In short, space is a practiced place" (p. 117).

    Following de Certeau's terminology, places do not exist 'in themselves,' or they exist only as a kind of potential not yet acted upon. We could perhaps think of the underlying computer technology of the Net, the materiality of the virtual, as the constitution of 'cyberplaces,' exceedingly existing, but not yet meaningful. Then, in the moment when the technology is put to use, cultural meanings can evolve and stories can begin to be told. When participants enter this world, engage with its textual surroundings, with each other, and with the activities of reading and writing, textual nodes and networks are transformed from places to spaces. But, there is something troubling about this picture in its reversal of more common understandings of 'place' and 'space' in cultural geography. It is hard to see how places, of whatever kind, could precede the imprint of cultural meaning, as if places could exist in a vacuum, passively awaiting the powers of spatializing/storytelling.

Moreover, the more time I have been spending online in general, and in Water-MOO in particular, the less relevant this conceptualization has proved. If for de Certeau, places become meaningful when their ordered stability is disrupted by the spatial practices of storytelling, then WaterMOO to its inhabitants rather seems to be characterized by a fundamental lack of stability. In this sense, these worlds do not represent a not yet meaningful order, but a not yet meaningful *dis*order, or void (absence of order). Reading de Certeau *backwards*, WaterMOO can be seen as containing a whole range of unstable 'spaces,' or of disordered potentials, which become meaningful through the structuring practices of place-making.

11. Bachelard (1958/1994), p. 8.
12. Bachelard (1958/1994), p. 9.
13. Bachelard (1958/1994), p. 22.
14. Bachelard (1958/1994), p. 18.
15. Bachelard (1958/1994), p. 19.
16. Bachelard (1958/1994), pp. 25–26.
17. Bachelard (1958/1994), pp. 211–212.
18. Bachelard (1958/1994), p. 212.
19. Bachelard (1958/1994), p. 221.
20. Both the hug and the smile in the last line are prewritten, standard hug and smile messages of a kind that frequently circulates in the MOO. Their rather high frequency, together with their status as automatons, makes them less emotionally loaded than they at first might appear to be.
21. Deleuze and Guattari (1980/1999), p. 478.
22. Nunes (1999), p. 71.
23. Deleuze and Guattari (1980/1999), p. 474.
24. For discussions on cybersex, see, for example, Branwyn (1994), Hamman (1996), and Reid (1994), pp. 75–95.
25. I will return to and analyze this excerpt (in an extended version) more at length in terms of textuality and desire in chapter 4, "Corporeal Obsession."
26. See Bechar-Israeli (1998) "From <Bonehead> to <cLoNehEAd>: Nicknames, Play and Identity on Internet Relay Chat" for a great story about the personal significance of nicks, and the identity crisis that might break out from realizing that someone else is using one's nick.
27. Slater (1998), p. 97.
28. Benedikt (1991), p. 10.
29. Baudrillard (1986), pp. 245–246. This passage is written in English in the French original.
30. Kolko (2000), p. 213.
31. Cf. Hayles (1997) for a similar account of the intricate dialectics between immersion, on one hand, and the visibly mediated, on the other. Hayles discusses the 'virtual book' ("books imagined on and through computer screens"), and argues: "As with film, the user is sometimes given the illusion that she is moving through the screen into an imagined world beyond. But unlike film, this imagined world contains text that the user is invited to open, read, and manipulate. Text is not left behind but remains in complex interplay with the perceived space into which the screen opens" (p. 191).

Chapter Four

1. Waldby (1995) p. 275.
2. See Sundén (2002b) for an earlier version of this chapter.
3. Holland (1995). Cf. Springer (1991, 1996).
4. In her essay "'Are You Male or Female?' Gender Performances on Muds," Kendall (1998) shows how the question "are you male or female?" is common enough to circulate as a joke among experienced MUD participants.
5. Danet (1996), under "Language, Writing and the Performance of Gender: Some Questions for Research." In the revised version of this article, Danet (1998), this phrase is slightly reformulated: "At least on the face of it, textual cross-dressing should be much easier than the RL variety. Nonetheless, it may be much more difficult than appears at first glance" (p. 145). For my purposes, I chose the online version that included a reference to 'textual passing.'
6. Garber (1993), p. 324.
7. Butler (1990), pp. 137–141.
8. Cherny (1999), p. 42.
9. Stone (1995), p. 71.
10. Cf. Ryan (2001).
11. One would perhaps expect a higher degree of suspicion regarding the sex of the typist of this 'girl,' especially from the point of view of somebody engaged in the activity of textual passing. Ironically, this is the way it usually seems to work. No matter how intricate the sex/gender games the typists are playing, it rarely strikes them that others might be doing the same thing. And, perhaps it rarely strikes online researchers that they too might be targets of the same kind of sophisticated displacements and alterations. . . .
12. Connell (1995), p. 74.
13. Adrienne Rich (1980) draws on the term 'compulsory heterosexuality' as a feminist critique of those powers that force women to devote themselves sexually to the model of reproductive heterosexuality. Butler (1990), in turn, uses the concept 'heterosexual matrix,' partly as a continuation of Rich's term to "designate that grid of cultural intelligibility through which bodies, genders, and desires are naturalized [. . .] that assumes that for bodies to cohere and make sense there must be a stable sex expressed through a stable gender (masculine expresses male, feminine expresses female) that is oppositionally and hierarchically defined through the compulsory practice of heterosexuality" (p. 151).
14. Butler (1993), pp. 88–89.
15. Butler (1993), p. 90.
16. Grosz (1995), pp. 153–171.
17. Grosz (1995), p. 170.
18. Connell (1995), p. 58.
19. Following Antonio Gramsci's theory of class relations, Connell's use of 'hegemony' points to the social and cultural dynamic by which a group occupies and maintains a leading position in society. Hegemonic masculinity is thus not a static concept, but a dynamic one that might be contested and subject to change. Connell defines hegemonic masculinity as "the configuration of gender practice which embodies the currently accepted answer to the problem of the legitimacy of patriarchy, which guarantees (or is taken to guarantee) the dominant position of men and the subordination of women" (p. 77).

20. In The Hite Report on Male Sexuality, Shere Hite (1981) states that "a large number of men said they liked or thought they would like a woman to be aggressive and dominate them" (p. 749). Among their answers were some stories very similar to the one involving kim and Wildman. Hite's investigation can of course not be regarded as a general statement regarding male sexuality, but it might serve as a sign of the occurrence of such fantasies in Western culture. A perhaps more interesting observation made by Roberta Perkins (1991) in her research on women prostitutes is that bondage and s/m prostitution services (where the female sex worker plays the dominatrix and the male client plays the dominated) is the most lucrative and rapidly growing domain of the sex industry.
21. I am indebted to Claudia Lindén for pointing me in this direction.
22. Deleuze (1967/1991), p. 21.
23. Deleuze (1967/1991), p. 22.
24. Waldby (1995), p. 272.
25. Waldby (1995), p. 274.
26. Waldby (1995), p. 274.
27. Plant (1998a), p. 30.
28. Foucault (1979), p. 145.
29. Barthes (1977), p. 148.
30. Barthes (1977), p. 147.
31. Foucault (1979), p. 158.
32. Barthes (1977), p. 142.
33. Grosz (1995), p. 19.
34. Derrida (1984/1986), pp. 5–6.
35. Grosz (1995), p. 21.

Chapter Five

1. Stone (1991), pp. 103–104.
2. An earlier version of this chapter was presented at the fourth international Digital Arts & Culture Conference in Providence, Rhode Island, April 26–28, 2001. I would like to thank participants at this conference, in particular Terry Harpold, for very useful comments. See also Sundén (2002c) for a more compressed discussion of the relationship between code and (corporeal) materiality in Swedish.
3. Cf. Wakeford (1996) about cyberspace as a series of partly overlapping performances.
4. Landow (1997).
5. Plant (1997), p. 10.
6. Bolter (1991), Landow (1997), Landow and Delany (1993), Lanham (1993), and Moulthrop (1988).
7. Moulthrop (1988), p. 1.
8. Cf. Aarseth (1997), pp. 1–23.
9. This might not be surprising considering that the same type of criticism has also been aimed at Barthes (1977) and his strong emphasis on the active and creative reader: "The reader is the space onto which all the quotations that make up writing are inscribed without any of them being lost; a text's unity lies not in its origin but in its destination" (p. 148). To speak about destination instead of origin is doubtlessly a neces-

sary and productive move, but if this shift in focus does not dissolve but merely transfers the qualities attached to the notion of authorial origin, of the sovereign subject, very little has been gained. According to Grosz (1995) while there is a shift in focus "perhaps decentring the sovereignty of the singular author, the multiplication of reading subjects remains governed by the norms of sovereignty. This becomes clear when the notion of the 'ideal reader' replaces that of multiplicity" (p. 17). Just as little as the hypertext reader is 'free' to create 'his' own text, the reader of any text is limited by the materiality of the medium. There are no such things as completely boundless journeys in textual landscapes. It is always a question of an intricate interplay between imagination and (material) regulation, between textual play and a resistance implied in the limit of the text itself.
10. Aarseth (1997, 1999). See also Grusin (1996) for a similar critique of American hypertext theory.
11. Aarseth (1997), p. 20.
12. Aarseth (1997), p. 21.
13. Ryan (1999b), p. 96.
14. Haraway (1991), p. 149.
15. Haraway (1991), p. 3.
16. Kolko (2000), p. 231n.
17. Butler (1997), p. 5.
18. In her examination of the relationship between interface and race in virtual worlds, Kolko (2000) acknowledges the fact that race as a feature of most MUD programs (except of the elf/dwarf variety in adventure MUDs) has been erased from the interface through various design choices. In short, there is no @race command. Kolko regards interfaces as mediating surfaces between users and technological artefacts charged with cultural and political assumptions: "The lack of an @race property means that the MUD is an environment where racial identity is presumed to be either irrelevant or homogenous. [. . .] The assumed homogeneity within cyberspace studies and cyberspace itself is staggering, as is the prevalence of 'we' vocabulary. And, quite simply, the lack of a writeable @race speaks volumes about the assumptions designers have, assumptions that tangibly affect the trajectory of technological development" (p. 218).
19. Perhaps it is not this scene that is impossible. The body 'itself' is certainly impossible to reach, in the same sense as the 'thing-in-itself' in Kantian discourse, but it is nevertheless possible to imagine that there is such thing as a body that cannot fully be captured in language—as something that at certain points resists cultural categorizations.
20. Butler (1997), pp. 33–34.
21. Irigaray (1977/1993), p. 26.
22. In an interview with Irigaray (1977/1993), the interviewer said: "Beyond a certain point I simply fail to understand the masculine-feminine oppositions. I don't understand what 'masculine' discourse means." To this Irigaray answered: "Of course not, since there is no other. The problem is that of a possible alterity in masculine discourse—or in relation to masculine discourse" (p. 140), pointing to the difficulty of recognizing a discourse that presents itself as self-evident and all-inclusive, in relation to which there is no outside, but perhaps an 'alterability' that might be explored and used from within.
23. Irigaray (1977/1993), p. 69.
24. Irigaray (1977/1993), p. 28.

25. Obviously, this brief reference to the work of Irigaray can give only a hint of its complexity. For good introductions to and critical discussions of her philosophy, see, for example, Burke, Schor and Whitford (1994); Duchen (1986); Grosz (1989); Moi (1987); and Whitford (1991).
26. Plant (1997), pp. 34–35.
27. See Plant (1998b), under "RosieX: Can I infer from your work that the term cyberfeminism implies that patriarchy is doomed?"
28. Zdenek (1999), p. 392.
29. Hayles (1999), pp. 192–207.
30. Hayles (1999), p. 198.
31. Hayles (1999) is careful to point out: "During any given period, experiences of embodiment are in continual interaction with constructions of the body" (p. 197). Taking the stress put on vaginal orgasm in the early 20th century as an example—found in domains as (seemingly) different as psychoanalysis and the novels of D. H. Lawrence—Hayles discusses how women's sexual practices interacted with this concept in ways that resulted in a wide range of experiences, some of them 'disciplined' along the lines of the concept while other experiences were very different altogether: "Because embodiment is individually articulated, there is also at least an incipient tension between it and hegemonic cultural constructs" (p. 197). I will return to and explore more closely the consequences of this observation that 'body' and 'embodiment,' although always engaged in an intense interplay, never quite collapse into each other.
32. Hayles (1999), p. 195.

Chapter Six

1. Butler (1993), p. 31.
2. Butler (1993), p. 68.
3. Butler (1993), p. 67.
4. Hayles (1999), pp. 196–197.
5. Hayles (1999), p. 197.
6. Hayles (1999), p. 197.
7. Grosz (1995), p. 21. My emphasis.
8. Derrida (1972/1982), p. 328. See also Derrida (1976/1984) for a more exhaustive account of the operation of signatures.
9. Grosz (1995), p. 21.
10. Dietrich (1997), p. 179.
11. Sofia (1992), p. 16.
12. Plant (1997), p. 46. My emphasis.
13. Hawthorne (1999), p. 217.
14. Hawthorne and Klein (1999), p. 8.
15. Coyne (1999). Cf. also Peters (1999).
16. Butler (1990), p. 7. My emphasis.
17. Grosz (1995), pp. 215–216.
18. Haraway (1991), p. 150.
19. For discussions on embodiment and race/ethnicity, see, for example, Bloodsworth (1999); Cranny-Francis (1995); Doyle (1994); and Zack, Shrage and Sartwell (1998).

20. Cf. Gedalof (2000); Ignacio (2000); and Kolko (2000), for discussions related to intersections of race/ethnicity and computer technologies.
21. For critical comparisons of these directions in feminist thought, see, for example, Cheah and Grosz (1998); Braidotti, with Butler (1997); Foster (1999); and Zakin (2000).
22. Braidotti (1994), p. 99. My emphasis.
23. Braidotti (1994), p. 99.
24. Braidotti (1994), p. 161.
25. Haraway, interview with Penley and Ross (1991), p. 20.
26. Cf. Bassett (2002), who argues for an understanding of the cybersubject as narrative and as narratable. Bassett makes narrative transformation the departure of a cyberfeminist politics in the sense that the subject is seen as someone who stretches out and exists "before and after" moments of technological intervention and connectivity. This view has some clear points of interference with the she-cyborg in terms of her attempts to bring together politics and imagination, as well as to rethink the subject 'as text' as a variety of material/corporeal mediations.
27. Haraway, interview with Markussen, Olesen and Lykke (2000), p. 12. Haraway puts forth that "gender is a verb, not a noun" and it is as such "always about the production of subjects in relation to other subjects, and in relation to artefacts" (pp. 12-13). In thinking about gender as an ongoing production or practice, it might be possible to use a term like post-gender differently, Haraway says. In relation to the understanding of the subject as process, post-gender does not refer primarily to a utopian universe in which gender is dissolving. Post-gender in this sense rather relates to how gender as something one does, need not be historically continuous: "It is the blasting of necessity, the no-necessity of this way of doing the world" (p. 13).
28. Hamming (2001).
29. Hamming (2001), p. 337.
30. Hayles (1999), for example pp. 1-24.
31. Cf. Lykke (2000, under "6. Conclusion"), who suggests a "queer cyborg" as a potent feminist ally: "While the cyborg deconstructs dichotomies and hierarchies between organism/machine, nature/culture, sex/gender etc., the queer breaks down dichotomies between different kinds of sexual orientation as well as the link between reproduction and sexual desires and identities. But when the two act in conjunction both kinds of tasks may be given equal weight and priority."

REFERENCES

Aarseth, Espen J. (1997). *Cybertext: Perspectives on Ergodic Literature*. Baltimore and London: The Johns Hopkins University Press.

Aarseth Espen J. (1999). "Aporia and Epiphany in *Doom* and *The Speaking Clock:* The Temporality of Ergodic Art." In Marie-Laure Ryan (ed.), *Cyberspace Textuality: Computer Technology and Literary Theory*. Bloomington and Indianapolis: Indiana University Press.

Agar, Michael H. (1980). *The Professional Stranger: An Informal Introduction to Ethnography*. Orlando and London: Academic Press.

Allen, Christina (1996). *Virtual Identities: The Social Construction of Cybered Selves*. Dissertation, Northwestern University.

Arnold, Josie (1996). "Colonising Cyberspace: The Politics of Cyberfeminism and Writing for Interactive Multi-Media in the IMMaterial World" [online]. Available: <http://www.swin.edu.au/ssb/media/staff/ja/cyberfem.htm>. Date accessed: April 26, 1998.

Austin, John L. (1962/1975). *How to Do Things with Words*. 2nd edition. J. O. Urmson & Marina Sbisà (eds.), Cambridge, Mass.: Harvard University Press.

Bachelard, Gaston (1958/1994). *The Poetics of Space*. Translated by Maria Jolas. Boston, Mass.: Beacon Press. Original title: *La poétique de l'espace*. Originally published by Presses Universitaires de France.

Balsamo, Anne (1996). *Technologies of the Gendered Body: Reading Cyborg Women*. Durham and London: Duke University Press.

Barthes, Roland (1977). *Image-Music-Text*. London: Fontana Press.

Barthes, Roland (1979). "From Work to Text." In Josué V. Harari (ed.), *Textual Strategies: Perspectives in Post-Structuralist Criticism*. Ithaca, NY: Cornell University Press.

Bartle, Richard (1990). *Interactive Multi-User Computer Games*. Colchester, UK: MUSE.

Bassett, Caroline (1997). "Virtually gendered: Life in an online world." In Ken Gelder & Sarah Thornton (eds.), *The Subcultures Reader*. London: Routledge.

Bassett, Caroline (2002). "Stretching Before and After." *Filozofski vestnik* 23(2).

Baudrillard, Jean (1986). *Amérique*. Paris: Bernard Grasset.

Baym, Nancy (1998). "The Emergence of On-line Community." In Steve Jones (ed.), *Cybersociety 2.0: Revisiting Computer-Mediated-Communication and Community*. Thousand Oaks, Cal.: Sage.

Baym, Nancy (2000). *Tune In, Log On: Soaps, Fandom, and On-line Community*. Thousand Oaks, Cal.: Sage.

Bechar-Israeli, Haya (1998). "From <Bonehead> to <cLoNehEAd>: Nicknames, Play and Identity on Internet Relay Chat." *Journal of Computer Mediated Communication* 1(2) [online]. Available: <http://www.ascusc.org/jcmc/vol1/issue2/index.html>. Date accessed: June 10, 2002.

Benedikt, Michael (1991). "Cyberspace: First Steps." In Michael Benedikt (ed.), *Cyberspace: First Steps*. Cambridge, Mass.: MIT Press.

Bloodsworth, Mary K. (1999). "Embodiment and Ambiguity: Luce Irigaray, Sexual Difference, and 'Race.'" *International Studies in Philosophy* 31(2).

Bolter, Jay David (1991). *Writing Space: The Computer, Hypertext, and the History of Writing*. Hillsdale: Lawrence Erlbaum.

Bolter, Jay David & Richard Grusin (2000). *Remediation: Understanding New Media*. Cambridge, Mass., and London: MIT Press.

Boumelha, Penny (1988). "Realism and the Ends of Feminism." In Susan Sheridan (ed.), *Grafts: Feminist Cultural Criticism*. London and New York: Verso.

Braidotti, Rosi (1994). *Nomadic Subjects: Embodiment and Sexual Difference in Contemporary Feminist Theory*. New York: Columbia University Press.

Braidotti, Rosi (1996). "Cyberfeminism with a difference." *New Formations* 29, autumn [online]. Available: <http://www.let.uu.nl/womens_studies/rosi/cyberfem.htm>. Date accessed: June 10, 2002.

Braidotti, Rosi (2001). *Metamorphoses: Towards a Materialist Theory of Becoming*. Cambridge: Polity Press.

Braidotti, Rosi, with Judith Butler (1997). "Feminism by Any Other Name: Interview." In Elizabeth Weed & Naomi Schor (eds.), *Feminism Meets Queer Theory*. Bloomington and Indianapolis: Indiana University Press.

Branwyn, Gareth (1994). "Compu-Sex: Erotica for Cybernauts." In Mark Dery (ed.), *Flame Wars: The Discourse of Cyberculture*. Durham: Duke University Press.

Bruckman, Amy (1992a). "Identity Workshop: Emergent Social and Psychological Phenomena in Text-Based Virtual Reality" [online]. Available: <ftp://ftp.media.mit.edu/pub/asb/papers/identity-workshop.rtf>. Date accessed: June 10, 2002.

Bruckman, Amy (1992b). "Gender Swapping on the Internet" [online]. Available: <http://www.cc.gatech.edu/fac/Amy.Bruckman/papers/index.html#INET>. Date accessed: June 10, 2002.

Bryld, Mette & Nina Lykke (2000). *Cosmodolphins: Feminist Cultural Studies of Technology, Animal, and the Sacred*. London: Zed Books.

Bukatman, Scott (1993). *Terminal Identity: The Virtual Subject in Postmodern Science Fiction*. Durham: Duke University Press.

Burke, Carolyn, Naomi Schor & Margaret Whitford (1994). *Engaging with Irigaray: Feminist Philosophy and Modern European Thought*. New York: Columbia University Press.

Butler, Judith (1990). *Gender Trouble: Feminism and the Subversion of Identity.* New York and London: Routledge.
Butler, Judith (1993). *Bodies that Matter: On the Discursive Limits of "Sex."* New York and London: Routledge.
Butler, Judith (1997). *Excitable Speech: A Politics of the Performative.* New York and London: Routledge.
Casey, Edward S. (1997). *The Fate of Place: A Philosophical History.* Berkeley and Los Angeles: University of California Press.
Castle, Terry (1986). *Masquerade and Civilization: The Carnivalesque in Eighteenth-Century English Culture and Fiction.* London: Methuen.
Cavallaro, Dani (2000). *Cyberpunk and Cyberculture: Science Fiction and the Work of William Gibson.* London and New Brunswick, NJ: The Athlone Press.
Cheah, Pheng & Elizabeth Grosz (1998). "The Future of Sexual Difference: An Interview with Judith Butler and Drucilla Cornell." *Diacritics* 28, spring.
Cherny, Lynn (1995). "'Objectifying' the Body in the Discourse of an Object-Oriented MUD" [online]. Available: <http://acorn.grove.iup.edu/en/workdays/toc.html>. Date accessed: January 17, 2000.
Cherny, Lynn (1999). *Conversation and Community: Chat in a Virtual World.* Stanford, Cal.: CSLI Publications.
Clifford, James (1986). "Introduction: Partial Truths." In James Clifford & George E. Marcus (eds.), *Writing Culture: The Poetics and Politics of Ethnography.* Berkeley and Los Angeles: University of California Press.
Clifford, James (1988). *The Predicament of Culture: Twentieth-Century Ethnography, Literature, and Art.* Cambridge, Mass.: Harvard University Press.
Clifford, James & George E. Marcus (1986). *Writing Culture: The Poetics and Politics of Ethnography.* Berkeley and Los Angeles: University of California Press.
Clynes, Manfred E. & Nathan S. Kline (1960). "Cyborgs and Space." *Astronautics* 14(9), September.
Cockburn, Cynthia (1983). *Brothers: Male Dominance and Technological Change.* London: Pluto.
Cockburn, Cynthia (1985). *Machinery of Dominance: Women, Men, and Technical Know-How.* London: Pluto.
Conboy, Katie, Nadia Medina & Sarah Stanbury (eds.) (1997). *Writing on the Body: Female Embodiment and Feminist Theory.* New York: Columbia University Press.
Connell, R. W. (1995). *Masculinities: Knowledge, Power and Social Change.* Berkeley and Los Angeles: University of California Press.
Correll, Shelley (1995). "The Ethnography of an Electronic Bar: The Lesbian Café." *The Journal of Contemporary Ethnography* 24(3).
Coyne, Richard (1999). *Technoromanticism: Digital Narrative, Holism, and the Romance of the Real.* Cambridge, Mass., and London: MIT Press.
Cranny-Francis, Anne (1995). *The Body in the Text.* Carlton South, Vic.: Melbourne University Press.
Curtis, Pavel (1992). "Mudding: Social Phenomena in Text-Based Virtual Realities." Proceedings of *Directions and Implications of Advanced Computing (DIAC'92).* Berkeley,

Cal. [online]. Available: <ftp://ftp.lambda.moo.mud.org/pub/MOO/papers/DIAC92.txt>. Date accessed: June 10, 2002.

Danet, Brenda (1996). "Text as Mask: Gender and Identity on the Internet" [online]. Available: <http://atar.mscc.huji.ac.il/~msdanet/mask.html>. Date accessed: June 10, 2002.

Danet, Brenda (1998). "Text as Mask: Gender, Play, and Performance on the Internet." In Steve Jones (ed.) *Cybersociety 2.0: Revisiting Computer-Mediated Communication and Community*. London: Sage.

Danet, Brenda (2001). *Cyberplay: Communicating Online*. Oxford: Berg.

Danet, Brenda, Lucia Ruedenberg & Yehudit Rosenbaum-Tamari (1998). "Hmmm ... Where Is That Smoke Coming From? Writing Play and Performance on Internet Relay Chat." In Fay Sudweeks, Margaret Mc Laughlin & Sheizaf Rafaeli (eds.), *Network and Netplay: Virtual Groups on the Internet*. Menlo Park, Cal.: AAAI Press: MIT Press.

de Certeau, Michel (1984). *The Practice of Everyday Life*. Berkeley, Los Angeles and London: University of California Press.

Deleuze, Gilles (1967/1991). "Coldness and Cruelty" in *Masochism*. New York: Zone Books. Original title: "Le Froid et le Cruel." In *Presentation de Sacher-Masoch*.

Deleuze, Gilles & Felix Guattari (1980/1999). *A Thousand Plateaus*. London: The Athlone Press. Translated by Brian Massumi. Original title: *Mille Plateaux*. Paris: Les Editions de Minuit.

Derrida, Jacques (1972/1982). *Margins of Philosophy*. Translated by Alan Bass. Chicago: University of Chicago Press.

Derrida, Jacques (1976). *Of Grammatology*. Translated by Gayatri Chakravorty Spivak. Baltimore: Johns Hopkins University Press.

Derrida, Jacques (1976/1984). *Signéponge/Signsponge*. Translated by Richard Rand. New York: Columbia University Press.

Derrida, Jacques (1984/1986). *The Ear of the Other: Otobiography, Transference, Translation: Texts and Discussions with Jacques Derrida*. Translated by Peggy Kamuf & Avital Ronell. New York: Schocken Books.

Dery, Mark (1994). "Back to the Future: Interviews with Samuel R. Delany, Greg Tate, and Tricia Rose." In Mark Dery (ed.), *Flame Wars: The Discourse of Cyberculture*. Durham and London: Duke University Press.

Dietrich, Dawn (1997). "(Re)-Fashioning the Techno-Erotic Woman: Gender and Textuality in the Cybercultural Matrix." In Steve Jones (ed.), *Virtual Culture: Identity and Communication in Cybersociety*. London and Thousand Oaks, Cal.: Sage.

Downey, Gary Lee, Joseph Dumit & Sarah Williams (1995). "Cyborg Anthropology." In Chris Hables Gray, with the assistance of Heidi J. Figueroa-Sarriera & Steven Mentor (eds.), *The Cyborg Handbook*. London and New York: Routledge.

Doyle, Laura Anne (1994). *Bordering on the Body: The Racial Matrix of Modern Fiction and Culture*. New York: Oxford University Press.

Duchen, Claire (1986) *Feminism in France: From May '68 to Mitterand*. London: Routledge Kegan Paul.

Escobar, Arturo (1994). "Welcome to Cyberia: Notes on the Anthropology of Cyberculture." *Current Anthropology* 35(3).
Ess, Charles & Fay Sudweeks (eds.) (2001). *Culture, Technology, Communication: Towards an Intercultural Global Village.* Albany, NY: State University of New York Press.
Featherstone, Mike, Mike Hepworth & Bryan S. Turner (eds.) (1991). *The Body: Social Processes and Cultural Theory.* London: Sage.
Featherstone, Mike & Roger Burrows (eds.) (1995). *Cyberspace, Cyberbodies, Cyberpunk: Cultures of Technological Embodiment.* London: Sage.
Fernback, Jan (1997). "The Individual Within the Collective: Virtual Ideology and the Realization of Collective Principles." In Steve Jones (ed.), *Virtual Culture: Identity and Communication in Cybersociety.* London and Thousand Oaks, Cal.: Sage.
Fiske, John (1987). *Television Culture.* London: Methuen.
Fiske, John & John Hartley (1978). *Reading Television.* London: Methuen.
Fornäs, Johan (1995). *Cultural Theory and Late Modernity.* London: Sage.
Fornäs, Johan (1998). "Digital Borderlands: Identity and Interactivity in Culture, Media and Communications." *Nordicom Review* 19(1).
Fornäs, Johan (2000). "The Crucial In Between: The Centrality of Mediation in Cultural Studies." *European Journal of Cultural Studies* 3(1).
Foster, Johanna (1999). "An Invitation to Dialogue: Clarifying the Position of Feminist Gender Theory in Relation to Sexual Difference Theory." *Gender and Society* 13(4).
Foucault, Michel (1979). "What Is an Author?" In Josué V. Harari (ed.), *Textual Strategies: Perspectives in Post-Structuralist Criticism.* Ithaca, NY: Cornell University Press.
Foucault, Michel (1986). "Of Other Spaces." *Diacritics* 16(1).
Frankel, Mark and Sanyin Siang (1999). "Ethical and Legal Aspects of Human Subjects Research on the Internet." American Association for the Advancement of Science (AAAS) [online]. Available: <http://www.aaas.org/spp/sfrl/projects/intres/main.htm>. Date accessed: June 10, 2002.
Friedman, Ted (1995). "Making Sense of Software: Computer Games and Interactive Textuality." In Steve Jones (ed.) *CyberSociety: Computer-Mediated Communication and Community.* London: Sage.
Fuller, Mary & Henry Jenkins (1995). "Nintendo® and New World Travel Writing: A Dialogue." In Steve Jones (ed.), *CyberSociety: Computer-Mediated Communication and Community.* London: Sage.
Garber, Marjorie (1993). "Spare Parts: The Surgical Construction of Gender." In Henry Abelove, Michèle Aina Barale & David M. Halperin (eds.), *The Lesbian and Gay Studies Reader.* New York and London: Routledge.
Gedalof, Irene (2000). "Identity in Transit: Nomads, Cyborgs and Women." *The European Journal of Women's Studies* 7(3).
Geertz, Clifford (1988). *Works and Lives: The Anthropologist as Author.* Stanford, Cal: Stanford University Press.
Gibson, William (1984). *Neuromancer.* New York: Ace Books.
Grosz, Elizabeth (1989). *Sexual Subversions: Three French Feminists.* London: Unwin Hyman.

Grosz, Elizabeth (1994). *Volatile Bodies: Toward a Corporeal Feminism*. Bloomington and Indianapolis: Indiana University Press.

Grosz, Elizabeth (1995). *Space, Time, and Perversion: Essays on the Politics of Bodies*. New York and London: Routledge.

Grusin, Richard (1996). "What Is an Electronic Author? Theory and the Technological Fallacy." In Robert Markley (ed.), *Virtual Realities and Their Discontents*. Baltimore and London: The Johns Hopkins University Press.

Hakken, David (1999). *Cyborgs@Cyberspace? An Ethnographer Looks to the Future*. London and New York: Routledge.

Halberstam, Judith (1991/1998). "Automating Gender: Postmodern Feminism in the Age of the Intelligent Machine." In Patrick D. Hopkins (ed.), *Sex/Machine: Readings in Culture, Gender, and Technology*. Bloomington and Indianapolis: Indiana University Press.

Hall, Kira (1996). "Cyberfeminism." In Susan Herring (ed.), *Computer-Mediated Communication: Linguistic, Social and Cross-Cultural Perspectives*. Amsterdam and Philadelphia: John Benjamins.

Hamman, Robin B. (1996). "Cyborgasms: Cybersex Amongst Multiple-Selves and Cyborgs in the Narrow-Bandwidth Space of America Online Chat Rooms." MA thesis, Department of Sociology, University of Essex [online]. Available: *<http://www.socio.demon.co.uk/Cyborgasms.html>*. Date accessed: June 10, 2002.

Hammersley, Martyn & Paul Atkinson (1983). *Ethnography: Principles in Practice*. London: Tavistock.

Hamming, Jeanne E. (2001). "Dildonics, Dykes and the Detachable Masculine." *The European Journal of Women's Studies* 8(3).

Haraway, Donna (1991). "A Cyborg Manifesto: Science, Technology, and Socialist-Feminism in the Late Twentieth Century." In Donna Haraway, *Simians, Cyborgs and Women: The Reinvention of Nature*. New York: Routledge [online]. Available: *<http://www.stanford.edu/dept/HPS/Haraway/CyborgManifesto.html >*. Date accessed: June 10, 2002.

Haraway, Donna (1997). *Modest_Witness@Second_Millennium: FemaleMan©_Meets_OncoMouse™*. New York and London: Routledge.

Hawthorne, Susan (1999). "Cyborgs, Virtual Bodies and Organic Bodies: Theoretical Feminist Responses." In Susan Hawthorne & Renate Klein (eds.), *Cyberfeminism: Connectivity, Critique and Creativity*. North Melbourne: Spinifex Press.

Hawthorne, Susan & Renate Klein (1999). "Cyberfeminism: Introduction." In Susan Hawthorne & Renate Klein (eds.), *Cyberfeminism: Connectivity, Critique and Creativity*. North Melbourne: Spinifex Press.

Hayles, N. Katherine (1996). "Embodied Virtuality: Or How to Put Bodies Back into the Picture." In Mary Anne Moser & Douglas MacLeod (eds.), *Immersed in Technology: Art and Virtual Environments*. Cambridge, Mass.: MIT Press.

Hayles, N. Katherine (1997). "The Condition of Virtuality." In Jeffrey Masten, Peter Stallybrass & Nancy J. Vickers (eds.), *Language Machines: Technologies of Literary and Cultural Production*. London and New York: Routledge.

Hayles, N. Katherine (1999). *How We Became Posthuman: Virtual Bodies in Cybernetics, Literature, and Informatics*. Chicago and London: The University of Chicago Press.

Herring, Susan (1993). "Gender and Democracy in Computer-Mediated Communication." *Electronic Journal of Communication* 3(2).

Herring, Susan (1996). "Two Variants of an Electronic Message Schema." In Susan Herring (ed.), *Computer-Mediated Communication: Linguistic, Social and Cross-Cultural Perspectives*. Amsterdam and Philadelphia: John Benjamins.

Hine, Christine (1998). "Virtual Ethnography." Paper presented at the Internet Research and Information for Social Scientists international conference, March 25–27 1998, Bristol, UK. [Online]. Available: <http://www.sosig.ac.uk/iriss/papers/paper16.htm>. Date accessed: June 10, 2002.

Hine, Christine (2000). *Virtual Ethnography*. London: Sage.

Hite, Shere (1981). *The Hite Report on Male Sexuality*. New York: Alfred A. Knopf.

Holland, Samantha (1995). "Descartes Goes to Hollywood: Mind, Body and Gender in Contemporary Cyborg Cinema." In Mike Featherstone & Roger Burrows (eds.), *Cyberspace, Cyberbodies, Cyberpunk: Cultures of Technological Embodiment*. London: Sage.

Hurley, Kelly (1996). *The Gothic Body: Sexuality, Materialism, and Degeneration*. Cambridge, MA: Cambridge University Press.

Huyssen, Andreas (1981). "The Vamp and the Machine: Technology and Sexuality in Fritz Lang's 'Metropolis.'" *New German Critique* 24/25.

Ignacio, Emily Noelle (2000). "Ain't I a Filipino (Woman)? An Analysis of Authorship/Authority through the Construction of 'Filipina' on the Net." *Sociological Quarterly* 1(4).

Irigaray, Luce (1977/1993). *This Sex Which Is Not One*. Translated by Catherine Porter. Ithaca, NY: Cornell University Press. Original title: *Ce Sexe qui n'en est pas un*. Paris: Les Editions de Minuit.

Ito, Mizuko (1997). "Virtually Embodied: The Reality of Fantasy in a Multi-User Dungeon." In David Porter (ed.), *Internet Culture*. New York and London: Routledge.

Jenkins, Henry & Justine Cassell (1998). *From Barbie to Mortal Combat: Gender and Computer Games*. Cambridge, Mass.: MIT Press.

Jones, Steve (1995). "Introduction." In Steve Jones (ed.), *CyberSociety: Computer-Mediated Communication and Community*. London: Sage.

Kendall, Lori (1996). "MUDder? I Hardly Know 'Er! Adventures of a Feminist MUDder." In Lynn Cherny & Elizabeth Reba Weise (eds.), *Wired Women*. Seattle: Seal Press.

Kendall, Lori (1998). "'Are You Male or Female?' Gender Performances on Muds." In Jodi O'Brien & Judith A. Howard (eds.), *Everyday Inequalities: Critical Inquiries*. Malden, Mass., Oxford: Blackwell Publishers.

Kendall, Lori (1999). "Recontextualizing 'Cyberspace': Methodological Considerations for Online Research." In Steve Jones (ed.), *Doing Internet Research: Critical Issues and Methods for Examining the Net*. Thousand Oaks, Cal., London and New Delhi: Sage Publications.

Kitchin, Rob (1998). *Cyberspace: The World in the Wires*. Chichester: John Wiley & Sons.

Kolko, Beth E. (2000). "Erasing @race: Going White in the (Inter)Face." In Beth E. Kolko, Lisa Nakamura, Gilbert B. Rodman (eds.), *Race in Cyberspace*. New York: Routledge.

Kolko, Beth E., Lisa Nakamura, Gilbert B. Rodman (eds.) (2000). *Race in Cyberspace*. New York: Routledge.

Kramarae, Cheris (1995). "A Backstage Critique of Virtual Reality." In Steve Jones (ed.), *Cybersociety*. Thousand Oaks, Cal.: Sage Publications.

Kramarae, Cheris & H. Jeanie Taylor (1993). "Women and Men on Electronic Networks: A Conversation or a Monologue?" In H. Jeanie Taylor, Cheris Kramarae & Maureen Ebben (eds.), *Women, Information Technology, + Scholarship*. Urbana, IL: University of Illinois Press.

Land, Nick (1995). "Meat (or How to Kill Oedipus in Cyberspace)." In Mike Featherstone & Roger Burrows (eds.), *Cyberspace, Cyberbodies, Cyberpunk: Cultures of Technological Embodiment*. London: Sage.

Landow, George P. (1997). *Hypertext 2.0: The Convergence of Contemporary Critical Theory and Technology*. Baltimore: Johns Hopkins University Press.

Landow, George P. & Paul Delany (eds.) (1993). *The Digital Word: Text-Based Computing in the Humanities*. Cambridge, Mass: MIT Press.

Lanham, Richard (1993). *The Electronic Word: Democracy, Technology, and the Arts*. Chicago: Chicago University Press.

Lanier, Jaron & Frank Biocca (1992). "An Insider's View of the Future of Virtual Reality." *Journal of Communication* 42(4).

Laurel, Brenda (1991). *Computers as Theater*. Menlo Park, Cal.: Addison-Wesley.

Lloyd, Genevieve (2001). *Feminism and History of Philosophy*. Oxford: Oxford University Press.

Lupton, Deborah (1995). "The Embodied Computer/User." In Mike Featherstone & Roger Burrows (eds.), *Cyberspace, Cyberbodies, Cyberpunk: Cultures of Technological Embodiment*. London: Sage.

Lykke, Nina (1996). "Between Monsters, Goddesses and Cyborgs: Feminist Confrontations with Science." In Nina Lykke & Rosi Braidotti (eds.), *Between Monsters, Goddesses and Cyborgs: Feminist Confrontations with Science, Medicine and Cyberspace*. London: Zed Books.

Lykke, Nina (1997). "To Be a Cyborg or a Goddess?" *Gender, Technology and Development* 1(1).

Lykke, Nina (2000). "Are Cyborgs Queer? Biological Determinism and Feminist Theory in the Age of New Reproductive Technologies and Reprogenetics." Paper presented at "Body, Gender, Subjectivity: Crossing Disciplinary and Institutional Borders" conference, September 28–October 1, Bologna, Italy [online]. Available: <http://www.women.it/quarta/workshops/epistemological4/ninalykke.htm>. Date accessed: June 10, 2002.

Markham, Annette N. (1998). *Life Online: Researching Real Experience in Virtual Space*. Walnut Creek, Cal.: AltaMira Press.

Markussen, Randi, Finn Olesen & Nina Lykke (2000). "Cyborgs, Coyotes and Dogs:

A Kinship of Feminist Figurations: Interview with Donna Haraway." *Kvinder, Køn og Forskning* 2.
Marsden, Jill (1996). "Virtual Sexes and Feminist Futures: The Philosophy of 'Cyberfeminism.'" *Radical Philosophy* 78.
McHoul, Alec (1987). "An Initial Investigation of the Usability of Fictional Conversation for Doing Conversation Analysis." *Semiotica* 67(1/2).
McLuhan, Marshall & Bruce R. Powers (1989). *The Global Village: Transformations in World Life and Media in the 21st Century.* New York: Oxford University Press.
McRae, Shannon (1996). "Coming Apart at the Seams: Sex, Text and the Virtual Body." In Lynn Cherny & Elizabeth Reba Weise (eds.), *Wired Women.* Seattle: Seal Press.
Mellström, Ulf (1995). *Engineering Lives: Technology, Time and Space in a Male-Centered World.* PhD thesis, Department of Technology and Social Change, Linköping University.
Meyrowitz, Joshua (1985). *No Sense of Place: The Impact of Electronic Media on Social Behavior.* New York: Oxford University Press.
Miller, Daniel & Don Slater (2000). *The Internet: An Ethnographic Approach.* Oxford: Berg.
Miller, J. Hillis (1995). *Topographies.* Stanford, Cal.: Stanford University Press.
Moi, Toril (ed.) (1987). *French Feminist Thought: A Reader.* New York: Blackwell.
Moi, Toril (1999) *What Is a Woman? And Other Essays.* Oxford: Oxford University Press.
Mooij, Jan J. A. (1993). *Fictional Realities: The Uses of Literary Imagination.* Amsterdam and Philadelphia: John Benjamins.
Moravec, Hans (1988). *MIND Children: The Future of Robot and Human Intelligence.* Cambridge, Mass.: Harvard University Press.
Moulthrop, Stuart (1988). "Containing Multitudes: The Problem of Closure in Interactive Fiction." *Association for Computers and the Humanities Newsletter* 10.
Mulkay, Michael (1985). "Agreement and Disagreement in Conversations and Letters." *Text* 5(3).
Mulkay, Michael (1986). "Conversations and Texts." *Human Studies* 9.
Murray, Janet H. (1997). *Hamlet on the Holodeck: The Future of Narrative in Cyberspace.* New York: The Free Press.
Nakamura, Lisa (1995/2000). "Race in/for Cyberspace: Identity Tourism and Racial Passing on the Internet." In David Bell & Barbara M. Kennedy (eds.), *The Cybercultures Reader.* London and New York: Routledge.
Nunes, Mark (1999). "Virtual Topographies: Smooth and Striated Cyberspace." In Marie-Laure Ryan (ed.), *Cyberspace Textuality: Computer Technology and Literary Theory.* Bloomington and Indianapolis: Indiana University Press.
O'Brien, Jodi (1999). "Writing in the Body: Gender (Re)production in Online Interaction." In Marc A. Smith & Peter Kollock (eds.), *Communities in Cyberspace.* London and New York: Routledge.
O'Farrell, Mary Ann & Lynne Vallone (eds.) (1999). *Virtual Gender: Fantasies of Subjectivity and Embodiment.* Ann Arbor: University of Michigan Press.

Oldenziel, Ruth (1999). *Making Technology Masculine: Men, Women and Modern Machines in America, 1870-1945*. Amsterdam: Amsterdam University Press.
Ong, Walter J. (1982). *Orality and Literacy: The Technologizing of the Word*. London: Methuen/ Routledge.
O'Riordan, Kate (2002). "Mediated Identities and The Ethics of Internet Research: Contesting the Human Subjects Research Model". Paper presented at "Crossroads in Cultural Studies: Fourth International Conference," June 29-July 2, Tampere, Finland.
Paccagnella, Luciano (1997). "Getting the Seats of Your Pants Dirty: Strategies for Ethnographic Research on Virtual Communities." *Journal of Computer Mediated Communication* 3(1) [online]. Available <http://www.ascusc.org/jcmc/vol3/issue1/paccagnella.html#rdanet>. Date accessed: June 10, 2002.
Pargman, Daniel (2000). *Code Begets Community: On Social and Technical Aspects of Managing a Virtual Community*. PhD thesis, Department of Communication Studies, Linköping University.
Paterson, Nancy (1996). "Cyberfeminism." [online]. Available: <gopher://echonyc.com/00/Cul/Cyber/paterson>. Date accessed: April 26, 1998.
Pearce, Lynne (1997). *Feminism and the Politics of Reading*. London: Arnold.
Penley, Constance & Andrew Ross (1991). "Cyborgs at Large: Interview with Donna Haraway." In Constance Penley & Andrew Ross (eds.), *Technoculture*. Minneapolis: University of Minnesota Press.
Perkins, Roberta (1991). *Working Girls: Prostitutes, Their Life and Social Control*. Canberra: Australian Institute of Criminology.
Peters, John Durham (1999). *Speaking into the Air: A History of the Idea of Communication*. Chicago: University of Chicago Press.
Plant, Sadie (1997). *Zeros + Ones: Digital Women + The New Technoculture*. New York: Doubleday.
Plant, Sadie (1998a). "Coming Across the Future." In John Broadhurst Dixon & Eric J. Cassidy (eds.), *Virtual Futures: Cyberotics, Technology and Post-Human Pragmatism*. London and New York: Routledge.
Plant, Sadie (1998b). Interview by RosieX [online]. Available: <http://206.251.6.116/geekgirl/001stick/sadie/sadie.html>. Date accessed: April 26, 1998.
Pratt, Mary Louise (1986). "Fieldwork in Common Places." In James Clifford & George E. Marcus (eds.), *Writing Culture: The Poetics and Politics of Ethnography*. Berkeley and Los Angeles: University of California Press.
Raymond, Eric S. (1991). *The New Hackers' Dictionary*. Cambridge, Mass.: MIT Press.
Reid, Elizabeth (1994). "Cultural Formations in Text-Based Virtual Realities" [online]. Available: <http://people.we.mediaone.net/elizrs/cult-form.html>. Date accessed: December 12, 1998.
Reid, Elizabeth (1995). "Virtual Worlds: Culture and Imagination." In Steve Jones (ed.), *CyberSociety: Computer-Mediated Communication and Community*. London: Sage.
Rheingold, Howard (1994). *The Virtual Community: Homesteading on the Electronic Frontier*. New York: HarperPerennial.

Rich, Adrienne (1980). "Compulsory Heterosexuality and Lesbian Existence." *Signs* 5(4).
Ricoeur, Paul (1969/1974). *The Conflict of Interpretations: Essays in Hermeneutics*. Don Ihde (ed.). Evanston: Northwestern University Press.
Ricoeur, Paul (1976). *Interpretation Theory: Discourse and the Surplus of Meaning*. Fort Worth: Texas Christian University Press.
Ricoeur, Paul (1991). *From Text to Action: Essays in Hermeneutics II*. London: Athlone.
Ryan, Marie-Laure (1999a). "Introduction." In Marie-Laure Ryan (ed.), *Cyberspace Textuality: Computer Technology and Literary Theory*. Bloomington and Indianapolis: Indiana University Press.
Ryan, Marie-Laure (1999b). "Cyberspace, Virtuality, and the Text." In Marie-Laure Ryan (ed.), *Cyberspace Textuality: Computer Technology and Literary Theory*. Bloomington and Indianapolis: Indiana University Press.
Ryan, Marie-Laure (2001). *Narrative as Virtual Reality: Immersion and Interactivity in Literature and Electronic Media*. Baltimore and London: The Johns Hopkins University Press.
Schaap, Frank (2000). *The Words That Took Us There: Not An Ethnography*. MA thesis, University of Amsterdam.
Scott Sørensen, Anne (1999). "New Texts and New Media in Global Youth Culture: The Fantasy Roleplaying Games." *Young* 7(3).
Seidler, Victor Jeleniewski (1998). "Embodied Knowledge and Virtual Space: Gender, Nature and History." In John Wood (ed.), *The Virtual Embodied: Presence, Practice, Technology*. London and New York: Routledge.
Silver, David (2000). "Looking Forwards, Looking Backwards: Cyberculture Studies 1990–2000." In David Gauntlett (ed.), *Web. Studies: Rewiring Media Studies for the Digital Age*. London and New York: Arnold.
Slater, Don (1998). "Trading Sexpics on IRC: Embodiment and Authenticity on the Internet." *Body and Society* 4(4).
Smith, Neil & Cindi Katz (1993). "Grounding Metaphor: Towards a Spatialized Politics." In Michael Keith & Steve Pile (eds.), *Place and the Politics of Identity*. London and New York: Routledge.
Sobchack, Vivian (1995). "Beating the Meat/Surviving the Text, or How to Get Out of This Century Alive." In Mike Featherstone & Roger Burrows (eds.), *Cyberspace, Cyberbodies, Cyberpunk: Cultures of Technological Embodiment*. London: Sage.
Sofia, Zoë (1992). "Virtual Corporeality: A Feminist View." *Australian Feminist Studies* 15. Adelaide: University of Adelaide.
Springer, Claudia (1991). "The Pleasure of the Interface." *Screen*, autumn.
Springer, Claudia (1996). *Electronic Eros: Bodies and Desire in the Postindustrial Age*. Austin, Tex.: University of Texas Press.
Stone, Allucquère Rosanne (1991). "Will the Real Body Please Stand Up? Boundary Stories about Virtual Cultures." In Michael Benedikt (ed.), *Cyberspace: First Steps*. Cambridge, Mass.: MIT Press.
Stone, Allucquère Rosanne (1992). "Virtual Systems." In Jonathan Crary & Sanford Kwinter (eds.), *Incorporations*. New York: Zone, distributed by MIT Press.

Stone, Allucquère Rosanne (1995). *The War of Desire and Technology at the Close of the Mechanical Age.* Cambridge, Mass.: The MIT Press.

Strate, Lance, Ronald Jacobson & Stephanie Gibson (eds.) (1996). *Communication and Cyberspace: Social Interaction in an Electronic Environment.* Cresskill, NJ: Hampton Press.

Suler, John (1996). "One of Us: Participant Observation Research at the Palace" [online]. Available: <http://www1.rider.edu/~suler/psycyber/partobs.html>. Date accessed: June 10, 2002.

Sundén, Jenny (2001a). "What Happened to Difference in Cyberspace? The (Re)turn of the She-Cyborg." *Feminist Media Studies* 1(2).

Sundén, Jenny (2001b). "The Virtually Global: Or, the Flipside to a Digital State of Being." Paper presented at "Global Networks: The Internet as a Medium of Cultural Globalization" conference, March 30–31, 2001, University of Copenhagen, Denmark. Working Paper in *Global Media Studies*, Copenhagen.

Sundén, Jenny (2002a). "Cyberbodies: Writing Gender in Digital Self-Presentations." In Johan Fornäs, Kajsa Klein, Martina Ladendorf, Jenny Sundén & Malin Sveningsson (eds.), *Digital Borderlands: Cultural Studies of Identity and Interactivity on the Internet.* New York: Peter Lang Publishing.

Sundén, Jenny (2002b). "'I'm still not sure she's a she': Textual Talk and Typed Bodies in Online Interaction." In Paul McIlvenny (ed.), *Talking Gender & Sexuality: Conversation, Performativity and Discourse in Interaction.* Amsterdam and Philadelphia: John Benjamins.

Sundén, Jenny (2002c). "Kön, kod och kropp i textbaserade virtuella världar" in Peter Dahlgren (ed.), *Internet, medier och kommunikation.* Lund: Studentlitteratur.

Sveningsson, Malin (2001). *Creating a Sense of Community: Experiences from a Swedish Web Chat.* PhD thesis, Department of Communication Studies, Linköping University.

Thapan, Meenakshi (ed.) (1997). *Embodiment: Essays on Gender and Identity.* New Delhi: Oxford University Press.

Thomsen, Steven R., Joseph D. Straubhaar & Drew M. Bolyard (1998). "Ethnomethodology and the Study of Online Communities: Exploring the Cyber Streets." Paper presented at the Internet Research and Information for Social Scientists international conference, March 25–27 1998, Bristol, UK. [Online]. Available: <http://www.sosig.ac.uk/iriss/papers/paper16.htm>. Date accessed: June 10, 2002.

Tuana, Nancy (1992). *Woman and the History of Philosophy.* New York: Paragon House.

Tuana, Nancy (ed.) (1994). *Feminist Interpretations of Plato.* University Park, Pa.: Pennsylvania State University Press.

Turing, Alan (1950). "Computing Machinery and Intelligence." *Mind* 59.

Turkle, Sherry (1995). *Life on the Screen: Identity in the Age of the Internet.* New York: Simon and Schuster.

Van Maanen, John (1988). *Tales of the Field: On Writing Ethnography.* Chicago: University of Chicago Press.

Wajcman, Judy (1994). "Technology as Masculine Culture." In *The Polity Reader in Gender Studies.* Cambridge: Polity Press.

Wajcman, Judy (1995). "Feminist Theories of Technology." In Sheila Jasanoff (ed.), *Handbook of Science and Technology Studies*. Thousand Oaks, Cal.: Sage.
Wakeford, Nina (1996). "Sexualized Bodies in Cyberspace." In Warren Chernaik, Marilyn Deegan & Andrew Gibson (eds.), *Beyond the Book: Theory, Culture, and the Politics of Cyberspace*. Oxford, UK: Office for Humanities Communication Publications.
Wakeford, Nina (1997). "Networking Women and Grrrls with Information/Communication Technology: Surfing Tales of the World Wide Web." In Jennifer Terry & Melodie Calvert (eds.), *Processed Lives: Gender and Technology in Everyday Life*. New York and London: Routledge.
Waldby, Catherine (1995). "Destruction: Boundary Erotics and Refigurations of the Heterosexual Male Body." In Elizabeth Grosz & Elspeth Probyn (eds.), *Sexy Bodies: The Strange Carnalities of Feminism*. London and New York: Routledge.
Weiss, Gail & Honi Fern Haber (1999). *Perspectives on Embodiment: The Intersections of Nature and Culture*. New York: Routledge.
Wellman, Barry (ed.) (1999). *Networks in the Global Village: Life in Contemporary Communities*. Oxford: Westview.
Whitford, Margaret (1991). *Luce Irigaray: Philosophy in the Feminine*. London: Routledge.
Wiener, Norbert (1948). *Cybernetics: Or Control and Communication in the Animal and the Machine*. New York: John Wiley & Sons.
Woodland, Randal (1995). "Queer Spaces, Modem Boys, and Pagan Statues: Gay/Lesbian Identity and the Construction of Cyberspace." *Works and Days* 13(1–2).
Zack, Naomi, Laurie Shrage and Crispin Sartwell (eds.) (1998). *Race, Class, Gender and Sexuality: The Big Questions*. Oxford: Blackwell.
Zakin, Emily (2000). "Bridging the Social and the Symbolic: Toward a Feminist Politics of Sexual Difference." *Hypatia* 15(3).
Zdenek, Sean (1999). "Rising up from the MUD: Inscribing Gender in Software Design." *Discourse & Society* 10(3).

INDEX

Aarseth, E. J., 25, 26, 44, 45, 156, 157, 159, 170
adventure MUDs, 20
Agar, M., 31
agency, 132
America
   and cyberspace, 115–19
   as "realized utopia," 119, 120
Amérique (Baudrillard), 119
@gender, 28, 29, 42, 51, 52, 53, 62, 83, 85, 86, 88, 126, 127, 128, 136, 139, 153, 166, 172
   help, 158–60
   in TinyMUD, 164
   morphs, 130
   'other,' 84
   swapping, 130
   virtual order in, 160–63
Austin, J. L., 29

Bachelard, G., 97, 99, 122
   phenomenology of the daydream, 98
Balsamo, A., 10, 69
Barthes, R., 8, 148, 149, 150, 154
Bartle, R., 20
Bassett, C., 80
Baudrillard, J., 119, 120
Billy, 102
Blade Runner, 9
bodies, 4
   dialectics, 165
   textual and material, 11
   textual dimension of online, 8, 20

Bodies that Matter: On the Discursive Limits of "Sex," (Butler), 53, 176
body writing, 150, 151
Bolter, J. D., 122
Braidotti, R., 9, 11, 186, 187
Butler, J., 11, 29, 53, 54, 130, 165, 166, 176, 177, 183, 184, 186
   hate speech and, 164
   lesbian phallus and, 141–43

Casey, E. S., 92
Castle, T., 68, 90
chatterbots, 169
Cherny, L., 27, 132
Clifford, J., 59
Clynes, M., 5
Connell, R. W., 138, 142, 143
corporeal feminism, 52
corporealization, 11
corporeal materiality, 177
Coyne, R., 183
cross-dressing, 129, 130
cultural geography, 16
Curtis, P., 21
cyberculture
   disembodiment in, 62
   studies, 57
cyberfeminism, 16, 81, 186
cyborgfeminism, 16, 180–83, 186
cybernetic, 157
   bedroom culture, 148
   disembodiment and, 7
cyberpunk, 4, 5, 66, 67

cybersex, 109
  example of, 110–11, 139–40
  "theme park" effect of, 147
cyberspace, 5
  bedroom, 146–48
  bodies in, 4, 19
  gender in, 15
  global connectivity and, 93
  male theorists and, 5
  technologies, 4
  women in, 168
Cyberspace: First Steps (Benedikt), 115
cyber-subjectivity, 3
Cybertext: Perspectives on Ergodic Literature (Aarseth), 157
cyborg, 6, 65, 127, 161, 182, 185, 187
  anthropology, 49
  cinema, 127
  female, 4–8
  imagery, 66
  'post-lesbian," 188
Cyborg Manifesto (Haraway), 188, 189

Danet, B., 129
Derrida, J., 47, 150, 151
  notion of the signature, 179
Deleuze, G., 107, 108, 144
Dietrich, D., 181
digitally mediated presence, 49
digital textuality, 156–58
disembodied characters, 59
drag, 130
Dungeons and Dragons, 20

electronic literature, 154
embodied
  communication, 108
  computer code, 152
  objects, 60–63
embodiment, 4, 172, 178
  deconstruction of, 74
encoded body-logics, 153
entrance messages, 106
ethnographic attitude, 18
ethnographic texts, 17
  definition of, 18
  and online culture, 48
Eve of Destruction, 127
Evelyn, 94, 95
exit messages, 106

Fate of Place, The (Casey), 92
feminism
  corporeal, 52
  queer theory and, 53
Feminism and the Politics of Reading (Pearce), 89
Foucault, M., 13, 93, 148, 149
Freud, S., 167
Friedman, T., 44

Garber, M., 129
gatekeepers, 36
gender
  language and, 51
  online issues of, 125–29, 129–33
  performance, theory of, 54
  software design and, 169
Gender Trouble (Butler), 184
Gibson, W., 4
Gilligan, 117
global youth culture, 63
Grosz, E., 11, 51, 52, 142, 150, 151, 179, 184, 186
Grusin, R., 122
Guatttari, F., 107, 108

Hamlet on the Holodeck: The Future of Narrative in Cyberspace (Murray), 59
Hamming, J. E., 188, 189
Haraway, D., 6, 11, 13, 18, 19, 28, 49, 64, 65, 127, 161, 185, 187
Hawthorne, S., 182
Hayles, N. K., 7, 11, 46, 170, 172, 178, 179, 189
heterosexual matrix, 11
heterotextual matrix, 137–40
heterotopia, 93
Hine, C., 48
Holland, S., 127
How We Became Posthuman: Virtual Bodies in Cybernetics, Literature and Informatics (Hayles), 7
human operator, 170
hyper-femininity, 81
hypermediacy, 122, 123
hypertext
  postmodernism and, 154–56
  theory, 153

imaginative bodies, 59–63
imitation game, 7
incorporation, 170, 171, 172, 179

inscription, 170, 171, 179
Internet, 11
Irigaray, L., 166, 167, 168
Ito, M., 14

Katz, C., 93
Kendall, L., 58
Kline, N., 5, 182
Kolko, B. E., 83, 122, 164

La Vie mode d'emploi (Perec), 156
LambdaMOO, 21, 28, 30, 134
    female characters on, 80–81
Landow, G., 154
Lang, F., 6
language and gender, 51
lesbian fetishism, 142
lesbian phallus, 141–43, 147
lexias, 154
location, 99
Lord of the Rings, The, 21
Lykke, N., 187

mapping, 16, 93, 94
Markussen, R., 187
Marsden, J., 6
Masculinities (Connell), 138
masquerade, 68
materiality of information, 14
materialization, 11
materialized deconstruction, 13
McHoul, A., 45
McRae, S., 65
Metropolis, 6
Miller, J. H., 94
MOO. *See* MUD, Object Oriented
Moulthrop, S., 155
MUD. *See* Multi User Dungeon
MUD$_I$, 20
MUD, Object Oriented (MOO)
    as a hypertext, 108
    as a striated space, 108
    being asleep in, 114
    character creation in, 32
    embodied communication and, 108
    heterotextual matrix in, 137–40
    hypertext fiction in, 158
    mapping the space of, 107
    physical locations in, 115
    themes in, 31, 32

Multi User Dungeon (MUD), 20
    adventure MUDs, 20
    anonymity of, 72, 73
    architecture of, 21–24
    communication, 24–27
    conducting research in, 35
    creating a character in, 27
    ethics of research in, 37–40
    grammatical distinctions in, 25
    newsgroups and, 38
    places and conversations, 39
    social interaction and, 44
    social MUDs, 20, 21
    speech in a social, 132
    "voice" in, 26
    wizards, 35
Murray, J., 59
mutation, 46

Nakamura, L., 27, 84
naturalization, online, 80
Neuromancer (Gibson), 4
neuters, 161–63
New Hackers' Dictionary, The (Raymond), 76
newsgroups, 38
Nunes, M., 107, 108

objectified bodies, 60–63
Olesen, F., 187
online
    bodies, 56–59
        and sexual categorization, 57
        and textual constructions, 62
    cross-dressing, 129, 130
    ethnography, 49
    masochism, 143–46
    naturalization, 80
    realism, 59
    textual embodiment, 51
organic reality, 6

Paccagnella, L., 43
paging/page messages, 106
Paterson, N., 81
Pearce, L., 89
Penley, C., 187
Perec, G., 156
performative, 29
Plant, S., 147, 155, 167, 168, 181
Poetics of Space, The (Bachelard), 97

politics of location, 16
postmodern utopianism, 109
poststructuralism, 13
Pratchett, T., 21
Professional Stranger, The (Agar), 31

queer theory, 16
quotations, 59

Race in Cyberspace (Kolko, Nakamura, and Rodman), 83
Raymond, E. S., 76
realism, 78
realistic determinism, 109
realized utopia, 119, 120
Reid, E., 28, 44, 45, 50
remediation, 122
Ricoeur, P., 10, 90
Robocop, 6
Rodman, G. B., 83
role-playing games, 63
Rose, T., 6
Rosencrantz & Gildenstern Are Dead (Stoppard), 85
Ross, A., 187
Rousseau, J. J., 183
Ryan, M.-L., 28, 158

Sacher-Masoch, L. von, 144, 145
Sade, M. de, 145
Sappho, 82, 83
science fiction, 4
    and fantasy characters, 69
    Hollywood and, 6
scriptor, 149
sex online. *See* cybersex
sexual textual talk, 140, 148–51
Shakespeare, W., 85
Slater, D., 74, 75, 113
Smith, N., 93
smooth space, 107, 108
Snow Crash (Stephenson), 31
social MUDs, 20, 21
Sofia, Z., 181
sonography, 165
Sørensen, A. S., 63
Spivak, G. C., 28
Star Trek, 21, 31
Stephenson, N., 31
Stone, S., 4, 57, 66, 80, 93, 133, 136
    gender performances and, 134

Stoppard, T., 85
striated space, 107, 108
structuralism, 18
subjectivity, 3
Suler, J., 32
supplement, 47

technological materiality, 170
technophoria, 156
Terminator, The, 6, 127
texts, 3, 8, 10
    as parody, 149
textual
    fluidity, 46
    machine, 157, 159, 170
    performativity, 53–55
    talk, 45, 95
TinyMUD, 20, 164
Tolkien, J. R. R., 21
topoanalysis, 97, 98
topography, 94
transgendered bodies, 66
Trubshaw, R., 20
Turing, A., 7
Turing test, 7
Turkle, S., 21, 72

virtual
    bodies, 50
    ethnography, 48
    gender, 50
    relationships, 135
    sex, 153
    topographies, 107

Wakeford, N., 82
Waldby, C., 146, 147
Walter, 134, 135, 136
War of Desire and Technology at the Close of the Mechanical Age, The (Stone), 57
WaterMOO, 2
    America as the dominant location in, 115–19, 121
    architecture in, 96
    as a visual culture, 90
    as a social MUD, 21
    as cultural production, 49
    @gender order in, 169
    bodies as 'signatures' in, 180
    body-writing in, 84
    body and place in, 121

character descriptions in, 19
construction of online bodies in, 153
creation of guest characters in, 30, 58
cyborg bodies in, 66
disappearance of characters in, 175
engendered pronouns in, 163–65
gender issues in, 126–29
hyper-femininity in, 81
limit of the body in, 178
nationality in, 71
notions of embodiment in, 14
placial geographies and, 111–13
race and, 83, 186
reading of texts in, 89
realism in, 78
selection for author's research, 31
sexuality in, 82
Spirits of, 33
textual bodies in, 15, 47
textual talk in, 68
topographic analysis of, 95, 121
writing and speaking in, 63
Winnie the Pooh, 31
wizards, 35
Woodland, R., 103
Woolf, V., 85

Xerox PARC, 21

Zdenek, S., 169

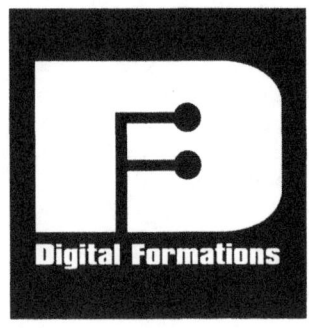

General Editor: Steve Jones

Digital Formations is the new source for critical, well-written books about digital technologies and modern life. Books in this series will break new ground by emphasizing multiple methodological and theoretical approaches to deeply probe the formation and reformation of lived experience as it is refracted through digital interaction. Each volume in *Digital Formations* will push forward our understanding of the intersections—and corresponding implications—between the digital technologies and everyday life. This series will examine broad issues in realms such as digital culture, electronic commerce, law, politics and governance, gender, the Internet, race, art, health and medicine, and education. The series will emphasize critical studies in the context of emergent and existing digital technologies.

For additional information about this series or for the submission of manuscripts, please contact:

    Acquisitions Department
    Peter Lang Publishing
    275 Seventh Avenue 28th Floor
    New York, NY 10001

To order other books in this series, please contact our Customer Service Department:

    (800) 770-LANG (within the U.S.)
    (212) 647-7706 (outside the U.S.)
    (212) 647-7707 FAX

or browse online by series:
    WWW.PETERLANGUSA.COM